CORPORATE STRATEGY

Lecturer's Guide

Richard Lynch

PITMAN
PUBLISHING

London · Hong Kong · Johannesburg · Melbourne · Singapore · Washington DC

PITMAN PUBLISHING
128 Long Acre, London WC2E 9AN
Tel: +44 (0)171 447 2000
Fax: +44 (0)171 240 5771

A Division of Pearson Professional Limited

First published in Great Britain in 1997

ISBN 0 273 60759 6

British Library Cataloguing in Publication Data
A CIP catalogue record for this book can be obtained from the British Library

10 9 8 7 6 5 4 3 2 1

Printed and bound by Bell and Bain Ltd., Glasgow

*Cover illustration: The chameleon is adaptable, innovative, sensitive to its environment,
possibly logical and certainly a survivor.*

Contents

Preface

The purpose of this *Lecturer's Guide* is to present you with a complete package of material for use with the book *Corporate Strategy*. The Introduction discusses the teaching issues presented by the text. The next section on Course Outlines provides some suggestions as to how the book might be adapted to different teaching needs. Each chapter is then discussed and explored with some indicative answers to the questions posed by the case studies and some comments on the Strategic Project for that chapter. Note that the summary of the chapter given in this *Guide* does not necessarily match that in the main text.

At the end of this *Guide* you will find a set of *overhead transparency masters* taken from the text for use during individual lectures. They are arranged to correspond with the Possible Lecture Structure outlined for each chapter.

With regard to the indicative answers to the case questions, lecturers hold differing views on distributing these to students. Some take the view that students should work out their own answers, while others believe that teaching notes can be handed out afterwards. I leave this entirely to your judgement, but would comment that the indicative answers have been prepared in a format that will allow copying if you wish.

If longer cases are required, use can be made of the cases in Chapters 5 and 6 regarding the ice cream market, of the Eurofreeze cases in Chapters 15 and 16 and a number of other linked cases - the list of case studies is given on pages xiii-xiv of the main book.

Both the publishers and I would warmly welcome your comments on the main text. The publishers' address is on the second page of this *Guide* and any comments and suggestions will be read with keen interest and noted for future reference.

Richard Lynch

Introduction: teaching programme issues

As *Corporate Strategy* represents a departure from previous student books on this subject, this section outlines some issues that may arise and explores their significance for teaching programmes.

Prescriptive and emergent approaches in corporate strategy

The underlying theme of the book is the need to consider not only the *rational* approach to strategic decision making but also the *creative* aspects of such decisions. The book uses two models of strategy to explain and explore this: the prescriptive and the emergent approaches. Arguably, the use of two models is a significant departure from existing texts in corporate strategy.

Over the last twenty years, the dominant mode has probably been to concentrate on the *prescriptive* approach: analysis, options, choice and implementation. There are a number of reasons for this which include:

- the prescriptive approach lends itself to a clear and simple teaching structure
- instant 'formula' for devising strategy
- integrative nature
- clear links with subjects such as financial and marketing analysis.

The structure has been so robust that it has been adopted by many texts, in spite of the problems that have become clear under the general heading of *crafting* corporate strategy, i.e. the *emergent* approach. This new text attempts to combine the two teaching approaches but several comments are necessary:

- *Oversimplification*: reducing the issues in corporate strategy to just two approaches oversimplifies the situation. This does not invalidate the method but it is important to be aware of its limitations. The basis of the text is that two divergent methods are better than one, even if more viewpoints are useful in reality.

- *Emergent strategy development*: for a number of reasons, prescriptive strategy approaches have more techniques associated with them than the emergent route: Five Forces model, Product Life Cycle and so on. Emergent strategy is less developed in this respect. This means that it is often possible to criticise emergent approaches from the viewpoint of practical application and they may be more difficult for students to understand and apply.

- *Balance between prescriptive and emergent throughout the text*: partly as a result of the greater development of prescriptive techniques, some topics are mainly explored using the prescriptive approach. A good example is Chapter 7 *Analysing Resources*, which is presented largely from a prescriptive perspective. In that example, the text contains an emergent approach Key Reading at the end of the chapter to provide some balance. More generally, certain business functions such as finance and operations also rely predominantly on a prescriptive approach. This has made it more difficult to develop a balanced text. The result is that certain chapters remain predominantly prescriptive in nature, e.g. Chapter 9 on finance and Chapter 15 on options selection. However, the latter part of the book concentrates on emergent issues. Therefore, taken as a whole, the text should present a balanced perspective.

Overall, the book has been designed in teaching terms to be *evolutionary rather than revolutionary*. It builds on the well-developed structures of prescriptive strategy while at the same time exploring the insights of emergent strategy. The text has been designed to allow lecturers to emphasise, explore and develop both approaches according to personal judgement and interest. The table below may prove helpful.

Chapter emphasis: prescriptive and emergent

Chapter	*Emphasis*
1 Corporate strategy	Prescriptive and emergent
2 A review of theory and practice	Prescriptive and emergent
3 Analysing the environment	Mainly prescriptive with emergent comments
4 Analysing the market	Prescriptive with emergent comments
5 Analysing competitors	Prescriptive with emergent comments
6 Analysing customers	Prescriptive with emergent comments
7 Analysing resources	Mainly prescriptive with emergent comments
8 Analysing human resources	Emergent with prescriptive comments
9 Analysing financial resources	Prescriptive with emergent comments
10 Analysing operations resources	Prescriptive with emergent comments
11 Background issues	Prescriptive and emergent
12 Mission and objectives	Prescriptive with emergent comments
13 Resource-based strategic options	Prescriptive with emergent comments
14 Market-based strategic options	Prescriptive with emergent comments
15 Strategy evaluation and selection - 1	Prescriptive
16 Strategy evaluation and selection - 2	Prescriptive
17 Finding the strategic route forward	Prescriptive and emergent
18 Strategy, structure and style	Emergent
19 Resource allocation, strategic planning and control	Prescriptive with emergent comments
20 Organisational structure and people issues	Emergent
21 Managing strategic change	Prescriptive and emergent
22 Building a cohesive corporate strategy	Prescriptive and emergent

Critical approach

It is possible that some students will find the *Comment* sections introduced in some chapters throughout the text to be puzzling. The formulaic certainties of some functional subjects are missing. The *Comment* section is designed to develop the student's critical faculties, but some may be daunted by the uncertainties that are explored. This needs careful handling by the lecturer if the student is to feel confident about the outcome and usefulness of corporate strategy.

For teaching purposes, therefore, the *Comment* sections have been highlighted and *can be ignored* if this is judged to be prudent from a teaching perspective. For example, it may be that for courses involving a simple treatment of corporate strategy little use is made of these sections: e.g. course modules for HNC/D or a second-year undergraduate foundation course in Business Policy.

Naturally, other students on more advanced programmes should find the *Comment* sections challenging and stimulating. In these circumstances, lecturers should not hesitate to encourage disagreement with the textual comments, which are deliberately designed to be provocative.

Focussed case approach

As mentioned in the main text, there are no long, integrative cases in the book. All the cases are *focussed* on specific strategic issues. Almost all of them provide some area of *contention or debate*, rather than merely presenting illustrations. Hence, each case has been written or chosen to go beyond a broad, strategic description of best practice and to supply material for lecturer presentation and class discussion.

Such a case approach may prove especially useful in coping with the newer lecturing and tutorial styles:

- larger class sizes
- followed up by separate, smaller seminar discussion sessions
- shorter attention-span and time availability of some students.

Importantly, the focussed case approach has the advantage that specific discussion and exploration of a topic can be undertaken. It also means that the cases can be introduced during the main lecture session to illustrate aspects of the topic. The *Minicases* may provide especially useful material here.

If longer integrative cases are required, then two books are recommended:

- John Hendry, Tony Eccles and others, *European Cases in Strategic Management*, Chapman & Hall, 1993.
- Colin Clarke-Hill and Keith Glaister (eds) *Cases in Strategic Management*, 2nd edition, Pitman Publishing, 1995.

This is not meant as an exhaustive list of suitable cases. In addition, there is an excellent range of cases available from the Case Clearing House based at the Cranfield University campus.

Key readings

Instead of cases being used in some seminar sessions, the Key Reading has also been chosen in many instances to form the basis of a useful class discussion. Again, these readings have been kept short, but students should be encouraged to read beyond the few words in the text. Key readings at the end of Chapters 2, 5, 7 and 22 may prove particularly useful as a source of discussion and even student essays. The chapter sections that follow in this text give some suggested questions for the readings. Other key readings can also be used to explore issues by examining the implications for corporate strategy given by the reading.

International aspects of strategy

For teaching purposes, international strategy has been treated as an *elaboration* of basic strategy, rather than taken as a topic to be explored in a separate chapter by itself. Thus international aspects are generally explored at the end of each chapter as additions to the basic topics of that chapter.

In some cases, this may oversimplify international strategy, e.g. tax treatments or national cultures, but it has the great merit of building a connection with the basic strategy elements. Moreover, it does mean that every student can be exposed to international aspects, if this is judged to be desirable. Equally, where some basic strategy courses do not require it, the international element can be ignored without jumping around the text. Lecturers will make their own judgements, in relation to their courses, on the emphasis that they wish to place in this area.

Flexibility in teaching schemes

The book has been designed to provide some flexibility in teaching schemes. For example, Chapter 17 is one of the more important chapters in the book. However, even this chapter can be treated in a variety of ways with perhaps two extremes.

- A *prescriptive* approach might emphasise the following: 'Now that we have examined the main elements of the prescriptive approach, it is relevant to explore the criticisms that have been made. These are contained in the opening part of Chapter 17 and represent areas that need to be considered before we move to implement the chosen strategy.'

- An *emergent* approach might emphasise the following: 'Now that we have examined the main elements of the prescriptive approach, we are in a position to consider its many weaknesses. Ultimately, these constitute a damning critique that undermines the basis of the approach and causes us to give much more weight to areas such as organisation structure and people issues, management style and strategic change, which we consider next.'

Course outlines for different teaching programmes

As explained in the main text, the book has been carefully designed to be used in a variety of ways. It can be studied from cover-to-cover but chapters have been written so that the text can also be used on other shorter programmes. The pages that follow give some suggestions.

Course outline 1: first-time, relatively easy strategy programme

10-week basic strategy course, such as HNC/D or a strategic management insert into a more general management programme. Ten lecture sessions plus a seminar after each lecture.

Session	Lecture session	Seminar
1	Introduction: Chapter 1	IBM *or* Electrolux
2	Chapter 3	Global steel *or* Benefon
3	Chapter 7	Resources at three European companies *or* Nolan Helmets
4	Chapters 11 and 12	Corning *and* Perrier
5	Chapter 13 and 14	News Corporation - 1 *and* 2 *or* Kodak
6	Chapter 15	Eurofreeze - 1 *and* 2 *or* Central heating
7	Chapter 17	Hutchison Mobilfunk *or* MCI
8	Chapter 19	Canon *or* Nestlé *or* Hanson, *or* compare all three
9	Chapter 21	United Biscuits *or* S G Warburg
10	Chapter 22 and conclusions	TomTec *or* Hanson

Assessment: Students might be asked to prepare an essay based on a Key Reading such as that at the end of Chapters 2, 5 or 22. Alternatively, they might be asked to undertake a written analysis of one of the longer cases such as: Case 4.3 World paper and pulp industry, Case 14.3 British Aerospace, Case 18.2 ASEA Brown Boveri, Case 21.3 S G Warburg or Case 22.2 Hanson.

Course outline 2: final level degree one-semester strategy programme

12-week basic course: Final year undergraduate BA in Business Studies or first semester MBA full-time programme. Twelve lecture sessions plus a seminar after each lecture.

Session	Lecture session	Seminar
1	Introduction: Chapter 1	IBM *or* Electrolux
2	Chapter 3	Global steel *or* Benefon
3	Chapter 7	Resources at three European companies *or* Nolan Helmets
First assessment	*Essay question from Chapters 3 or 7, e.g. question 7 from Ch 3 or questions 5 or 11 from Ch 7*	
4	Chapter 11	Corning *and* Perrier
5	Chapter 12	Ford Motors *and* Pink Elephant
6	Chapter 13	News Corporation - 1 *or* Kodak
7	Chapter 14	News Corporation - 2 *or* British Aerospace
8	Chapter 15	Eurofreeze -1 *and* 2 *or* Central heating
9	Chapter 17	Hutchison Mobilfunk *or* MCI
Second assessment	*Essay question from Chapter 17, e.g. questions 1 or 9*	
10	Chapter 19	Canon *or* Nestlé *or* Hanson, *or* compare all three*
11	Chapter 21	United Biscuits *or* S G Warburg*
12	Chapter 22 and conclusions	TomTec *or* Hanson*

* These three sessions might be replaced by course presentations of *Strategic Projects* based possibly on those suggested in the chapters of the book. Typically, the project presentations might be assessed, with immediate comment and feedback, before a written report is presented after session 12.

Final assessment: Paper-based either on the end-chapter questions or on a case-based analysis.

Course outline 3: year-long programme across two semesters

24-week or two-semester course: final year undergraduate BA in Business Studies or two semester MBA Programme. Twenty-four lecture sessions plus a seminar after each lecture.

Session	Lecture session	Seminar
1	Introduction: Chapter 1	IBM *or* Electrolux
2	Chapter 2	Spillers -1 *and* 2 *or* Saes Getters
3	Chapter 3	Global steel *or* Benefon
First assess-ment	*Essay question from Chapter 3, e.g. question 7, or Assessment of Key Reading from Chapter 2. Or written case analysis*	
4	Chapter 4	South African oil *or* World paper and pulp
5	Chapter 5	Compare footwear, telecomms and grocery, *or* Mars *and* Nestlé
6	Chapter 6	Ice cream segmentation *or* Boeing 777
7	Chapter 7	Resources at three European companies *or* Nolan Helmets
Second assess-ment	*Essay question from Ch 7, e.g. questions 5 or 11, or Assessment of Key Reading from Chapter 5. Or written case analysis*	
8	Chapter 8	BP *or* Rank Xerox
9	Chapter 9	Brewers' growth *or* MorphoSys
10	Chapter 10	Toyota *or* SKF *or* ISS
11	Chapter 11	Motorola, Corning *and* Perrier
12	Chapter 12 and conclusions	Business in the Community *or* Pink Elephant
	Mid-year break	
13	Chapter 13	News Corporation - 1 *or* Kodak
14	Chapter 14	News Corporation - 2 *or* British Aerospace
15	Chapter 15	Eurofreeze -1 *and* 2 *or* Central heating
16	Chapter 16	Nokia *or* Eurofreeze - 3
17	Chapter 17	Hutchison Mobilfunk *or* MCI
Third assess-ment	*Essay question from Chapter 17, e.g. questions 1 or 9. Or assessment of Key Reading from Chapter 22 (or some other guru such as Porter or Mintzberg)*	

18	Chapter 18	General Motors *or* ABB
19	Chapter 19	Canon *or* Nestlé *or* Hanson, *or* compare all three
20	Chapter 20	Telepizza *or* Ford Motors*
21	Chapter 21	United Biscuits *or* S G Warburg*
22	Chapter 22 and conclusions	TomTec *or* Hanson*
23	Strategic project presentations	
24	Strategic project presentations	

* These three sessions might also be used for course presentations of *Strategic Projects,* based possibly on those suggested in the chapters of the book. Typically, the project presentations might be assessed, with immediate comment and feedback, before a written report is presented after session 24.

Final assessment: Two papers, one based on theory questions perhaps adapted from the end of chapter questions, the other based on a case analysis.

Course outline 4: first semester basic programme with topic-based second semester

24-week or two-semester course: final year undergraduate BA in Business Studies or two-semester MBA Programme - but a course in which the basic strategy programme needs to be covered in Semester 1, since some students move on to other topics.

Semester 1: 12 lecture sessions plus a seminar after each lecture in first semester.
Semester 2: *Only some students* advance to a second semester.

First semester: See **Course outline 2.**

Second semester: **Option 1**: Fill in the missing chapters in sequence.
            or
            Option 2: Topic-based.

In the latter case, the text can be used as a source book of material that will encourage further exploration of topics. The outline below is based on Option 2. Clearly students might be invited to suggest topics: for the purposes of this outline, some subjects have been chosen.

Some lecturers might take the view that *fewer topics* are required, since they all present rich sources of strategy development, especially when coupled with the recommended readings and references contained in the text. Essentially, the book can be used in a more creative way as a basis for a second semester strategy course.

Option 2: Second semester only

Session	Topic	Chapters
13	Inter-relationships between government and strategy	Chapters 3, 4 and 16 (stakeholders)
14	Competitive warfare strategies and techniques	Chapters 3, 5, 14 and 16
15	The benefits and problems of a customer-driven strategy	Chapters 3, 6 and 14
First assess-ment	*Essay questions based around the above themes*	
16	Importance and role of leadership in strategy development	Chapters 7, 8, 18 and 19
17	Vision and innovation in strategy	Chapters 11, 20 and 21
18	The role of technology, including information technology, in strategy development	Chapter 3 (environment), 11 and 19 (resources)

Session	Lecture session	Seminar
19	Managing strategic change	Chapters 7, 8, 20 and 21
20	The opportunities and problems of empowerment in the development of strategy	Chapters 8, 18, 19, 20
21	The inter-relationship between strategy and organisational structure	Chapters 8, 17, 18 and 20
Second assess-ment	Essay questions based around the above themes	
22	Strategy in public organisations	Chapters 3, 4, 5, 6, 19 and 20
23	Strategy in small businesses	Chapters 3, 4, 5, 6, 19 and 20
24	Conclusions and course review	Perhaps important to prepare an overall survey when the course might be considered to lack shape

Final assessment: essay-based examination with wide selection of topics and a choice of questions.

Course outline 5: International corporate strategy

12-week international strategy course: Final year undergraduate BA in Business Studies or first semester MBA Programme. Twelve lecture sessions plus a seminar after each lecture.

Session	Lecture session	Seminar
1	Introduction: Chapter 1	IBM or Electrolux
2	Chapter 3 plus global issues from Chapter 4	Global steel or Benefon
3	Chapter 7 plus international culture from Chapter 8	Resources at three European companies (Case 7.1) and Industry groups in Japan, Korea, Hong Kong and Italy (Case 8.2)
First assess-ment	Essay question from Chapters 3, 4, 7 or 8	
4	Chapters 9 and 10	Interbrew and Toyota
5	Chapters 11 and 12	Corning and Ford global
6	Chapters 13 and 14	News Corporation -1 and 2 or British Aerospace
7	Chapter 15	European central heating or Nokia (from Chapter 16)
8	Chapter 17	Hutchison Mobilfunk or MCI or Chapter 18 cases: Sony, General Motors
9	Chapter 19	Canon, Nestlé and Hanson
Second assess-ment	Essay question from Chapters 15, 17 or 19	
10	Chapter 20	Telepizza and Ford global*
11	Chapter 21	United Biscuits and ABB (from Chapter 18)*
12	Chapter 22 and conclusions	TomTec and Hanson*

* These three sessions might be replaced by course presentations of *Strategic Projects* based possibly on those suggested in the chapters of the book. Typically, the project presentations might be assessed, with immediate comment and feedback, before a written report is presented after session 12.

Final assessment: as Course outline 2.

Chapter 1
Corporate strategy

Synopsis of chapter

This chapter introduces the basic concepts of corporate strategy. It explores why corporate strategy is important before covering the core areas of the subject. It then goes on to introduce prescriptive and emergent strategy before making some comments on particular strategic situations: strategy development in public, non-profit and international contexts. Most lecturers will probably choose to spend some time on the prescriptive and emergent models because of their importance to the subject.

Summary

- The chapter explores the nature of corporate strategy - the linking process between the organisation and its environment - which focusses particularly on competitive advantage, the distinctive capabilities of the organisation and the need to be innovative. Adding value is of particular importance to most organisations, though for non-profit and government organisations this is not necessarily the case.

- Corporate strategy is important because it deals with the major, fundamental issues that affect the future of the organisation. It integrates the functional areas of the organisation, covering the range and depth of its activities.

- There are three core areas of corporate strategy: strategic analysis; strategy development; and mission and strategy implementation. Although the three core areas are often presented as being strictly sequential, they interlock and overlap in practice. There are two important qualifications to the three core areas: the use of judgement and values to derive the strategy and the need to make highly speculative assessments about the future. Unless handled carefully, these may give a false sense of direction about the future.

- In developing corporate strategy, there is a need to distinguish between process, content and context. Process is the method by which the strategies are derived; content is the strategic decisions then made; context is the environment within which the organisation operates and develops its strategies. Process is usually the area that presents most problems because it is difficult to measure precisely.

- There is a fundamental disagreement among strategists regarding how corporate strategy can be developed. There are two basic routes: the *prescriptive approach* and the *emergent approach*. The prescriptive approach takes the view that the three core areas are linked together sequentially. The emergent approach regards the three core areas as being inter-related. The two approaches have some common elements in the early stages - the analysis and the development of a mission for the organisation. Beyond this, they go their separate ways and lead to two different models for the corporate strategy process.

- In public, government-owned organisations, the strategy is usually governed by broader public policy concerns, rather than profits. In non-profit institutions, strategy needs to reflect the values of the organisation concerned. Beyond these issues, the basic strategic principles can then be applied.

- In international terms, the development of corporate strategy is more complex. There are a number of reasons including the impact on trade between nations, financial issues, economies of scale in global production and differing cultures and beliefs. All these make international corporate strategy more difficult to develop.

Possible lecture structure

The following structure is based on the *Learning outcomes* in *Corporate Strategy* at the beginning of Chapter 1:

- Start with a comparison of the profitability of Hewlett-Packard during the same period as IBM was making huge losses: why? Differences in strategy, not just about products, market share, etc. but also about company culture, etc.
- Define corporate strategy and explain its five key elements: the main elements are shown on the two pages which follow for use as overheads.
- Outline the main reasons for the importance of corporate strategy: an overhead page follows showing the main elements.
- Explain the core areas of corporate strategy and how they link together: use Figures 1.5 and 1.7 from *Corporate Strategy* in the set of Overhead Transparency Masters at the end of this *Guide*.
- Distinguish between process, content and context of a corporate strategy: use Figure 1.6 from the set of overheads.
- Explain prescriptive strategy: use Figure 1.8. You could also use Figure 2.1 to explain the principle.
- Explain emergent strategy: use Figure 1.8. You could also use Figure 2.3 to explain the principle.
- If required and time is available, describe the extent to which corporate strategy is different in public and non-profit organisations. Comment on international strategy.

Strategic project

Various strategic themes are possible in the computer industry: rapid market change, the influence of technology, global involvement, the shift in value added from IBM to Microsoft and Intel, the ability of the smaller companies to survive. It would probably be wise to pick an individual company in order to provide focus to such a study: the revolution at IBM under its new chief executive, Lou Gerstner, might be interesting, especially if the over-confident culture of the company was also explored.

What is corporate strategy?

No universally agreed definition

One example of a definition:

'Corporate strategy is the pattern of major objectives, purposes or goals and essential policies for achieving those goals, stated in such a way as to define what business the company is in or is to be in and the kind of company it is or is to be.'

Strategy is developed by a consideration of the resources of the organisation in relation to its environment, the prime purpose being to add value.

Five key elements to strategy:

- Sustainability
- Distinctiveness
- Competitive advantage
- Exploitation of linkages between the organisation and its environment
- Vision

Why is corporate strategy important?

Because it deals with the fundamental issues that affect the future of the organisation.

Corporate strategy ...

... involves the entire organisation

... is likely to concern itself with the *survival of the business* as a minimum objective

... and the *creation of value added* as a maximum objective

... covers the range and depth of the organisation's activities

... directs the changing and evolving relationships of the organisation with its environment

... is central to the development of distinctiveness in the organisation

... is crucial to adding value

Corporate Strategy Lecturer's Guide, Pitman Publishing
© Aldersgate Consultancy Limited 1997

The three core areas of corporate strategy

Strategic analysis

- Environment
- Resources
- Vision, mission and objectives

Strategic development

- Options
- Rational selection
- Finding the strategic route forward

Strategy implementation

- Resource allocation
- Strategic planning and control
- People issues and strategic change

Case notes

Corporate strategy at Hewlett-Packard

This is a highly successful company that has a consistent profit record over many years. Significantly, the company strategy has always emphasised excellence and innovation. Yet the company has not had some major vision of where it is headed over time. This may be because the company is operating in a market where it has been exceptionally difficult to identify the long-term trends: for example, who could clearly have foreseen the development of the laser printer thirty years ago? Yet Hewlett-Packard laser printers are a fundamental part of its highly successful product range.

1. How important to corporate strategy is profit or a similar quantified objective?

Without profits, commercial operations cannot survive. Hence this demonstrates the importance of profitability and should be reflected in the corporate strategy of the company. However, beyond the matter of mere survival, the issue is not the need to deliver profit so much as *how* this is to be achieved.

In delivering profits, there may be a need to develop other activities such as *market dominance* in computer printers. If such an activity is to be undertaken then there is a strong case for testing after time whether this has been achieved, i.e. there is a need to measure the market share of Hewlett-Packard to see whether it dominates the market or not. Quantifying the objective is the starting point to testing whether it has been achieved. In this sense, market dominance may be considered as a quantified objective in addition to the profits of the company and is important in developing the strategy of the company.

2. To what extent does management style also matter? Are these compatible?

Hewlett-Packard presents a particular style of management - informal and open - which was set by the two founders of the company from its inception. They certainly believed that management style mattered. Other companies may develop different approaches where management style would appear to matter less: for example, profits and payments to the shareholders of the company may be more important than an open style in some companies.

Management style may not be compatible with the delivery of profit. In the case of Hewlett-Packard, *share options* were given to employees in order to reward them and encourage them to remain with the company. These would dilute the share interests of existing shareholders and in the *short term* reduce dividends per share to such existing shareholders. In this sense, there may be some incompatibility. However, others would argue that, in the long term, the satisfied employees will deliver higher profits, particularly where such profits are highly reliant on the individual skills and commitment of such people. In this sense, they may not be incompatible.

Corporate Strategy Lecturer's Guide, Pitman Publishing
© Aldersgate Consultancy Limited 1997

Corporate profit disaster at IBM

Over the last twenty years, there have been few companies that have equalled the profit disaster that befell IBM during the early 1990s. However, it should be recognised that the seeds of the problem were sown during the 1980s and were not simply the fault of the management at the time when the difficulties were declared.

Important strategic mistakes were made at IBM during the 1970s and 1980s. Even though some of them had been recognised, it is not always possible in corporate strategy to provide instant solutions: large corporations develop conflicting interests that are not always easy to reconcile and cannot make rapid changes because of the size of the organisation. For example, at IBM there was a conflict between the need to preserve the highly profitable mainframe computers and the need to develop the smaller machines that might steal business from the larger models. Moreover, with a very large company, it takes time to discuss and agree any changes that need to be made.

1. What was the strategic significance of IBM's decision to obtain supplies of computer chips and software from other manufacturers rather than make them itself?

This allowed the suppliers to develop their business on the basis of the reputation of IBM. The mistake made by IBM was not to buy in supplies, but to allow their suppliers to sell the same goods to competitors of IBM. As IBM established the market, it was developing a common standard - the IBM-compatible computer - that was ready-made for its suppliers to use as the basis of developing their business.

2. How big a part did the change in computer technology play in IBM's problems? Could this have been predicted by IBM? What is the significance of your answer for corporate strategy?

Developing computer technology was one of the major problems that IBM faced during the 1980s: small computers were becoming more powerful and more able to compete with at least some of IBM's products. Technology may be difficult to predict where it is revolutionary. However, in the case of IBM, it was essentially evolutionary so might have been predicted. Where something such as technology cannot be predicted, it makes it difficult to develop rigid corporate strategy for many years ahead. Prescriptive approaches may be impossible in fast changing environments.

3. How important was the decision of IBM's suppliers to spend marketing funds on branding their products? What strategic significance does this have for the late 1990s in computer markets?

It has proved vital: value added has shifted from the assembler of computer components such as IBM to the supplier of exclusive, branded supplies such as Intel and Microsoft. Branding has been a method of delivering that exclusivity: the *Pentium* chip and *Windows 95* have locked customers into Intel and Microsoft respectively and provided real competitive advantage.

4. Can you think of any reason why companies like Hewlett-Packard could continue to make adequate profits during this period?

They had differentiated products that could not be easily imitated by their competitors. They were also more innovative and used this to reduce costs, increase value for money for their customers and provide genuinely new products.

Importantly, Hewlett-Packard was more adaptable as a company. The company was able to change with the market more easily than IBM. Moreover, H-P was less complacent than IBM and more willing to work to improve its products as a result. It is important to realise that IBM's problems were partly the result of its *culture and style*, just as much as technology and marketing.

5. Use the five key elements of strategy to evaluate IBM's corporate strategy. What conclusions do you draw for these and added value?

- *Sustainability*: the company's strategy was only partially sustainable over time. It worked well at the mainframe level but not for smaller computers.
- *Distinctiveness*: the small computers had no distinctive features beyond being branded and sold by the largest computer company in the world. This gave them some advantages but they were not technically as advanced nor as cheap to produce as their competitors.
- *Competitive advantage*: this was in decline over the years.
- *Exploitation of linkages between the organisation and its environment*: IBM never really exploited the linkages that it undoubtedly had in earlier years with, for example, its suppliers and its customers. It allowed others to muscle in and take share.
- *Vision*: the IBM vision was very clear in earlier years but seemed to be one of catching up during the 1980s. By contrast, other companies had a much clearer sense of their direction and purpose.

Added value has been reduced, as some of the profitable parts of the computer manufacturing process have moved outside IBM: software to Microsoft and computer chips to Intel. Arguably, this was a major strategic mistake by IBM.

It has to be said that the above comments are made with all the wisdom of hindsight. They were not so easy to identify at the time, which is why corporate strategy is not always simple or straightforward.

Corporate Strategy Lecturer's Guide, Pitman Publishing
© Aldersgate Consultancy Limited 1997

Electrolux plans for growth

Over the last thirty years, the Swedish company Electrolux has built a major strategic position around the world in electrical domestic appliances: washing machines, refrigerators and so on. The purpose of this case is to explore the language of strategy, as practised in a company, and assess its implications. It is possible to identify the company's mission and objectives from the text.

1. How would you summarise the company's mission and objectives? Where do garden equipment and forestry fit into this picture?

It is typical of many companies that there is some discussion of its mission and objectives in its Annual Report and Accounts. This is often available in libraries, through the Internet and directly from the company itself.

Mission: to be devoted mainly to household goods for indoor and outdoor use.

Objectives: good growth in net worth and dividends to our shareholders plus being the largest or second largest in the world in its major product areas.

Garden equipment and forestry do not readily fit here at all. They are in the company for historical reasons but have contributed little to its international growth. Companies may hold on to products for sentimental reasons and for reasons associated with the protection of employees who have been loyal over many years. This would be regarded as 'wrong' if the prime purpose of a company was to serve its shareholders, but not all companies around the world take this viewpoint.

2. What strategies has it followed to achieve these? With what results?

In a similar way, it is also possible to identify the strategies that the company has used to pursue the above mission and objectives:

- Acquisitions
- Restructuring
- New products
- Investment in new production facilities

The results have included becoming first or second in many of the world's major markets for electrical domestic appliances. There has been a concentrated attempt by the company to develop world brands, locate factories to suit local demand and pursue market share. All such activities cost finance and some may costs jobs as employment is rationalised and economies of scale are realised. Moreover, the investment has had some impact on short-term profits and dividends to shareholders.

3. Thinking back to your knowledge of the various functional areas of a business (marketing, finance, etc.), what in your opinion would have been the main problems that the company faced over the period? To what extent do you judge that they should form part of the formal corporate strategy of the company? Why?

The various functions of the company will all have been influenced by the acquisitions, restructuring and so on. For example in the case of an acquisition:

- finance may have been involved in undertaking the assessments that are needed before a company can be acquired;
- production will have needed to consider the type and age of production facilities that have been purchased;
- marketing will make an assessment of the strength and relevance of any brand names that might have been purchased along with the source and stability of the sales from the newly-acquired company;
- Human resources will wish to assess the quality, skills and culture of employees in the company that has been acquired and estimate the changes that will be necessary for its new owners.

Corporate strategy is concerned with the overall direction of the company, rather than individual functional areas. However, it is bound to be influenced by aspects of the individual functions: for example, the Electrolux objective of gaining a leading market share in its main markets is bound to have an impact on marketing, who have the responsibility for share building, and finance, who will need to make the appropriate funds available. Production will also be involved because of the need to rationalise plant and human resources will be concerned with the implications for people in the organisation: redundancy, training, new employees and so on. All must make a contribution to the corporate strategy of the company.

4. Are there any areas of the Electrolux strategy that are perhaps not fully covered in the 1993 Report that you would consider to be important?

The strategy areas not fully covered in the 1993 Electrolux report concern such matters as the future for some existing businesses which do not seem to fit with its international ambitions, such as garden equipment, its employee policies as it expands and where and how it will gain competitive advantage beyond mere size in the market place.

Corporate Strategy Lecturer's Guide, Pitman Publishing
© Aldersgate Consultancy Limited 1997

Chapter 2
A review of theory and practice

Synopsis of chapter

The chapter has three main parts. The first traces the development of corporate strategy over the twentieth century and relates it to changes in the environment. The second explores the main elements of the prescriptive and emergent approaches to strategy development. Finally, the two approaches are explored in more detail with some of the main theories associated with each of these being outlined.

Summary

- Prescriptive and emergent strategies can be contrasted by adapting Mintzberg's analogy:

  Prescriptive strategy is Biblical in its approach: it appears at a point in time and is governed by a set of rules, fully formulated and ready to implement.

  Emergent strategy is Darwinian in its approach: an emerging and changing strategy that survives by adapting as the environment itself changes.

- Given the need for an organisation to have a corporate strategy, much of this chapter is really about the *process* of achieving this strategy. As has been demonstrated, there is no common agreement on the way this can be done.

- At one extreme, there is the *prescriptive* process which involves a structured strategic planning system. There is a need to identify objectives, analyse the environment and the resources of the organisation, develop strategy options and select among them. The selected process is then implemented. There are writers who caution against having a system that is too rigid and incapable of taking into account the people element in strategy.

- At the other extreme, there is the *emergent* process that does not identify a final objective with specific strategies to achieve this. It relies on developing strategies whose final outcome may not be known. They will rely more on trial and error and experimentation to achieve the optimal process.

- In the early part of the twentieth century when industrialisation was proceeding fast, the prescriptive process was the main recommended route. As organisations came to recognise the people element and its importance to strategic development during the middle part of the century, emergent strategies were given greater prominence. In recent years, emphasis has switched between market-based routes and resource-based routes in the development of strategy. Social and cultural issues have also become more important as markets and production have become increasingly global in scale.

- Within the *prescriptive* route, three main groups of strategic theory have been identified:

  - *the profit maximising, market-based route*: the market place is vital to profit delivery;
  - *the resource-based route*: the resources of the organisation are important in developing corporate strategy;
  - *the socio-cultural-based route*: this focusses on the social and cultural dimensions of the organisation, especially for its international implications.

  Each of these has different perspectives on the development of strategy.

- Within the emergent route, three main groups were also distinguished:

  - *the survival-based route*: this emphasises the "survival of the fittest" in the jungle of the market place;
  - *the uncertainty-based route*: this regards prediction as impossible because of the inherently unstable nature of the environment;
  - *the human resource-based route*: this places the emphasis on *people* in strategic development. Motivation, politics, culture and the desires of the individual are all important. Strategy may involve an element of experimentation and learning in order to take into account all these factors.

Possible lecture structure

Based on the *learning outcomes* from the beginning of the chapter:

- Outline the political and economic background to the development of corporate strategy in the twentieth century: outline chart follows.
- Describe and evaluate prescriptive strategic practice: use Figure 2.1.
- Describe and evaluate emergent strategic practice: use Figure 2.3.
- Identify the main theories associated with *prescriptive* corporate strategy: use Figures 2.4, 2.5, 2.6.
- Identify the main theories associated with *emergent* corporate strategy: use Figures 2.7, 2.8, 2.9.

Strategic project

The food industry is characterised by slower levels of growth. Organisation cultures are also more settled and traditional. However, tastes have become more international and the food industry has been attacked both by new technologies and by the power of the retail supermarkets in many western countries. These issues could easily be explored in such a project.

Corporate Strategy Lecturer's Guide, Pitman Publishing
© Aldersgate Consultancy Limited 1997

Possible conclusions on corporate strategy from its development during the twentieth century

- Corporate strategy responds to the environment existing or developing at that time.

- The early twentieth century was characterised by the greater use of science and technology. This was reflected in greater structuring of management and strategy. Mass production of quality products became possible.

- In the mid-twentieth century, the accelerated rate of technological change and greater spread of wealth led to new demands for formal strategy development.

  In the late twentieth century, there were four distinct pressures on corporate strategy:

  - free market competition
  - the rise of the Asia-Pacific economies
  - global competition
  - greater knowledge and training of managers and employees

  All four elements in the environment have directed the development of corporate strategy.

Case notes

Attacking a dominant competitor: a joint venture strategy by Nestlé and General Mills

Using the description of prescriptive and emergent strategies from Chapter 1 (and Chapter 2 if you need it), decide the following: was CP pursuing a prescriptive strategy, an emergent strategy or both?

Prescriptive strategy elements

- Quantified objectives, such as a 20 per cent share of the European market by the year 2000.

- Background analysis of different markets.

- Common products and branding across many markets with a centralised joint venture HQ.

Emergent strategy elements

- Variation of product ranges to keep Kelloggs guessing and to suit local tastes.

- Different market entry methods that were adjusted to suit the individual markets and strategic opportunities, e.g. acquisitions in the UK and Poland but new product launches in many other countries.

- Continued desire to adapt to local market opportunities, tastes and circumstances within the context of the global brand, Nestlé, and the global product range 'Golden Grahams', 'Cheerios', etc.

Conclusion: the company was adopting elements from *both* approaches.

Corporate Strategy Lecturer's Guide, Pitman Publishing
© Aldersgate Consultancy Limited 1997

Prescriptive strategic planning at Spillers plc

At the time of the case in 1979, prescriptive strategic processes were regarded as an important part of corporate strategy. Even in the late 1990s, many companies still operate some form of planning process that is not dissimilar to that introduced at Spillers. Chapter 19 describes such processes at three more companies and the Cereal Partners company from the beginning of Chapter 2 also successfully operates a form of strategic planning. The introduction of strategic planning at Spillers was an important new initiative that was probably in advance of many companies. However, this is not to deny that there can be significant weaknesses in such an approach.

1. Using Mintzberg's critique of prescriptive processes, what are the main weaknesses of the Spillers' proposals?

Exploration of the following possible areas of weakness:

Assumption that the future could be predicted: this was a problem when investment was needed in a new venture over several years such as that at Reading Abattoir. If circumstances changed, then the investment might be wasted. However, this needed to be set against the difficulty that some investments take this length of time to develop. In the case of the food industry, markets were relatively predictable and the assumption was workable. However, in other markets such as computers, such an assumption would be more dubious.

Better to forgo the short-term benefit: Spillers had been largely planning on a short-term basis up to that point, so the prescriptive approach was a new departure. It was probably beneficial for the reasons given in the case.

Strategies logical and capable of being managed as proposed: this is a real area of weakness as the Spillers main board only had limited information on the individual groups.

The Chief Executive Officer has the knowledge and power to choose between options: the case claims that rational debate was possible for the first time as a result of introducing the new system. In the case of Spillers, this is probably correct but it still needs to be tempered by a realisation that not all the facts will be readily available at the centre.

Strategic decisions do not require to be modified as the environment changes: in any fast-moving market, this is unlikely to be valid. Even at Spillers in the slow-moving food industry, there were areas such as the Restaurant group where the situation could change with new competition opening up or the surrounding area being redeveloped. Prescriptive approaches are always open to this criticism.

Implementation is separate and distinctive: the Spillers planning process was geared to the initial decision but really needed to have much more involvement as the strategy then unfolded. This was a weakness, however; the system was new and could be adapted.

2. Bearing these in mind, was it a worthwhile exercise for Spillers in your judgement?

Given the previous total lack of information at the centre and the resource demands being made upon it, the exercise was certainly worthwhile. It was possibly over-elaborate, possibly incomplete. It would certainly have needed modification over the years.

The really surprising aspect was that Spillers could have muddled along for many years without some mechanism for allocating resources. Perhaps the centre was contributing little and not really required at all: the parts of the group would have been better floated off as independent companies. As an alternative strategy, this would certainly have been worth investigating.

Note: Because of the nature of the question, no suggested answer has been provided in this Guide for Case study 2.2 Prescriptive strategy at Otto Versand.

Corporate Strategy Lecturer's Guide, Pitman Publishing
© Aldersgate Consultancy Limited 1997

Emergent strategy at Spillers Baking

The case examines a fierce competitive battle that took place over nearly ten years. Spillers was the underdog in this process. Its strategies were essentially to copy the moves made by its larger competitors. However, it had neither the resources nor the skills to make a success of such an approach. Over a ten-year period, it tried three different strategies with the third one - divestment - being forced upon it when the other two failed.

1. The Spillers' emergent approach to strategy development required at least a year to elapse between each phase. What might be the reasons for this? Are there any disadvantages in this timing from a strategic perspective?

The reasons were that it was simply not possible to develop and implement a new strategy overnight. Large companies with substantial investment cannot be suddenly adjusted: new plant has to be ordered and installed, workers have to be trained and so on. Even the later phases of development required time for them to be undertaken: for example, it took months of negotiation for the divestment strategy to be completed.

The obvious disadvantage is that it is not possible to respond immediately to market change. Large oil tankers change course slowly. Crafting emergent strategy needs to be both imaginative, which following the market leader clearly was not, and flexible. Such flexibility is difficult in industries that have large amounts of capital and plant.

2. Critically evaluate the Spillers Bakeries' strategies during the 1970s. Was the company wise to spend nearly ten years pouring funds into such an operation? What would you have done?

The strategies were clearly unsuccessful. The key decision was that made to merge with rivals in 1970. Once this move was made, the die was cast and the company was forced into a series of moves that were increasingly desperate over the period. With all the wisdom of hindsight, this was the wrong strategic decision.

An alternative strategy might have been to break up the company and turn it into a series of smaller, more responsive bakeries. This might have worked but for the constant pressure from a highly aggressive market leader and for the time required. It is arguably a real weakness of emergent strategic processes that they assume that organisations can respond quickly to market change and competitive pressure.

Dalgety corporate strategy continues

1. For much of this period, Dalgety concentrated on acquisitions. Is this approach prescriptive or emergent?

It depends on the nature of the acquisitions. If they follow a logical pattern such as those to build market share at Electrolux (*see* Chapter 1), then there is clearly a master-plan and overall objective associated with a dominant market share that would be prescriptive in its approach. If there is little pattern other than to seize market or business opportunities as they occur, then this is much more likely to be emergent.

Within this approach, can you identify any particular strategy route? What does this tell you about the Dalgety strategy?

Dalgety clearly kept within the food industry in the broadest sense. For example, it never acquired steel mills or car companies. However, its acquisitions during the 1980s, even in the food industry, appeared haphazard and opportunistic to many outside commentators. There was no attempt to build economies of scale or strength in particular areas of business. It was only towards the end of the decade and into the 1990s that the company decided to focus on what it called three core areas. Even then, pig breeding and animal feeds required quite different skills and expertise so it is arguable that the company was still muddled.

This all adds up to a strategy that was ill-defined for a lengthy period during the 1980s. It was probably neither prescriptive nor emergent, just lacking in focus. In fairness, it should be said that the strategy for the 1990s now has much greater direction based on the three (or four) core areas. It is being pursued with a much greater sense of vision and determination.

2. During the 1990s, Dalgety decided to concentrate on 'three legs'. What is the main danger that comes from focussing its strategic resources?

The main danger is that it picks the wrong areas and one of the three legs fails. As soon as resources are concentrated in a few product categories rather than spread across many, the areas chosen may be inherently weak or overtaken by technology. For example, any company relying on animal feeds will undoubtedly suffer if cattle have to be slaughtered and no longer require feeding. The Europe-wide BSE crisis of 1994 onwards will impact on the strategic decision by Dalgety to concentrate partly in this area, even though it was made with the best information available at the time in the late 1980s.

Corporate Strategy Lecturer's Guide, Pitman Publishing
© Aldersgate Consultancy Limited 1997

Strategy at Saes Getters

This company was for many years a *one-product company* with all the strategic risks associated with that approach. For a small company in an industry where economies of scale and product innovation are important, the strategy of concentrating resources may be a risk worth taking. In the case of the Saes company, this was clearly the case. However, it should be recognised in assessing the strategy that there was a risk involved.

1. How would you categorise the company's strategy?

With its focus on a small part of every television and its investment in further low-cost development, it is certainly prescriptive.

In addition, it appears to have a high percentage share of the small and specialised market for *getters*. It has used its high share and its innovative technology to develop new products with higher performance and lower costs than its customers can make for themselves. This combination of strategies might place it in two areas within the general prescriptive approach:

- profit-maximising, competition-based strategy;
- resources-based strategy.

It is probable that the company uses both approaches, but the sheer concentration of the one-product company suggests that it is resources that are the crucial ingredient in its undoubted success.

2. What are the implications for its future strategy development?

The company has already recognised the need to diversify so that it is not so reliant on a single item, the *getter*, that may well disappear from televisions over the next ten years. This is one area of future strategy.

The issue then becomes *how* it diversifies. According to the resource-based approach, it should analyse carefully the skills and resources that it possesses and attempt to utilise these in its search for new products. This may need a leap of imagination and creativity for success: the emergent strategic approach has much to commend it to the company.

Chapter 3
Analysing the environment

Synopsis of chapter

The chapter presents the main elements of an analysis of the environment. It identifies six areas that will be familiar to most lecturers:

- Basic environmental influences
- PEST Analysis
- Key Factors for Success
- Five Forces analysis
- Competitor profile and portfolio analysis (growth/share matrix)
- Customer analysis.

This is a summary chapter which is then developed in more depth in the following three chapters.

Lecturers may like to note that *Key Factors for Success* are explored further in Chapter 7 because they also relate to the resources of the organisation. Any reference here could usefully be coupled with a comment on a return to the same topic later.

Summary

In analysing the environment surrounding the organisation, six main factors are important:

- *A general consideration of the nature of the environment and, in particular, the degree of turbulence.* When events are particularly uncertain and prone to sudden and significant change, corporate strategy needs to become more flexible and organise its procedures to cope with the situation.

- *A general analysis of the factors that will affect many industries.* This can be undertaken by using two procedures: the PEST analysis and scenarios. The PEST analysis explores political, economic, socio-cultural and technological influences on the organisation. It is important when undertaking such an analysis to develop a shortlist of only the most important items, not a long list under every heading. In developing scenarios, it should be recognised that they provide a *different view* of conceivable future events, rather than predict the future.

- *The identification of the key factors for success.* Moving toward an analysis of the environment surrounding the organisation itself, it is useful to establish the key factors for success in the industry (not the organisation). This also requires a consideration of the resources of the organisation (see Chapter 7).

Corporate Strategy Lecturer's Guide, Pitman Publishing
© Aldersgate Consultancy Limited 1997

- *A Five Forces analysis*. This will involve an examination of buyers, suppliers, new entrants, substitutes and the competition in the industry. The aim is to analyse the balance of power between each force and the organisation in the industry.

- A *product portfolio analysis*. This plots market growth and relative market share for the organisation's main group of products. It identifies four major categories of products: stars, cash cows, dogs and problem children. It permits some consideration of their contribution to the organisation and a comparison with competition.

- *A study of customers*. This final area of analysis is concerned with actual and potential customers and their importance to the organisation. Segmentation of markets derives from customer analysis and plays an important role in corporate strategy development.

Possible lecture structure

Essentially, there are a number of concepts that analyse the environment which need to be explained:

- Explore the *main environmental forces* surrounding the organisation and relate the degree of change to prescriptive and emergent strategic approaches: use the Usinor-Sacilor material to illustrate the points: see the chart on page 22 of this *Guide*.
- Summarise the main elements of the topic: use Figure 3.1. Comment on prescriptive and emergent approaches: *predictable* environment in the prescriptive approach, *understanding* the environment, but no prediction in the emergent.
- Undertake a *PEST analysis* of the general influences on the organisation: use Exhibit 3.1, making the point about the weaknesses of checklists.
- Understand the importance of *key factors for success* in the environment. You may wish to make only a brief reference to this and return to it in the context of the analysis of resources in Chapter 7.
- Carry out a *Five Forces analysis* of the specific influences on the organisation. Use Figure 3.3. Probably worth taking some time to explain and explore this area.
- Explain the *competitor profile analysis:* see the chart on page 23.
- Outline the *product portfolio analysis* of the organisation and its competitors. Use Figure 3.4.
- Explore the *customers* and their relationship with the organisation: see the chart on page 24.

Strategic project

Massive production overcapacity, cyclical markets, traditional working practices, organisation cultures that have only changed slowly, the threat of cheap international steel and of new, smaller steel plant: all these represent possible themes in this area. Many European countries have leading iron and steel companies: page 188 of my book *European Business Strategies*, 2nd edition, Kogan Page, lists these and possibly provides a starting point for a strategic study.

Environmental influences surrounding the organisation

Changeability: the degree to which the environment is likely to change

Changeability comprises:

- *Complexity*: the degree to which the organisation's environment is affected by such factors as internationalisation and technological, social and political issues

- *Novelty*: the degree to which the environment presents the organisation with new situations

Predictability: the degree to which such changes can be predicted

Predictability compromises:

- *Rate of change* of the environment from slow to fast

- *Visibility of the future* in terms of the availability and usefulness of the information used to predict the future

Corporate Strategy Lecturer's Guide, Pitman Publishing
© Aldersgate Consultancy Limited 1997

Competitor profile analysis

The following aspects of the competitor's organisation need to be explored:

- Objectives

- Resources

- Past record of performance

- Current products and services

- Present strategies

Customer analysis

Main considerations:

- **Identification of the customer and the market**

  Immediate customer base

  Wider customer franchise

- **Market segmentation and its strategic implications**

  Market segmentation: the identification of specific parts of a market and the development of different market offerings that will be attractive to those segments

  Strategic implications: strength in a segment may deliver competitive advantage

- **Role of customer service and quality**

  Superior service may deliver competitive advantage

  Superior quality, as perceived by the customer, may also deliver real advantages

Corporate Strategy Lecturer's Guide, Pitman Publishing
© Aldersgate Consultancy Limited 1997

Case notes

Usinor-Sacilor copes with a difficult environment

Most of the major European steel companies have major investment in plant and machinery: making steel is a capital-intensive business. Profits are made when the machinery is utilised as near as possible to its capacity. Losses are made when it is not possible to run the plant at capacity, because plant such as a blast furnace can only be run at full power and there are heavy fixed costs which need active working to recover them. This makes steel plant exceptionally vulnerable to changes in the environment: it can move from healthy profit to significant loss with relatively small changes in factors outside the company.

1. What were the main changes in the environment of Usinor-Sacilor? What was their impact on company strategy?

The main environmental changes and their impact on strategy were:

- **Economic downturn**
  Impact: attempt to reduce the number of workers so that costs were reduced. Also retrain those that remained so that they were more skilled and the company culture was more flexible.

- **European Union and national government interference**
  Impact: negotiate with the French national government and the EU to attempt to obtain extra support as workers were made redundant. A further point is made in Case 3.1 about steel: the competition from other EU steel producers that do not need to make a profit because they are subsidised by the state. Companies such as Usinor-Sacilor attempted to influence the EU to have the subsidised companies closed down. This is a part of corporate strategy.

- **Major changes in technology**
  Impact: Usinor-Sacilor invested in new technology when it had the funds but was clearly reliant on its shareholders such as the French government for support. Nevertheless, the company made a start in this area.

- **Increasing low-cost competition from outside Western Europe**
  Impact: potentially an important threat to the company. Negotiations with the EU and with the French government to restrict imports of steel would reduce the level of competition. The company also decided to develop its product range so that it no longer competed directly against the low-cost producers. It undertook this by a series of acquisitions, alliances and new product launches that took it into special steels where low-cost production was not so important and it could charge higher prices for its special products.

2. Which single factor seems to have been more important than any other? What implications, if any, does this have for corporate strategy at the company?

From all the many factors, the evidence suggests that the company moved back into profit as the steel market moved into a cyclical upswing in 1994. This suggests that the most important factor is change in the economy in the countries in which the company is operating. In this case, the French economy was probably the most important environmental factor likely to influence its profits because the majority of its sales were in France.

The implication for corporate strategy is that it is important for the company:

- *either* to understand and work with the changes in the French economic cycle
- *and/or* to move outside France so that its sales are less dependent on that country.

Strategy might therefore be adjusted to build more flexible French capacity that could be adjusted as the economy changed. It might also seek acquisitions and other entry into such countries as Germany and the USA which follow their own cycles of development. In fact, Usinor-Sacilor acquired both German and American companies in deals in the early 1990s.

Corporate Strategy Lecturer's Guide, Pitman Publishing
© Aldersgate Consultancy Limited 1997

Steeled for global action

The case explores the possibility of steel companies selling their products in one global market, rather than relying on regional markets that are protected behind trade barriers.

1. What particular aspects of the environment does the case highlight?

- Government involvement
- Government ownership and investment in the industry
- Relationship to economic growth
- Ability of currency fluctuation significantly to alter profitability
- Possibility that technology may have a strong bearing on future strategies

*2. According to the case, the main alternative to **national** steel companies is the **global** steel company. What arguments and data, if any, does the case contain to justify this position? Given the case is only a summary of a more detailed analysis, what would you expect such an analysis to contain?*

The arguments to justify the global company are the trend towards privatisation, the changing nature of the steel market and the growing importance of developing countries. However, there is little convincing argument, rather a description of the moves to privatisation and the growth of steel manufacture in developing countries. There is also little data in the case to justify the global steel company.

More data is needed on steel production, steel demand, barriers to trade, labour costs and competitive plans for steel investment. It would require a major analysis to assess the full impact. In fairness, this is simply not possible in a limited case.

3. The case argues that one of the problems in the European steel industry is production over-capacity. How does the case suggest that the strategy of moving onto a global scale can help overcome this problem? Do you find this strategy persuasive?

The case argues that over-capacity has arisen at least partially out of the government subsidies that have allowed inefficient steel companies to survive. As privatisation has been introduced, so such companies will be forced to reduce their capacity and modernise in order to survive in a free market. All this will make the European steel industry more able to compete in world markets.

What the companies making this argument fail to recognise is the substantial differences in wage costs between Europe and some developing countries. In bulk chemicals, it is this problem that has forced much of the world's production to shift to Asia-Pacific. The same may well apply to steel, which has some of the same structural characteristics: heavy plant investment, labour costs as an important element of total costs, relatively limited technology, and transport costs which are only one element of the total cost picture. The strategy is not persuasive.

Benefon keeps in touch

1. Given the limited resources and geographical spread of Benefon, how would you approach the task of analysing the environment for corporate strategy development? What process would you recommend and what data would you collect?

With a fast growing environment such as mobile telephones, it is important to recognise that it is highly *changeable*. However, it is arguably not complex in the sense that the main elements are understood but it could still be subject to novelty as new technologies are developed and refined. For similar reasons, the environment is probably fairly *predictable*, even though there is a fast rate of change with the future being reasonably visible.

Having established this situation, it would then be appropriate to identify the underlying causes. This could take the form of the PEST analysis and Five Forces analysis shown in outline below. Importantly given the small size of the Benefon market share, it will be necessary to consider competition carefully in terms of its likely impact on the company. The wide geographical spread and the limited resources to undertake any analysis suggest that it would be quite unrealistic to expect a detailed analysis of every market.

2. Undertake a PEST analysis and a Five Forces analysis for this company's future development.

PEST analysis
Probably the two most important factors are:

- the pace of economic development because the company relies so heavily on high-priced mobile telephones, which rely in turn on economic growth;
- the rate of technological change, because this could either undermine the company or provide real competitive advantage over the next few years.

Five Forces analysis
In brief:

- Competition is clearly high.
- Buyer bargaining power is probably medium to low because of its fragmented nature.
- Supplier bargaining power may be high in some cases: there is insufficient information in the case to be sure. There may be some items that the company buys in and relies upon that are exclusive to one or a few suppliers.
- Potential entrants pose some threat. However, the market is growing so fast that they are unlikely to be anything more than an irritant at this stage, unless they possess totally new technology.
- Substitutes: some alternative forms of telephone and radio communication could form a real threat here, especially as Benefon's prices are high.

Corporate Strategy Lecturer's Guide, Pitman Publishing
© Aldersgate Consultancy Limited 1997

3. From the many possible environmental factors, choose the three *which you consider to be the most significant in preparing a corporate plan. Why?*

Given the small size of the company and its need to position itself at the high quality end of the market, the three items might be:

- the economic development;
- totally new technologies; and
- new equally high-priced competitors.

However, it should be noted that there are no conclusive answers in the above. Turbulence makes the environment essentially partially unpredictable.

Chapter 4
Analysing the market

Synopsis of chapter

The chapter covers three main areas that, purely for learning purposes, have been summarised under the letter 'G'. *Growth issues* explore the strategic implications of growing and mature markets through the product life cycle. *Government issues* examine the relationships between government and corporate strategy. *Global issues* investigate global and international issues in the environment and their impact on corporate strategy.

Summary

In any market analysis, the chapter identified three key areas for investigation: growth characteristics, government influence and global trends.

- *Growth characteristics* can be explored using the industry life cycle concept. Markets are divided into a series of development stages: introduction, growth, maturity and decline. In addition, the maturity stage may be subject to the cyclical variations associated with general economic activity or other factors over which the company has little control.

- Different stages of the life cycle demand different corporate strategies. The early stages probably require greater investment in R&D and marketing to develop and explain the product. The later stages should be more profitable on a conventional view of the life cycle. However, there is an argument that takes a more unconventional stance: it suggests that it is during the mature phase that investment should increase in order to restore growth.

- The *role of government* can be seen through its involvement in both political and economic issues. Politics has been an important driver of industrial growth. Corporate strategy needs to consider the opportunities and difficulties that derive from such government influences. Government policies can be broadly classified as *laissez-faire*, free-market, or *dirigiste*, more centrally directed. More specifically, policies on such matters as public expenditure, competition and taxation will all influence organisations and their corporate strategies. Organisations may wish to develop links and influence government policy on relevant aspects of corporate strategy.

- Government policies also influence national economic growth and may affect the market growth of particular sectors. Both these areas need careful study when developing strategy.

- Over the last ten years, *global trade* has increased faster than manufacturing output: countries are trading more with each other. It has come to represent a significant factor in corporate strategy.

- Theories of international trade provide a framework within which to develop corporate strategy. The role of government in providing economic stability and sound infrastructure development has been emphasised. To stimulate growth, governments also need to encourage an increasingly competitive home market with low barriers to international trade. Corporate strategy needs to identify the relevant trends in its own product groups.

- In developing international corporate strategy, one of the main issues is the relationship of the state with companies. State support and encouragement may be both beneficial and problematical for individual companies. In international markets, companies may also wish to develop relationships with governments as part of the development of corporate strategy.

Possible lecture structure

- Summarise the main elements of the topic: use Figure 4.1. Comment that both prescriptive and emergent approaches desire to understand the market better.
- Explain the implications of market growth and maturity for corporate strategy: use the product life cycle, Figure 4.2. Emphasise the strategic implications of *early market entry* into new markets, *market share fragmentation* as markets mature and the possibility of *different strategies for different market segments*.
- Identify the specific strategic issues associated with cyclicality in a market: use Figure 4.4.
- Outline the role that governments can play in the development of corporate strategy: see the two charts that follow this page.
- Examine the inter-relationships between governments, nations and companies in the development of global corporate strategy: see the chart that follows on page 34.
- Identify the main elements of an analysis of international markets.

Strategic project

Strategic areas of investigation might include: cyclical markets, specialisation in profitable product categories, the involvement of governments in company investment and takeover decisions, new technology. From an international competitive perspective, it may be more appropriate to identify three areas of the world: the Americas, Europe, Asia-Pacific. One aspect that might warrant further investigation is the use of the takeover mechanism to build economies of scale, market share, market dominance, etc. over the last twenty years: *European Business Strategies*, 2nd edition, Kogan Page, Chapter 21, will provide a starting point.

Five political trends that have affected corporate strategy

- The decline of the centrally directed command economies of Eastern Europe coupled with the move towards democracy and freer markets.

- The absence of world wars and the more recent end of the Cold War.

- The relative weakness of African and South/Central American economies.

- The rise of international trade, global companies and new trading nations.

- The emergence of supportive international finance and economic institutions such as the World Bank and International Monetary Fund.

Corporate Strategy Lecturer's Guide, Pitman Publishing
© Aldersgate Consultancy Limited 1997

Government and industrial policy

Basic policy

- *Laissez faire*: free-market approach

- *Dirigiste*: centrally directed approach

Broader aspects of government policy and state institutions

- *Public expenditure*

- *Competition policy*

- *Taxation policy*

- *Regional policy*

Analysis needed at two levels

- *National economy on macroeconomic level*: to determine economic growth, inflation and policy

- *Industry level*: to establish government attitudes to specific industries

Global developments and their relationship with corporate strategy

- Over the last ten years, global trade has increased faster than manufacturing output. International trade has become a driver of output for companies.

- Theories of international trade and the development of nations provide the framework within which to analyse corporate strategy:

  - *Theory of comparative advantage*

  - *Competitive advantage of nations* (Porter): four main factors plus government policy and chance

  - *Limited state intervention* (World Bank) to develop the infrastructure and open competition

- Global political developments have enhanced world trade over the last 25 years, e.g. GATT Uruguay Round negotiations. Corporate strategy needs to analyse and determine the relevant trends for its relevant product groups or businesses.

Corporate Strategy Lecturer's Guide, Pitman Publishing
© Aldersgate Consultancy Limited 1997

Case notes

Stora expands through acquisition and internal growth

In the early 1980s, Stora set itself the task of becoming Europe's largest pulp and paper company. By 1995, it was the second largest and had achieved major growth in sales over the intervening period of years.

1. How important was the objective for Stora's strategy development? Should the company be disappointed that it was still only the second largest?

From the strategies pursued by the company over the period since the objective was agreed, it is evident that the target focussed the company on its future in a dramatic and realistic way. The company has been quite single-minded in its pursuit of its objective to become Europe's largest pulp and paper company. The strategies have all largely been focussed in this area, e.g. acquisitions and divestments.

In spite of the objective, it was overtaken during the 1990s by the Finnish company, UPM/Kymmene. There is always the possibility in strategic development that the unexpected will happen: in this case, the merger of two major rivals. The development could not have been halted by Stora, so it cannot really have been disappointed that the precise objective was not achieved.

Importantly in analysing Stora, it should be recognised that *size itself is no guarantee of business success*, even in the pulp and paper industry. To be the largest company in an industry in cyclical markets and amidst fierce competition will assist survival, but it will not ensure it. Large companies can still be unprofitable. An exploration of why and how such an objective was set is therefore important but is beyond the scope of the case material.

2. Is growth important in itself in corporate strategy? Give reasons for your views.

Growth is useful in corporate strategy because it provides opportunities for renewal and development. Some commentators argue that growth is essential but this will depend on the size of the business and the nature of the ownership. For example, if a business is small, has a single owner who is satisfied with a low-growth objective and has no desire to expand, then growth may not be important.

However, for many companies growth is useful. Shareholders, managers and employees may all desire growth, even if their reasons do not necessarily coincide. For example, shareholders may want to see their investment grow, managers may like the concept of managing larger enterprises and employees may obtain easier promotion if new growth opportunities are created. In the case of Stora, the reasons for setting a growth objective are given at the beginning of the case.

Coping with politics after apartheid

1. Should Shell South Africa seek actively to support the end of the controlled market on the basis that it is well placed to make higher profits, or should its policy simply be to accept what is decided by the government?

As with much of corporate strategy, there are merits in both approaches and it is not easy to decide the best route forward. Reasons for actively supporting the end of the controlled market might be:

- The company has a large market share and is therefore able to benefit from any relaxation.
- If lower controls are inevitable, then those companies especially able to benefit should encourage it to happen sooner.

Arguments against might include:

- The current market is profitable so that it makes no sense to encourage the demise of such a regime.
- The government might regard it as unwarranted interference in its policy making role if the company were to attempt to influence events.
- The consequences of such an important change are not entirely clear and carry some risk.

2. How will this influence its corporate strategy?

Clearly, relationships with the government have been important for the company over the last few years. This is typical of many companies around the world and is not unique to South Africa.

Because the government is clearly an important determinant of company profitability, the corporate strategy of the company will therefore need to involve close contact with the government and an attempt to influence it. Such a situation is typical of many companies that either have the government as customers, e.g. health and defence, or have the government as a major sponsor of industry development initiatives, e.g. information technology. There may even be occasions where government funds are an important determinant of research policy.

Corporate Strategy Lecturer's Guide, Pitman Publishing
© Aldersgate Consultancy Limited 1997

Corporate strategy in the world paper and pulp industry

This is a lengthy case that can be explored in a number of ways. These notes focus only on the case questions and would benefit from further exploration than is possible here.

1. Which of the possible strategies in the industry were followed by Stora?

Stora made a series of *acquisitions* in the 1980s and 1990s. They included companies involved in every aspect of the generation of added value as pulp and paper are manufactured: forests, pulp, specialist papers, distribution of paper products, etc. The company was aiming to build economies of scale and market strength in its chosen markets.

Other strategies included:

- *building distribution strength* through the acquisition of distributors in order to counter the bargaining power of customers;
- *investment in modern plant* so that costs could be reduced below those of competitors;
- *the development of new higher added-value products* in order to move away from those with low margins and develop competitive advantage.

2. In which strategic areas will it be important to gain government involvement? How would you approach this task?

Government involvement is often necessary for acquisitions if significant market share is acquired. There is a concern that a company may come to dominate the market and restrict free competition. National government offices such as the Monopolies Commission in the UK and the Bundeskartelamt in Germany may be involved. For larger activities inside the European Union, the European Commission itself has responsibility. Other countries around the world have similar institutions.

In addition, governments can also be useful in many other areas: investment in infrastructure projects such as transport or telecommunications, education and training of employees, taxation issues and protection of home industries from foreign competition may all be important.

The task of obtaining government involvement often starts with lobbying the government on an informal basis. It may also involve working with an industry-wide trade institution to represent views more formally.

3. Most pulp and paper companies are strong in regions of the world. Is there a case for developing a global strategy? What elements might it contain?

Global strategy has to involve real commercial benefits. In some markets such as cars and soft drinks, such advantages can be identified: for example, cost savings that arise from economies of scale in development (see Case 20.2 on Ford) or in global branding such as Sony (see Chapter 18, Minicase). There are also costs involved in global strategy: for example, the costs of coordination and communications between the various parts of the world. In the case of pulp and paper, it is not at all clear that the benefits will outweigh the costs because of the high cost of transport for some heavy paper products around the world. However, certain *branded* paper products certainly justify such costs because the profit margins are usually higher on branded products: one example is the market for disposable baby paper nappies (diapers in North America). *Pampers* from Procter & Gamble and similar brands from other manufacturers are certainly available globally.

Corporate Strategy Lecturer's Guide, Pitman Publishing
© Aldersgate Consultancy Limited 1997

Chapter 5
Analysing competitors

Synopsis of chapter

The chapter examines *six subjects* relating to competition: competitive advantage, the intensity of competition in an industry, aggressive competitive strategies (competitive warfare), strategic groups within an industry, individual competitor analysis, distributor analysis.

Summary

- *Sustainable competitive advantage* has been placed at the centre of the development of corporate strategy. The real benefits of developing this area derive from those aspects of the organisation that cannot easily be imitated and can be sustained over time. Such advantages can take many forms: differentiation, low costs, niche marketing, high performance or technology, quality, service, vertical integration, synergy and the culture, leadership and style of the organisation.

- In exploring the intensity of competition in an industry, it is useful to commence by exploring the *degree of concentration* in a market. This may range from perfect competition to pure monopoly. The concentration ratio itself can also be calculated: it is the percentage of an industry turnover or value added controlled by the largest four, five or eight firms.

- Military language and concepts are often used to describe the *aggressive strategies* of competitors. The four main attack strategies are: head-on, flanking, totally new territory and guerrilla. In addition, *innovatory strategies* may be employed, especially those that rewrite the rules of the game in a market.

- Within the context of competitive analysis, it is often helpful to explore groups of immediate competitors more extensively: the *analysis of strategic groups*. In addition, it is usually useful to identify one or more *immediate competitors* for detailed analysis. Such a study will examine the competitor's market share, resources, cost structures, objectives and current strategies.

- Another area of investigation is that concerning *distributors*, i.e. those companies that purchase the product and then resell it to small end-consumers. In some markets, distributors are a vital part of the chain of sale and need to be analysed in detail: service levels, quality, pricing and discounts and the support from the distributor are subjects for investigation.

- *International competition* has increased over the last twenty years. This has taken many forms but three areas can be usefully highlighted: the ambition of some companies for global expansion; low costs through careful sourcing of production; and global strategies to integrate worldwide operations.

Possible lecture structure

Competitor analysis can usefully begin with a consideration of general concepts before moving to those more specifically related to the industry.

- Begin the lecture by cross-comparison between the fragmented footwear market, the monopolistic telecommunications services market and the oligopolistic grocery retailing market: see Case studies 5.1, 5.2 and 5.3.
- Summarise the main elements of the topic: use Figure 5.1. Comment that the whole approach is probably more *prescriptive* than emergent in its emphasis.
- Explain the importance of sustainable competitive advantage: use the chart that follows.
- Explore the intensity of competition in an industry: reminder of Five Forces analysis coupled with more general comments (or a reminder for those students who have studied microeconomics) on perfect competition and pure monopoly. Explore through concentration ratio: use the chart that follows.
- Assess aggressive competitive strategies: use the overheads for Figure 5.2 and Exhibit 5.2 at the end of this *Guide*. In addition, mention the importance of *innovatory strategies*.
- Analyse strategic groups: use Exhibit 5.3.
- Examination of individual competitors: use the chart from Chapter 3 of this *Guide*.
- Examination and importance of distributors: use the chart that follows.

Strategic project

Unilever, Nestlé and Mars are all developing world businesses: they have been investing in China, the Philippines, Malaysia, the USA and many other countries around the world. Strategies have often been using acquisition as a starting point. Häagen-Dazs and Ben & Jerry Ice Creams are continuing to move into Europe although neither seems to be able to make significant profits up to 1996. Competitive issues include the elements of Porter's Five Forces, the use of attack and defence strategies and the benefits of the uniqueness derived from branding. This particular competitive battle is by no means over.

Corporate Strategy Lecturer's Guide, Pitman Publishing
© Aldersgate Consultancy Limited 1997

Sustainable competitive advantage

- Advantages over competitors that cannot easily be imitated

- Sustainable over time by being deeply embedded in the organisation

Sources:

- Differentiation
- Low costs
- Niche marketing
- High performance or technology
- Superior quality
- Superior service
- Vertical integration
- Synergy
- Culture, leadership and style of an organisation

Intensity of competition in an industry

Measured by:

- Degree of concentration of companies in the industry

- Range of aggressive strategies of competitors in the marketplace

Degree of concentration is often summarised in the *concentration ratio* - the degree to which value added or turnover is concentrated in the hands of a few or a large number of firms in an industry.

Concentration ratio: the percentage of industry value added or turnover controlled by the largest four, five or eight firms in an industry -

the C4, C5 or C8 ratio respectively.

Corporate Strategy Lecturer's Guide, Pitman Publishing
© Aldersgate Consultancy Limited 1997

Distributor analysis

How the product or service is distributed to the customer and the costs that are involved

Strategic opportunity: to distribute the product differently

Strategic problem: to obtain any significant distribution at all for the product

Analysis will cover:

- *Distributor objectives*: beyond price, distributors will specify a level of service, quality and technical support. Distributors will also be seeking to meet their own profit objectives

- *Service levels*

- *Technical and quality specifications*

- *Distributor pricing and discounts*

- *Distributor support for the product or service*: product is often not 'sold' until it has moved off the shelf of the distributor. Promotion can help this process

Case notes

Unilever Ice Cream defends its European market share

1. What is the source of Unilever's advantages over its competitors?

Unilever has three main advantages: its investment over many years in its national brands, its well developed distribution service and its sheer size in the market place, which delivers economies of scale. More recently, the company has been investing in pan-European brands such as *Cornetto*, *Magnum* and *Carte d'Or*. It has also continued to acquire smaller competitors in order to consolidate its hold on the market. It has also launched new products to ensure that it is represented in every segment of the market and no competitor gains a foothold in an undefended segment.

Because of its structure a series of national companies, it is well placed to respond to local customer demand and competitive initiatives.

2. What are Unilever's main strengths? Where do its weaknesses lie? What, if anything, would you do about its weaknesses?

The main strengths are summarised in the outline to Question 1 above. Its weaknesses are:

- its lack of a strong range of branded confectionery which it could turn into ice cream;
- its poor record on product innovation: most of the main initiatives have come from the competition;
- its national company structure which makes it difficult for the company to react quickly to pan-European initiatives.

Investment in confectionery is probably too late for Unilever. The area of product innovation is one that Unilever should address: there is no excuse for its relatively poor record in this area. The national company structure has advantages as well as disadvantages: see above. However, it could perhaps react faster to any pan-European initiatives by its competitors by greater coordination measures from the centre.

3. Should Unilever go further in launching truly pan-European products, like those associated with Mars Ice Cream or Nestlé Kit Kat Ice Cream? How important, if at all, are such products to overall Unilever strategy?

Because of its basic weakness in this area, it is difficult for Unilever. It would probably be more productive for the company to concentrate on its strengths rather than build on its weaknesses so it should not pursue confectionery brands. However, it has the resources to build pan-European ice cream brands like Magnum and should continue to undertake this. Their branding differentiation will provide competitive advantage in the future for the company, even though it has a significant cost in the short term.

Corporate Strategy Lecturer's Guide, Pitman Publishing
© Aldersgate Consultancy Limited 1997

The fragmented European footwear market

1. What strategies would you be seeking, as a small shoe company, to develop sustainable competitive advantage?

In exploring this area, it is useful to use the material developed earlier in the chapter. In addition, it is important to consider the strengths and weaknesses of small companies in a fragmented industry. It is notable that some branded companies now import nearly all their footwear from low labour cost countries. For the purposes of this answer, it is assumed that the small shoe company is located in Europe. However, there is no reason why it should not be a small company located in south-east Asia, such as Indonesia or the Philippines, though in this case it would have even lower labour costs that might allow some further strategies.

Using the items identified in Table 5.2 for small businesses and applying the logic of the shoe industry, we have:

- *Quality*: explore superior quality that larger mass-manufactured shoes cannot match.
- *Prompt service*: offer a level of rapid turnaround on orders that could never be matched by companies producing products thousands of miles away.
- *Personalised service*: offer a level of service that is individual to the customer.
- *Keen prices*: low overheads and the need for branding might help but it will be difficult to compete in the shoe industry against very low labour costs from other countries.
- *Local availability*: develop and deliver products that match local customer demand, e.g. special types of shoes for industry and other local customers.

None of the above is conclusive as a strategy, but several may be worth considering.

2. How does market fragmentation affect corporate strategy for such companies?

Market fragmentation is the division of markets into ever-smaller shares as new companies enter a mature market: see Chapter 4, page 128. Because entry into the footwear market has relatively low costs, many small companies have entered or have only remained in the market by keeping their costs low. In particular, companies have entered from the low labour-cost economies of the Far East. For some European smaller companies, this may lead to a downward spiral that is difficult to exit: as costs are put under greater pressure through fragmentation, there is a tendency to cut back and thus forgo the investment that might pull the company out of the downward pressure. This is not a full description of the mechanism or its strategic consequences but indicates the type of problem that needs to be overcome.

Monopoly in Europe's national telecommunications companies

1. What strategies would you be seeking, as a monopolistic telephone company, to develop sustainable competitive advantage?

It is clearly in the interests of such companies to preserve the monopoly as long as possible. The first strategy has therefore to be to lobby government on this matter. Most of the companies were owned by their respective governments, so the links were close and such activity was also in the interests of the government concerned.

Lobbying was the corporate strategy followed during the 1980s with some success. The fact that customers were paying higher prices than was necessary was not the prime consideration of such companies. In fairness, governments and some companies recognised this issue: the strategy was really buying time for their national monopolies to increase their efficiencies so that they could withstand the blast of greater competition in the 1990s.

2. How might this advantage change as competition opens up across Europe?

During the 1990s as the liberalisation of the market came closer, the strategy needed to shift towards cost cutting and increased efficiency if the companies were to survive. It also encompassed international linkages through joint ventures, etc. in order to service international customers. Case study 17.1 gives more details on this latter point.

In fact, many of the companies listed in the case were also expected to be privatised over this period. This would have the effect of breaking their strong links with their governments and increasing the competitive pressure. There was even more reason to increase efficiencies and lower prices before the competition arrived.

Corporate Strategy Lecturer's Guide, Pitman Publishing
© Aldersgate Consultancy Limited 1997

Oligopoly in European grocery retailing

1. What strategies would you be seeking, as a large grocery retailing company, to develop sustainable competitive advantage?

Where possible, it would be useful to build market share by increasing the concentration even further. This would create further economies of scale and take out the smaller players. In addition, it would be important to retain existing customers since the total market is changing only slowly. In the UK, it would be wise for companies to avoid price competition. In other European countries where price competition was already present, then retailers would probably need to invest in order to keep costs at the lowest possible level. Attempting to differentiate their product range and service may be an insufficient response to a determined price battle.

2. How does the degree of concentration in this industry influence corporate strategy?

Higher grocery concentration has focused the competitive battle and reduced costs. It has also tended to put increased pressure on manufacturing suppliers to cut their prices. It has raised the cost of entry for potential new retailers.

Mars ice cream: distribution strategy problems

1. How would you summarise the strategies adopted by Mars to launch its ice cream products?

- Differentiation through branding
- Building on its strengths in grocery retailing and confectionery branding
- New innovative products
- Premium pricing for higher quality ingredients
- Attempting to buy distribution through licensing or giving away freezers

2. Do you think that Mars will ever make significant profits from its ice cream operations? Why? How?

Taking on the industry giants, the Mars company has several real strategic problems:

- Distribution will never be cheap beyond the large grocery outlets. The way that other companies reduce the costs by selling a wider range of products is not really available to a company that is locked into a narrow, branded-range strategy.

- Product range will always be narrow and may not attract some retail customers, who need a broader range of products that Mars can supply: bulk packs, dessert ice creams, etc.

- Competitors are beginning to develop their own brands that replicate the Mars brand values. Mars itself needs to support its branded ice cream range with advertising but has not been able to generate the profits to justify this.

There is no easy answer to the questions: Mars themselves will be wondering what to do. One solution would be to extend the product range but this would be expensive and against the Mars overall approach. Another would be to seek distribution mainly through grocery outlets but this would reduce total sales.

Nestlé ice cream: attacking through acquisition and branding

1. What are the advantages and disadvantages of the strategies adopted by Nestlé?

- *Advantages*: acquisitions can build market share fast; the company was also building on its strengths in confectionery and food.
- *Disadvantages*: good companies are usually expensive to acquire because of the goodwill payment. Such a strategy is also dependent on companies being available.

2. From Unilever's viewpoint, how would you summarise the main Nestlé strengths and weaknesses?

- *Strengths*: strong share in some European markets, confectionery branding.
- *Weaknesses*: difficult to develop a pan-European operation, many Nestlé operations still unprofitable.

3. Is Nestlé following a clear international strategy, or is it just being opportunistic?

Probably a combination of both. Its international strategy depends on the availability of suitable acquisitions and the funds needed to make such purchases. The clarity of the international strategy would be more convincing if it had acquired companies in the countries where it was clearly weaker or, alternatively, launched its own companies and products in those countries.

Corporate Strategy Lecturer's Guide, Pitman Publishing
© Aldersgate Consultancy Limited 1997

Chapter 6
Analysing customers

Synopsis of the chapter

The chapter has five main themes: the *relationship* of customers to the development of corporate strategy, the *analysis* of customers and market segments, the *communication* with customers, the *pricing/value for money* relationships with customers and the *complex relationship* between customers, products and competitors. There is also an important section on the internationalisation of customer demand and its strategic implications for those involved in international strategy development.

Summary

- Customers are important because they buy the products or services of the organisation and therefore turn its products into profits. At its most basic level, corporate strategy will wish to determine the levels of demand for its goods. In addition, corporate strategy may wish to investigate the customer needs that are currently not being met by existing products: they may provide possible future opportunities. Some companies have oriented their strategy towards developing the customer-driven organisation.

- In analysing customers, both prescriptive and emergent approaches are useful. In addition, customers need to be carefully defined from a broad and a narrow perspective: if this is missed, important areas of customer need and competitor attack may be missed.

- Market segmentation is the identification of specific groups of customers who respond differently from other groups to competitive strategies. The advantages of segmentation in corporate strategy relate to the development of sustainable competitive advantage and to the ability to target products to that segment.

- Communicating with customers is important both to inform them and persuade them about the organisation's products and services. Cost effectiveness is the main criterion when it comes to assessing the methods to employ. Costs are relatively easy to determine but the effects of some forms of promotion may be more difficult to judge.

- Pricing is important because of its short-term impact on profits, because it allows a product to be positioned against others and because it is a measure of the value for money delivered by the organisation. To develop pricing strategy, it is necessary to examine both costs and competitive prices. The result also needs to be balanced with a number of other factors in the market place, such as price elasticity, the position in the product life cycle and the role of pricing in the product. Target pricing is one approach to pricing strategy: it places the emphasis on matching competitive prices.

- The customer/competitor matrix is one method of drawing together some of the strategy issues that arise out of these two areas. It combines the extent to which customers have common needs with the possibilities of achieving competitive advantage in the market place. Four main types of strategic situation result.

- Business is undoubtedly becoming more international. Customer analysis therefore needs to follow this trend. It has been argued that, although there are national differences in taste and culture, it is more important to seek out the similarities than to examine the differences. The greater economies of scale from operating internationally will be reflected in lower prices that will overcome any lingering problems over differences in taste.

Possible lecture structure

- Begin by contrasting some of the different types of customer, drawing out some strategic implications: use Table 6.1 (from the set of overhead masters at the end of this *Guide*) as a reminder. Ask students to suggest other examples for each category.
- Summarise the main elements of the topic: use Figure 6.1. Comment that both prescriptive and emergent approaches wish to understand customers.
- Explore the importance of a customer-driven organisation and the significance of unmet customer needs: use Exhibit 6.1.
- Analyse customers and the segments to which they belong: use the two charts that follow this page on characteristics of customers and on key segmentation criteria.
- Outline the basic principles involved in communicating with customers and their strategic implications: use Figure 6.1 which shows the communications mix.
- Explore the main elements of pricing strategy: use Figures 6.3 and 6.4.
- Explain the customer/competitor matrix and its importance for strategy development: use Figure 6.5.
- Identify some of the main international issues in customer strategy: Exhibit 6.3.

Strategic project

Production over-capacity versus international demand is the starting point for analysing the strategic problems in regional aircraft. However, the interesting question is *why* such capacity has arisen: a national desire to have an aircraft industry, the ease of entry into the market, the reliance on the business customer, the competitive pricing needed to achieve sales, the fragmented nature of the industry, and many other areas all deserve to be investigated. The culture of companies in the industry also represents an interesting field of study: the Fokker deal and Daimler-Benz, the disaster at Dornier, the difficulties at British Aerospace are all recorded in various articles: *see* the *Financial Times* 27 July 1992, p15; 6 April 1993, p23; 21 October 1993, p25; 3 February 1994, p23; 30 June 1994, p36; 27 January 1995, pp1 and 17; 17 May 1996, p28. One of many case studies that never made it into the final text!

Corporate Strategy Lecturer's Guide, Pitman Publishing
© Aldersgate Consultancy Limited 1997

Some categories of customers

Domestic customers
- Buy products for themselves and their families
- Individual bargaining power usually low
- Often grouped together into segments

Large industrial customers
- Tend to buy for more rational and economic reasons
- Buying power of individual customers sufficient to justify special attention

Small business customers
- Tend to buy for rational reasons
- But order size may not justify individual attention

Large service customers
- Often sell products/services to domestic customers
- 'Product' includes the service

Public service customers
- Similar to large service customers
- But profit may not be the prime motive

Not-for-profit charities
- Also involve service but strong sense of mission
- Need to keep volunteers happy

Market segmentation

Market segmentation: the identification of specific groups (or segments) of customers who respond differently from other groups to competitive strategies.

Criteria for selecting useful market segments:

- *Distinguishable*: customers must be sufficiently distinctive so that they can be isolated in some way

- *Relevant* to purchasing needs of customer

- *Sufficient in size* to justify special strategies and their associated costs

- *Reachable* so that it is possible to direct the strategy to the segment

Corporate Strategy Lecturer's Guide, Pitman Publishing
© Aldersgate Consultancy Limited 1997

Case notes

Estimating demand for the Airbus SuperJumbo

The pan-European large aeroplane consortium, Airbus, has developed a successful strategy to compete with the US market leader, Boeing, in the global market for large passenger aircraft. The company is now faced with assessing the commercial attractiveness of a new generation of aircraft, the SuperJumbo. Would there be sufficient demand to make a profit?

1. How should Airbus go about estimating demand?

The obvious route forward is to ask its customers. It has already sold aircraft to around 130 customers world-wide so it would not be a massive task to contact each of them again.

Clearly, the answer is clear if all the airlines respond negatively. The difficulty is to assess the positive responses that are received. Most airline companies will want to know the price and performance of such an aircraft, so even a positive response is likely to be cautious and incomplete. Moreover, each potential airline customer would be well aware that there is usually much bargaining on the precise specifications that it requires: in negotiating terms, it is unlikely therefore to give away its position by an enthusiastic response in advance of such discussions. These considerations would make such a simple piece of research difficult to assess.

Another more generalised approach would be to assess the trends in demand for airline travel and the associated pressures on airport capacity. There would also be a need to examine the pressure for seats on individual routes where the new aeroplane might be used and the prices that are being charged. It might also be appropriate to examine the pressure for 'green' environmental issues: a larger aircraft might use fuel more efficiently. These issues are more complex to assess but might provide an indicator of the background demand for the larger aircraft.

2. Should they even try to estimate demand, or just go ahead for strategic reasons?

This clearly involves greater risk: the development costs could be as high as US\$ 12 billion. However, given the complexity of estimating demand and the likelihood of expanded air travel in the twenty-first century, there is a clear case for going ahead anyway.

To keep up with Boeing, it is likely that Airbus will need at some stage to build a bigger aircraft than the company currently supplies. It might be better to take the strategic initiative and start now on the next generation of machines. This is a strategic decision that goes beyond the strict estimation of customer demand. However, unless a totally new technology emerges for transporting people around the world, it is likely that the company will have the justification for such an aircraft without major customer research.

Two ways of segmenting the European ice cream market

The case describes two methods of undertaking this task: by purchase intention and by a price/quality relationship.

1. What other methods of segmenting the ice cream market are available?

Quite deliberately, the case does not mention the most obvious method of segmenting the market: by age group. Ice creams bought by children are substantially different from those purchased by adults. As a result, there have been *children's* products around for many years. What is much more recent is the launch of *adult* products, or at least products presented in an adult context: *Magnum* and the presentation of *Häagen-Dazs* ice creams are examples of this.

Such approaches present opportunities for corporate strategy because they allow a company to develop and then dominate a new segment of the market. Having the leading share of a market segment allows the company to secure loyal customers, distribution and the economies of scale that come from larger sales. All these and other benefits make successful market segmentation attractive for strategic purposes.

2. Using the tests for segmentation, what conclusions do you draw on the usefulness of the two methods above?

Segmentation test	Purchase intention method of segmentation	Price/quality method of segmentation
Distinguishable	No: the two divisions are very broad and cover too many areas to provide useful strategic routes forward	Yes
Relevant to purchasing	Yes	Yes
Sufficient size	Yes	Yes, but possibly not super-premium segment?
Reachable	No: there are no special media for each segment	Yes: advertising media are segmented by quality, age group and lifestyle

From a strategy perspective, both segments are useful but only the second fully matches the criteria. On this basis, only the second segmentation method is worth pursuing.

The conclusion might be taken to imply that the take-home/impulse distinction serves little useful purpose. This would be incorrect. It simply has limited value for market segmentation. When coupled with other elements, it might form the basis of new product introductions, e.g. *children's* take-home or *children's* impulse purchases.

Corporate Strategy Lecturer's Guide, Pitman Publishing
© Aldersgate Consultancy Limited 1997

Different communications approaches at Häagen-Dazs and Boeing

1. What brand image do you derive from the advertisement? How important is such communication to the overall strategy of the brand?

In practice, research would reveal an accurate image of the brand conveyed by the advertisement. Nevertheless, it would be reasonable to conclude that the image is likely to be:

- Adult and challenging
- Uninhibited and carefree
- Middle class, rather than working or upper class
- Enjoying the luxurious aspects of life

Given the premium price position of the brand and the high quality ingredients, the advertising presents a new aspect of eating such products. This differentiates it from other ice creams and relies largely on advertising. The communication is therefore an important element in the overall brand strategy.

2. Is brand building part of the basic corporate strategy of Häagen-Dazs? If so, how should its contribution be assessed?

The advertisement clearly demonstrates that brand building is an essential element of the corporate strategy for the product. Clearly, the contribution of such activities must ultimately be assessed in terms of the profit delivery to its parent company, Grand Metropolitan (UK).

The parent does not publish detailed profit information on individual product groups. However, in 1996 the company was reported as saying about Häagen-Dazs that it was still only 'verging on breakeven' and this was partly as a result of the costs of lavish advertising (*Financial Times*, 6 September 1996, p19). Such a statement only makes the strategic issue more acute: the brand was launched in Europe in 1990, so how long should the company continue investing before a profit is achieved? The issue remains unresolved at the time of writing.

3. How precisely should the company decide the level of advertising investment in this product and estimate the price premium to be charged?

It might be argued that these are essentially marketing questions and are not the concern of corporate strategy. This is not correct. If brand investment is important to the overall strategy, then such questions deserve wider exploration than debate within the marketing function.

The accepted marketing response is to set up three guidelines:

- *by advertising to sales ratio*, i.e. a comparison of advertising expenditure on the brand and competing brands in relation to the sales delivered (advertising divided by sales expressed as a ratio);

- *by share of voice*, i.e. the share of advertising as a percentage of the total advertising in the category (the argument being that essentially brands need to spend in excess of competition if they wish to build their market share);

- *by the funds needed to undertake the task*, i.e. the absolute level of advertising to achieve a degree of awareness of the brand.

None of the above take into account the impact of truly creative advertising, which can boost the cost-effectiveness of a campaign but is difficult to measure.

More fundamentally, none of the above mechanisms really answers the fundamental issue raised in the question above: they only provide guidelines which can be broken. For example in the case of Häagen-Dazs, it is likely that the company has outspent its rivals on advertising in terms of its existing brand share and it is still only breaking even. Should it stop in 1996, after six years? Or should it carry on? If it does carry on, when should it then stop? The parent company is funding this investment through the reduced profits available for distribution to its stakeholders, so it is a legitimate question for corporate strategy.

Corporate Strategy Lecturer's Guide, Pitman Publishing
© Aldersgate Consultancy Limited 1997

Boeing's customer and competitor strategies for its new airliner - the Boeing 777

1. What was the customer strategy of Boeing for the 777? What had it been previously? Why?

The 777 customer strategy was to involve the airline customers in the design of the new aircraft. This was because the company had made some mistakes in the way it had designed earlier models and the expense of these had been borne by the customer, at least in part.

The previous approach had been to use engineers to develop the designs. The reason given in the case was that airlines had to be especially concerned about safety and also because it is difficult for the customer to be fully aware of new engineering technical developments.

Although these were the reasons given by Boeing, readers might also like to consider the following additional points:

- Involving the customer in the design might predispose such a customer to purchase the product afterwards.
- Competition had increased over the previous ten years and customers were able to be more choosy.
- Technology was less radical for the 777 model, so engineering input was likely to be lower.

2. Do you agree with the Airbus comment that the new customer strategy was nothing special? Or do you take the view that Boeing could hardly have become the leading aircraft manufacturer in the world if it had little idea of customer needs?

Listening to customers was clearly new at Boeing. The company itself acknowledged the previous dominance of engineers and the United Airlines experience of previous aircraft deliveries left something to be desired. However, like many competitive comments, the Airbus retort was probably an exaggeration: Boeing had clearly been producing customer-friendly products for many years.

3. How significant do you regard the desire of Boeing and its customers to adopt the 'fly-by-wire' technology of its rival? To what extent was this just a catching-up process? How, if at all, might it give a competitive design edge to Boeing?

Highly significant in the sense that its competitor already had the technology and Boeing customers wanted it as well. At Boeing, this was entirely a catching-up process and was most unlikely to give a design edge to the company. It was essential for the company to develop this technology in order to ensure that it kept pace with its rival.

Technology can sometimes deliver real competitive advantage. In this case, there was some advantage for Airbus but it was not so great that the customers were persuaded to shift from Boeing. Technology is perhaps more likely to deliver competitive advantage where the customers make their purchase decisions on the basis of rational rather than emotional triggers. For its industrial customers, Boeing's strategy therefore had to be factually persuasive and technologically advanced if it was to be successful.

4. How convincing do you find the Boeing estimate of 15 000 sales over the next 20 years? What does this imply with regard to its investment of US$5 billion?

No company can make an *accurate* estimate of sales over such a lengthy period of time. In the case of aircraft, it is dependent on continued growth in the world economy, the absence of major wars, the relative price of fuel and so on. The precision of the sales estimate may therefore be unconvincing on this basis alone.

We do not have precise data on the sales to the present to be able to comment on the more general level of predicted sales. For example, how does 15 000 sales compare with aircraft sales over the last ten or twenty years? For this reason also, the comment is not in itself convincing. This does not mean that it is wrong, rather that we must remain unconvinced on the basis of what we know.

If the figure is correct, then a simple multiplication of numbers of aircraft by the price of an individual aircraft and profit margin will quickly show that the development cost of US$5 billion will rapidly be recovered during the lifetime of the model at a relatively modest sales margin. At a price of US$120 million (see Minicase) and a (guessed) sales margin of 20 per cent, the development costs would be recouped by selling just over 200 aircraft - almost nothing compared to the market of 15 000.

$$US\$5 \text{ billion} \div [US\$120 \text{ million} \times 20\,\%] = 208 \text{ aircraft}$$

5. If you were working in corporate strategy at Airbus Industrie and had read the article in the Financial Times *on which this case study is based, what would it indicate about the strategies that Airbus needed to adopt over the next five years?*

It should be noted that this question is entirely realistic. Such articles do provide useful guidance for the competition.

It would suggest that Airbus needs to develop its products closer to its customers, if it is not already adopting such a procedure.

Airbus had a competitive edge with its technology. This was clearly impressive to its potential customers. If it can do this once, then it can do it again: it should therefore explore further its technology strategies.

The article also suggests that there is a real market for this size of aircraft: the company might therefore need to consider how the A340 should be modified, if at all, to compete more directly and aggressively.

Three major companies had not yet ordered the 777: why? Even those customers that had ordered the aircraft might be persuaded to change. Was there any further evidence for Airbus on customer demand that the company could develop a new or modified rival that would outsell the 777 in the long term? These questions deserve exploration.

Corporate Strategy Lecturer's Guide, Pitman Publishing
© Aldersgate Consultancy Limited 1997

Chapter 7
Analysing resources

Synopsis of chapter

The chapter explores the six main areas involved in undertaking a basic resource analysis: *key factors for success*; how the main resources *add value* and lead to the *value chain*; the routes to *cost reduction*; the analysis of *core competences;* and a *SWOT analysis*. This last subject clearly covers elements of market analysis as well as resources and is used to summarise the basic analytical process.

Summary

- For both prescriptive and emergent strategists, the resources of the organisation are an important element in strategy. Prescriptive approaches emphasise the need to build on strengths, whereas the emergent view favours flexibility and harnessing the more unpredictable human element. This chapter concentrates on the prescriptive view.

- In seeking to understand the *key factors for success* in an industry, the 'three Cs' can be used as a basis for analysis: customers, competitors and company. The purpose of such an approach is to identify those strategic factors that are common to most companies in an industry and are essential to delivering the objectives of such companies. The key factors for success can be used to focus on other areas of strategy development.

- Resources add value to the organisation. They take the inputs from suppliers and transform them into finished goods or services. The *value added* is the difference between the market value of outputs of an organisation and the costs of its inputs. It is possible to calculate this accurately for an overall company but very difficult for individual parts of the company. When used in developing competitive advantage where parts of the company are important, the concept is therefore often left unquantified.

- In order to develop sustainable competitive advantage, it is necessary to consider the various parts of the organisation and the value that each part adds, where this takes place and how the contribution is made. The *value chain* undertakes this task. It identifies where value is added in different parts of the organisation.

- It may also be necessary to consider the *value system*, i.e. the way that the organisation is linked with other parts of a wider system of adding value involving suppliers, customers and distributors. Unique linkages between elements of the value system may also provide competitive advantage.

- Cost reduction is a major way to increase value added through resource-based strategy. There are five main areas of cost reduction: designing-in such reductions, supplier relationships, economies of scale and scope, the experience curve and capacity utilisation.

- Resource analysis will also seek to determine the core skills and competences of the organisation. These add up to a group of skills and technologies that allow the organisation to gain long-term advantage over competitors. They may take many years to develop fully but represent a major resource area for corporate strategy development.

Possible lecture structure

- Use Case study 7.1 and compare three quite different industries: pharmaceuticals, construction and the railway industry. Relevant national companies might be identified by students to replace those in the case, along with the resources that each contains. I have also used Figure 7.2 successfully here. The Exhibits and Figures appear in the final section of this *Guide*.
- Comment on prescriptive and emergent approaches to resources: *see* summary above.
- Explore briefly the *key factors for success* in an industry. Reminder of Chapter 3 on *market* factors before considering the *resources* inside the company. Use Exhibit 7.1.
- Explore how resources *add value*: use Figure 7.3. This whole section is a much fuller explanation than often appears in strategy texts and overcomes the problems that many students have in understanding about added value before considering the value chain.
- Explain the *value chain* of an organisation and comment on its strategic significance: use Figure 7.4.
- Explain the *value system* of an organisation: use Figure 7.5.
- Explain how the value chain and value system can lead to *competitive advantage*: use Figure 7.6.
- Explore the main routes for *cost reduction* in an organisation: use chart that follows. You may also like to use Figure 7.7 on the experience curve.
- Outline the *core resources* of an organisation, including its core competences. Use the chart that follows, together with Figure 7.8.
- Undertake a *SWOT analysis* for the organisation. Use Table 7.2.

Strategic project

There have been two main routes for the leading global pharmaceutical companies over the last five years:

- the acquisition of distributors of drugs (especially in the US); and
- the purchase of competitors or a merger with rivals.

See *Financial Times*: Pharmaceuticals Survey, 25 March 1996.

The two routes have largely different objectives, depending on what is perceived to be the main strategic issue: the need for distribution or the economies of scale in terms of research and development and marketing. Another route to growth has been the purchase of biotechnology companies with their exceptional growth prospects. A further strategy has been the development of *over-the-counter* branded drugs which have higher profit margins and are less prone to price negotiation. This can be contrasted with *ethical* pharmaceuticals, where large hospitals, government health authorities and other bodies have begun to put real pressure on the drug companies.

Routes to cost reduction

- **Designing-in cost reduction**: before the product ever reaches the factory floor, redesign of its components may save substantial costs.

- **Supplier relationships**: negotiating better prices for the same quality will reduce costs for a manufacturer.

- **Economies of scale**: unit costs may reduce as the size of a plant increases.

- **Economies of scope**: it may be possible for different products to share some functional costs, e.g. common services, and so reduce costs.

- **The Experience Curve**: as a company becomes more experienced at production, it should be able to reduce costs.

- **Capacity utilisation**: where plant has a high fixed cost, there may be cost reductions to be obtained by running the plant as close to capacity as possible.

Core resources of an organisation

- **_Architecture_**: the network of relationships both within and outside the firm.

- **_Reputation_**: the standing of the firm in the community at large.

- **_Innovative ability_**: the structures, skills, procedures and rewards that allow some organisations to innovate better than others.

Core competence: a group of production skills and technologies that enables an organisation to provide a particular benefit to customers.

Core competences can be built up in a variety of ways in existing and new products to deliver competitive advantage to the organisation.

Three distinguishing features of major core competences:

- **_Customer value_**: must make a real impact on how the customer perceives the organisation.
- **_Competitor differentiation_**: competences must be unique against competition.
- **_Extendable_**: core competences need to be capable of providing the basis for products or services that go beyond those currently available.

Corporate Strategy Lecturer's Guide, Pitman Publishing
© Aldersgate Consultancy Limited 1997

Case notes

Utilising resources at Glaxo Wellcome Pharmaceuticals

1. What are the major resources of a company like Glaxo Wellcome?

- Range of unique, patented products: for example, Zantac in the case.
- Research and development: successful development will deliver competitive advantage.
- Promotion and marketing: individual doctors and hospitals need to be persuaded to purchase the drugs from Glaxo Wellcome rather than rivals. This is a skilled task.
- Product manufacturing coupled with good quality control.

2. What were the strategic implications for those resources of the acquisition of Wellcome by Glaxo?

New drugs from Wellcome were added to the Glaxo portfolio. Research and development, marketing and manufacturing were combined together to obtain substantial cost savings. These were mainly through reductions in the numbers employed. The other strategic implication was that employees felt threatened by the uncertainty of the merger process after the acquisition.

3. What were the risks involved? Did the results justify the risk?

Until the results of the merger and job-cut review were announced, many employees felt threatened. This was a risk because employees could have left. Their skills, especially in R&D, were hard to replace in the short term.

The results were expected savings of US$ 1 billion. Since the period of acute uncertainty was only a few months, it could be argued that such a substantial saving justified the risks that were involved.

4. The case suggests that other pharmaceutical companies are following alternative strategies. What are these? Do they involve lower risk?

There were two main alternative strategies: the move into drug distribution and the acquisition of biogenetic drug companies. Ostensibly, they might involve lower risk. However, this is not necessarily the case:

- The distribution companies were acquired at a substantial premium over their asset values. Unless substantial savings or extra sales can be gained, such extra payment will not be justified.
- Biogenetic companies are working at the forefront of medical development and the fancy prices paid for such companies has to be justified in products that remain to be developed and proven in the market place.

How three European companies attempt to utilise their resources

Three totally different companies are compared in terms of the resources that each possesses and the way that these are deployed to generate value added.

1. An examination of the cost profiles of the three companies reveals that research and development (R&D) features more prominently in Glaxo than in the other two companies. Why is this? What risks, if any, are associated with heavy R&D expenditure? What implications might this have for strategic decisions?

R&D is particularly important to pharmaceutical companies because it can be a major source of competitive advantage. Unique, patented drugs such as *Zantac* at Glaxo and the anti-AIDS drug *Retrovir* at Wellcome provide a major source of profits for the drug companies. By contrast, rail companies do not have the same opportunities for unique, patented products: for example, it is not possible to patent the journey by rail from Amsterdam to Maastricht. Equally, it is not possible for CGE to patent its road-building programme.

The downside of the large investment in R&D by the drug companies is the risk of failure: not all drug developments are successful. The costs of failure can be hundreds of millions of dollars. Glaxo Wellcome itself withdrew from several drug developments at the time of the 1995 merger and simply wrote off the costs that had been incurred.

The implication for strategic decisions is that there is always an attempt to reduce the risk of failure. This might be undertaken in a number of ways:

* Early review of some routes with limited prospects.
* The pursuit of a large number of routes on the principle that this will raise the probability of at least one major success.
* Funding of university research so that the companies stay in contact with other sources of new knowledge.

2. Marketing and related expenditures are much higher as a proportion of sales in Glaxo than Nederlandse Spoorwegen. What are the reasons for this? Can you make out a strategic case for higher levels of marketing expenditure at the Dutch railway company?

As covered earlier, pharmaceutical companies spend heavily on marketing because of the important and difficult task of persuading medical staff to adopt their drugs rather than those of their rivals. By comparison, the sums spent at the railway company under the same heading are rather smaller.

The strategic case for higher marketing expenditure at Nederlandse Spoorwegen can be made in the following way. The major investment in a rail company is the track and rolling stock. Once this has been made, higher profits are generated by increasing the usage of such stock: more people carried by trains that are running anyway will clearly bring in more revenue which goes straight into profit. Therefore, a heavier

Corporate Strategy Lecturer's Guide, Pitman Publishing
© Aldersgate Consultancy Limited 1997

expenditure on marketing to persuade more people to use the train will increase profits. The argument is probably a little simplistic in practice, but has some validity. The main difficulty is that Dutch railways already carry full trains at peak periods, so the real issue is to increase passengers during off-peak periods, which by definition are less popular.

3. The case suggests that holding companies have a more complex task in managing their resources. Do you agree?

CGE manages a wide range of products and services, but it does not undertake this task solely from the centre: part of the strategy is decided and implemented in the operating subsidiaries concerned with a particular area of the business. The centre is mainly concerned with raising overall finance, cash management and allocating resources. In this sense, the task of the centre may not be so complex because it leaves some of the key strategic decisions to the operating subsidiaries.

The task of holding companies is therefore not necessarily more complex, just different. Part 6 of *Corporate Strategy* further examines holding companies.

Nolan Helmets

The case describes how a small company has developed its strategy over the last thirty years. After a degree of instability, the company is now investing for its future aimed at revitalising the brand and cutting costs.

1. What would you estimate to be the key factors for success for the industry in which Nolan is located?

Nolan makes motorcycle helmets. Demand is therefore derived from the motorcycle industry and any legislative demand for riders to wear helmets. Its demand is also dependent on at least two main geographic markets: Germany 32% and Italy 20% of total sales. The case does not indicate if other markets are also important. Demand for Nolan mid-range helmets is based on three main areas:

- Technical features
- Helmet detail
- Brand image

Nolan needs to be successful in all these three areas, but the case suggests that two other areas are important:

- Production efficiency, e.g. the reduction in factory size
- Distribution to motorcycle shops, i.e. the point-of-sale edge mentioned in the case.

2. Undertake a value-chain analysis for this company and point out the most likely areas where value is being added. What value linkages does the case suggest this company might have? How important might they be?

- *Inbound logistics*: no major significance.
- *Operations*: major importance in terms of profitability.
- *Outbound logistics*: unclear, possibly significant given the international transport costs that are clearly involved.
- *Marketing & sales*: branding and in-store display are clearly major factors.
- *Service*: unclear but possibly important for distributors.
- *Firm infrastructure*: no major significance.
- *Human resource management*: a few key individuals but not especially important.
- *Technology development*: major significance in terms of helmet design and also surface colour design.
- *Procurement*: could be important. Unclear from case.

Value linkages exist with helmet distributors through their shareholding in the company and with financial institutions to fund further growth. These have clearly been important in the more recent development of the company.

Corporate Strategy Lecturer's Guide, Pitman Publishing
© Aldersgate Consultancy Limited 1997

3. How would you characterise the company's resources? How have they changed over the last four years? With what result?

- *Architecture*: links with motorcycle retailers
- *Reputation*: brand name, design
- *Innovation*: unclear, possibly rather limited.
- *Core competences*: not entirely clear from the case, but likely to include helmet shell design and assembly, plastic technologies, surface design skills.

Over the last four years, the designs have been revamped, branding strengthened and the production redesigned to reduce costs. The results of this process have been that the company has stabilised in terms of direction with substantial new funds invested. The results of such a process have still to be seen in terms of increased sales and profitability.

4. What are the core strengths of the company? How has the company exploited these over the last few years? What does the case suggest about exploiting them further in the future? Do you judge these arguments to have any merit?

The core strengths clearly lie in helmet design, production efficiency, branding and helmet distribution. The company has exploited these with some success over the last few years in that profits have risen significantly and are expected to rise further. But this has to be set against what was clearly a poor profit record up to the period 1993/94.

The case suggests that the core strengths can be exploited further into other sports and markets, such as Eastern Europe. It does not say which sports but those requiring helmets such as rock climbing, pedal cycling (in some countries), and canoeing would suggest openings. Given the increased profitability of the last two years, this does suggest that the company is beginning to improve. However, there is no hard evidence in the case that it has the resources required to tackle new sports areas, which may well require new distributors, nor new countries which will certainly require new distributors. The arguments at this stage are no more than ideas and are backed by little real substance. In fairness, the company may have more substantive proposals than it was prepared to make public in the case study.

Chapter 8
Analysing human resources

Synopsis of chapter

The chapter has four main themes: an *audit of the human resources* of an organisation, an assessment of its *organisational culture*, an exploration of the organisation's ability to prompt and handle *strategic change* and an examination of the *power and politics* of the organisation.

For those interested in international strategic issues, the chapter has a final section on international culture. Strategic change is also examined in more depth in Chapter 21 of the book.

Importantly, the chapter begins with the assertion that people are a vital strategic resource and cannot simply be left as a task to be considered after other aspects of the strategy have been agreed. Human resources are a major *input* to strategy development.

Summary

- The analysis of human resources is important for strategy development for two reasons. People are a vital resource. In addition, strategy development often involves change and some people may put up resistance. There are four areas to explore in the analysis of this area: resource audit, organisational culture, strategic change and its implications in terms of the power and politics of the organisation.
- Human resource-based analysis emphasises the emergent approach to corporate strategy. Sustainable competitive advantage will often depend on human resources. In fast moving markets, the adaptability of people inside the organisation becomes a special and important skill. Coping with strategic change is a vital element in the development of corporate strategy.
- The human resource audit will have two main elements: *people* in the organisation and the *contribution* of human resources to the development of corporate strategy. A basic analysis will reflect these two areas but also needs to consider key factors for success, competitive comparisons and possibly international issues.
- Culture is the set of beliefs, values and learned ways of managing the organisation. Each organisation has a culture that is unique. In analysing culture, there are four main areas: environment, cultural factors specific to the organisation, the basic cultural type of the organisation and the strategic implications.
- Factors within the organisation influencing culture include: history and ownership, size, technology and leadership. These can be coupled with the cultural web of the organisation to provide a method of summarising the main cultural influences. The cultural web includes stories, routines and rituals, symbols, organisation structure and control systems.

Corporate Strategy Lecturer's Guide, Pitman Publishing
© Aldersgate Consultancy Limited 1997

- The four main types of culture are power, role, task and personal. Their importance for corporate strategy lies in the ability of each type to cope with strategic change and to deliver competitive advantage.
- Analysis of strategic change needs to consider three areas: the type of organisation, the phase of organisation growth and the strategic pressures for organisational change. Four types of organisation have been identified with each having a different response to strategic change. The age and size of an organisation will provide information on its phase of growth. The strategic pressures for organisational change need careful assessment. They may include such concepts as delayering - the reduction of the number of reporting layers in an organisation - and business process re-engineering - the use of new technology to reduce the administrative task and reduce costs.
- Strategic change needs to take into account what is possible in terms of change in the organisation, rather than what is theoretically desirable. Political issues in the organisation therefore need to be carefully explored - the political network.
- International cultures may have a profound impact on corporate strategy. They may even make some strategy proposals very difficult to implement.

Possible lecture structure

- Compare Shell and BP: the need for new strategies and the importance of the human resources aspects of such issues.
- Comment that human resource analysis concentrates on the emergent aspects of strategy development: use Figure 8.1.
- Explain the human resource audit of an organisation and explore its strategic implications: use Exhibit 8.1.
- Outline the strategic issues involved in organisational culture and analyse the culture of the organisation: use Figure 8.3 (Overview on culture), Figure 8.4 (Cultural Web) and Table 8.1 (Four types of culture). Perhaps emphasise that cultural analysis needs to go beyond analysing the six elements of the Cultural Web, which seems to satisfy some students?
- Analyse strategic change: use Figures 8.5 and 8.6 to outline the three main areas.
- Possibly a comment on the impact of downsizing and business process re-engineering in the context of human resources.
- Assess the political network of an organisation and assess its strategic implications: use Figure 8.7.
- Appraise the impact of international cultural aspects on strategy development: use the chart that follows.

Strategic project

By the early 1990s, Repsol was more profitable than Elf. The Spanish company was more focussed geographically, had a well-developed monopoly interest in gas distribution to complement its dominance of the Spanish market and was more prudent in its policy of acquisitions. Elf had embarked on a costly acquisition spree in the late 1980s and early 1990s that left the company with major problems: see *Financial Times,* 2 September 1994, p22; 27 January 1995, p24. For Repsol, see Lynch, R (1993) *Cases in European Marketing*, Chapter 2, plus its related teaching note.

International cultural perspectives

International culture: 'The collective programming of the mind which distinguishes the members of one human group from another. ... Culture, in this sense, includes systems of values; and values are among the building blocks of culture.' *Hofstede*

Five dimensions of culture:

- *Power distance*: the extent to which those who are poorest in society are willing to accept their position.

- *Individualism/collectivism*: the extent to which societies are collections of individuals or are bound together into a cohesive whole.

- *Masculinity/femininity*: masculine societies see a sharp distinction in roles between the sexes; female societies see more equality.

- *Uncertainty avoidance*: the extent to which members of a culture feel threatened by the unknown.

- *Confucian versus dynamism*: long-term outlook versus living-for-today.

Corporate Strategy Lecturer's Guide, Pitman Publishing
© Aldersgate Consultancy Limited 1997

Case notes

Barons swept out of fiefdoms at Royal Dutch/Shell

1. What were the reasons given for the reorganisation? Were they sufficient to justify the upheaval involved?

- Company profitability was not high enough to sustain the company in the long term: cuts in employee numbers were required.
- The committee culture of the company made change slow and bureaucratic.
- There were a number of regions around the world that were run too independently of the global interests of the company.
- The main product groups were given insufficient attention.

According to the evidence in the case, the problems *were* sufficient to justify the upheaval.

2. What problems, if any, did Shell foresee in implementing the proposed changes? How did it propose to solve them?

Problems were clearly foreseen relating to the existing areas of power controlled by the managing directors in charge of regional empires: the barons in their fiefdoms. The company also appeared to have some idea that employees might resist being sacked, but it did not appear to have recognised this in any substantive way, e.g. by providing reassurance or support during this period. By implication, the company seemed to be taken by surprise: for example, 'Considerable resistance to change. ... It had proved more time consuming ...'

As a consequence, it appeared to have little idea in advance on how to tackle such issues, which many would argue were highly predictable. One result was that the planned cost savings were proving harder to achieve: the savings in *staff cuts and wages*, which are quite specific and can be calculated, were to be replaced by *increases in performance*, which are much more difficult to estimate and guarantee.

3. How would you describe the previous culture and values of people in Shell? In what way might they change with the new organisation? What effect, if any, would you expect the announced changes to have on morale in the organisation?

The previous culture and values might be characterised as committee-oriented, highly structured, report-and-analysis oriented - the *role culture* of Section 8.3.4. It is not surprising that such a culture found it difficult to cope with the proposed changes and chose to react by careful analysis, discussion and a desire for extensive consultation.

Beyond the obvious point that people might fear for their jobs, it is not clear whether there was likely to be any change in the fundamental culture of the company as a result of the cuts. The whole process was not likely to encourage a new culture: it might just cut the numbers employed and make employees more careful of their own positions. If this is the case, morale was likely to be adversely affected.

Culture, crisis and power at British Petroleum

The case describes the arrival of a new chairman at BP and his attempts to change the culture and shake up what he regarded as a large and over-bureaucratic organisation. It then tracks these changes over a three-year period, culminating in the departure of the chairman.

Clearly, Bob Horton (subsequently Sir Robert Horton) made a number of enemies and arguably made some mistakes. However, it would be wrong simply to view the case as a description of failed strategic change: all the senior managers supported the appointment of Mr Horton and many of the major changes that were proposed. There was a difficult strategic situation at BP during this period which needed to be tackled urgently. Many of the changes originally identified by Mr Horton were implemented over this period.

1. What was the significance of involving 35- to 40-year-old managers for Horton? And his fellow board members?

For Mr Horton, they represented the new wave of managers who would identify and see through proposed changes. They were the new guard.

For his fellow board members, they must have represented something of a potential threat. They had the power to cause trouble and were not locked into the existing power structures. However, it could be argued that they also represented fresh blood and the chance to allow some of the brighter managers a chance to present their ideas for change. In the end, the board still had the power to accept or reject the proposals.

2. How important do you regard the comment to be by Horton about the over 40-year-old managers?

Very important indeed.

From one viewpoint, just put yourself into the shoes of any manager of that age, even those who would welcome change. They were being told by their chairman that he did not trust them and his starting point was that they might attempt to sabotage his new ideas. At a more cynical level, they might also have enquired about the age of Mr Horton.

From another viewpoint, Mr Horton was setting out his position: he wanted radical change and needed to signal this to everyone in the organisation. He had considerable experience of resistance from senior older managers to this process and was determined to stop this at an early stage.

3. What is your assessment of the cultural changes that took place in the period 1990-92 as against the cultural change models outlined in the chapter?

In this short note, it is not possible to provide a full analysis. However, Figure 8.5 can be used as the basis of the main headlines:

Corporate Strategy Lecturer's Guide, Pitman Publishing
© Aldersgate Consultancy Limited 1997

Type of organisation. Clearly BP was not a *prospector* organisation. It was either a *defender* or an *analyser* in the Miles and Snow classification, probably the latter. This meant that strategic change would inevitably be a slow and long process that could not easily be hurried, as had been proposed over the period 1990-92. This was bound to lead to problems.

Phase of organisational growth. The company was old and large. In Greiner's phases of growth, it clearly rested somewhere in phase 4 . It was possibly going through the 'crisis of red tape' before achieving new success in collaboration. However, caution should be used in such a simple interpretation of the changes and pressures. Large organisations are more complex than this. Certainly at BP, the whole way that change was introduced and developed went considerably beyond this simple typology.

Pressure for change. There were clear pressures for strategic change related to the profitability of the business. There were also perceived pressures for change related to the desire to introduce a new style to the business.

The politics of strategic change. As Chairman of the organisation, Mr Horton wielded considerable power. He used this on occasions to bring about change, but he also appeared to ignore the political power structures of the company.

For example, after he had held his briefing meeting in December 1989, another meeting of the Managing Directors took place to which Mr Horton was not invited. This entirely unofficial gathering appeared to have the power to overturn everything announced the previous day! The fact that the decisions were allowed to proceed appears to have been fortuitous rather than planned. Mr Horton appeared to have largely ignored the power structures that clearly existed in BP. The manner of his subsequent departure suggests that he did not take such important elements of strategic change sufficiently seriously. For leaders, it is important to carry the majority of senior managers with you.

4. Horton took the view that his decisions may have been autocratic but were for the good of the company. Moreover, the board knew his personality when it appointed him. On this basis, he was entitled to expect more support than he received. Do you agree with this view of the politics of BP?

Clearly, the answer to this question is subject to personal judgement. However, as implied, chief executives cannot operate without the support of those around them. Conversely, Horton may have failed to give his senior managers support when they needed it. If this is correct, then it follows that there was a two-way breakdown in mutual support. Both parties needed to change.

Note: Because of the nature of the questions, no suggested answers have been provided here to Case study 8.2 Industry groups in Japan, Korea, Hong Kong and Italy.

How Rank Xerox shifted its strategy and changed its organisation

After being overtaken by the successful strategy of Japanese photocopying companies in the 1970s and 1980s, Rank Xerox was potentially in considerable trouble in the 1990s. The case describes how it tackled these issues. It relates strategy and human resources as they were developed during this period.

1. How would you summarise the strategies adopted by Rank Xerox in the face of strong Japanese competition? Do you think they will be successful?

The strategies included:

- Remaining in the high-end part of the photocopying market, rather than extending down in any major way.
- Redefining the mission to provide a broader service than merely photocopying: the document company.
- The creation of CBUs which involved splitting up the larger country organisations.
- Devolving power to the CBUs.
- Re-engineering processes to cut costs.
- Benchmarking to identify and set standards.

These strategies build on the strengths of the company and provide relevant distinctiveness to customers, and so there is a reasonable chance of success. However, this is not assured: the data in the case is vague in some important areas, e.g. Italian profitability was 'in sight'.

2. The company argued that there were real benefits from moving to CBUs: what were they? Is it possible that the company has lost out on central control and economies of scale as a result of these moves? Do you think CBUs will still be around in five years' time?

CBU benefits: smaller size was better for customers, though it was not clear exactly what this meant, i.e. better in what way? Importantly for Rank Xerox, there seemed to be a correlation between smaller size and increased profitability but this was not conclusive. The smaller size was also associated with individual smaller countries, so that the real benefits might have come from being associated with being identified with an individual country.

It is highly likely that the company has lost out on central control and this is possibly also true of economies of scale. However, economies of scale rely on manufacturing processes and manufacturing was still concentrated and specialised in certain locations across Europe. This latter point is not fully explored in the case. CBUs existed more at the customer end rather than the manufacturing end of the company.

CBUs may still be around in five years' time, but they could equally have been replaced by some other organisation structure. The culture of the company would be to see them as only one step in the evolution of its organisation over time: the company rather liked change.

Corporate Strategy Lecturer's Guide, Pitman Publishing
© Aldersgate Consultancy Limited 1997

3. Rank Xerox laid great emphasis in its strategy initiatives on re-engineering *and* benchmarking: *what organisational, morale and human resource problems might arise as a result?*

Both these techniques involve significant strategic change, especially in terms of new jobs and responsibilities and possibly even job losses. Some employees may feel threatened by such moves and resist the changes that have been proposed.

Organisational issues might therefore include the redefinition of reporting structures in the organisation, the provision of new jobs and new responsibilities. These are not necessarily problems for everyone: some may gain from such changes. However, there may well be an attempt to resist and negotiate as well as involve more subtle moves in the political power battles of the organisation.

Morale will clearly suffer in *re-engineering* if the changes are poorly handled. As far as *benchmarking* is concerned, this should have more positive aspects: the aim is to actually help people perform better by comparison with those already achieving better results. Explored correctly, benchmarking could well raise morale.

Human resource problems need not arise if the potential issues are explored in *advance* of the strategy being decided. This is more likely to happen where workers are empowered to make changes and therefore they can own the decisions that they have made. It could even be argued that giving workers such power is more likely to lower resistance and therefore make the strategic changes more effective and lasting. This issue is explored further in Parts 5 and 6 of this book under the general heading of *Learning Strategy*.

4. How would you characterise the company culture of Rank Xerox from the material in the case and using the categorisation in Section 8.3?

In brief only, for reasons of space:

Environment
- Highly competitive
- Innovative
- Need for high degree of service

Cultural factors specific to the organisation
- Large company with many subsidiaries needing international co-ordination.
- Complex with a changing mission and strategies that needed to be communicated both to employees and to customers.
- Relatively sophisticated technology along with high degrees of service, which will require training and monitoring.

Basic cultural style
Strong elements of the *task* style when cultural change was required but also elements of the *role* culture typical of large organisations.

Analysis of the strategy implications

- *Both prescriptive and emergent*. Prescriptive in such decisions as the change of mission statement and the move to CBUs. Emergent in the use of empowerment, the investigation of benchmarking.
- *Competitive advantage*. The company still had trouble coping with the competitive moves of its rivals which suggests that its competitive advantage was still related to power rather than a task culture.
- *Coping with strategic change*. In spite of the above, the company had encouraged a culture that was able to cope with strategic change.

Chapter 9
Analysing financial resources

Synopsis of chapter

Finance is treated in this chapter principally as a source of funds for other strategy developments. The main *sources of funds* are analysed and then the *constraints* on each source explored. The costs of different sources of finance and the capital structure of organisations are then investigated in order to establish the *cost of capital* in the organisation. The *financial appraisal of strategy projects* is then examined. Finally, a comparison is made between *financial and corporate objectives*.

There is a separate section on international finance at the end of the chapter. In the section on cost of capital, there is a description of the algebraic derivation of the cost of capital.

Summary

- Organisations need to finance their existing and proposed new strategies. There are six main sources of funds for such activities, each with its own merits and problems. *Retained profits* are the first source of finance for most organisations: probably the largest and cheapest source of funds. *Equity finance* - that is the issuance of new shares to either existing or new shareholders - is another way of raising funds. *Long-term debt finance* is simpler and cheaper than equity but there are limits to the amount that can be raised. There are also major constraints on debt finance. These relate to the need to pay interest on the debt regardless of the profit fluctuations in the business.

- Other sources of finance include *leasing* (renting) of plant and machinery, *savings* from reductions in short-term debt and the *sale of existing assets*. They all have their advantages and problems.

- All capital raised by the organisation has a cost associated with it. Calculating the cost matters because it reassures the stakeholders that their efforts are worthwhile and because it provides a benchmark for assessing the profitability of future strategies.

- The cost of equity capital can be calculated using the Capital Asset Pricing Method, but it really only works where there is wide public shareholding. The cost of debt is calculated from the weighted average of the individual loans to the company. For the company overall, the combined cost of debt and equity is called the Weighted Average Cost of Capital (WACC).

- When assessing new strategic proposals, it is normal to undertake a financial appraisal. Discounting techniques are often used as part of this in Western companies. They reduce future net cash flows back to their value in today's terms.

Several difficulties have been identified with this approach. Probably the most substantial is the problem of producing accurate projections of future profitability.

- Basic cash flow analysis is also undertaken. It should not be confused with the discounting techniques above. Analysing cash flow is essential to ensure that the company avoids bankruptcy.

- To define objectives purely in terms of the organisation's short-term financial profitability would be over-simplistic and incomplete. A distinction needs to be drawn between strategic and financial objectives.

When international operations are involved, financial resource analysis becomes more complex. Probably the greatest source of risk for many companies is currency fluctuation. Taxation and the cost of capital are both subjects that require in-depth and possibly specialist financial analysis.

Possible lecture structure

- Explore the sources of finance at Heineken and the purposes to which such funds are put: use Figure 9.2 and ask students to summarise some of Heineken's related strategies from the Minicase.
- Explain the role of finance in providing funds for the development of strategic initiatives: use Figure 9.1.
- Comment that, by its precise and quantified nature, financial analysis tends to be *prescriptive* rather than emergent in its approach. Nevertheless, many financiers recognise the uncertainties and judgements involved in the process. *See* page 331 for further comment.
- Explore the sources of finance available to the organisation: use the chart that follows and Table 9.3.
- Examine the constraints on these sources of finance: use the chart that follows.
- Explore an organisation's potential for further funding through its cost of funds and capital structure: use the chart that follows.
- Show how the financial appraisal of strategy is undertaken: use the chart that follows and Figure 9.3.
- Explain the importance of balancing the organisation's financial objectives with its other corporate objectives: use Table 9.4.

Strategic project

The purchase by Interbrew of the Canadian brewer, John Labatt, is commented upon in the *Financial Times*, 6 July 1995, p25 and 16 October 1995, p23. The global strategies of leading brewers can also be examined by reading the Heineken and Carlsberg Annual Reports and Accounts for the mid-1990s. The issues of globalisation, its benefits and problems are illustrated by these and other companies. Asia-Pacific readers might like to explore San Miguel, the Philippines, and its growing links with western brewing companies. North American students might prefer to research the international ambitions of Anheuser Busch.

Corporate Strategy Lecturer's Guide, Pitman Publishing
© Aldersgate Consultancy Limited 1997

Sources of finance available to the organisation

There are five main sources of finance for strategic activities. Each has its merits and problems.

- *Equity finance*, i.e. the issuing of new shares to either existing or new shareholders, is one clear route but it has numerous disadvantages associated with the costs of issue and the possible loss of control in the company.

- *Long-term debt finance* is simpler and cheaper, but there are limits to the amount and there are major difficulties if the company defaults on paying the interest charges.

- *Leasing (renting) of plant and machinery* has some specialist uses and attractions: it can have tax benefits and lower costs; but the equipment remains the property of the lessor at the end of the period.

- *Savings from reductions in short-term debt* can be a substantial source of funds to a company. But they can only usually be made once.

- *The sale of some existing assets* to fund development elsewhere is useful but drastic.

Constraints on sources of finance available

- There are three main constraints on debt financing:

  1. The need to fund the interest payment regardless of profit fluctuations.

  2. The company with debt is more exposed to profit fluctuation than the one without.

  3. The reluctance of banks to offer finance that would gear companies above 100%.

- The main constraint on equity financing is the need in many companies to establish a steady increase in dividend payouts, regardless of profit variations.

- As a result of the debt and equity payout constraints, fluctuations in profit impact disproportionately on the funding needed for strategic change.

Corporate Strategy Lecturer's Guide, Pitman Publishing
© Aldersgate Consultancy Limited 1997

Cost of funds and capital structure

- The cost of equity of capital can be calculated using the Capital Asset Pricing Method but it only really works where there is wide public shareholding.

- An alternative method starts with the cost of risk-free government bonds and then adds a factor for the risk of owning shares.

- The cost of long-term debt is calculated from the weighted average of the individual loans made to the company.

- For the company overall, the combined cost of debt and equity is called the Weighted Average Cost of Capital (WACC). It combines equity and debt in proportion to their use in the company.

- The optimal capital structure for a company will also involve the assessment of risks, in addition to the costs estimated above.

- Calculating the cost of capital matters because it reassures the stakeholders that their efforts are worthwhile and because it provides a benchmark for assessing the profitability of future strategies.

Financial appraisal of strategy

- Strategic expansion is often analysed using discounting techniques (DCF Analysis) to reduce future projected cash flows back to their value in today's monetary terms.

- Several difficulties have been identified with this approach. Probably the most substantial is the difficulty of producing accurate projections of future profitability and cash flows.

- DCF is not to be confused with a basic cash flow analysis, which is not discounted but projects the net cash flows during the life of the project. Cash flow analysis is essential for project assessment in order to identify and avoid bankruptcy.

- Overall, while there are certain difficulties involved in the techniques, it is probably better to undertake rather than ignore them.

Corporate Strategy Lecturer's Guide, Pitman Publishing
© Aldersgate Consultancy Limited 1997

Case notes

Global expansion: brewing at Heineken NV

1. Using the following information, estimate the order-of-magnitude finance required by Heineken for new strategies in a typical year.

	Cost per annum: US$ million
One company every three years	16.6
One new Far Eastern plant per annum	5.0
Ten events sponsored per annum for the new speciality beers	10.0
Research and development costs as stated in the case	5.0
Joint ventures and licenses	10.0
Total	46.6

2. Compare this with the Heineken balance sheet and profit and loss statement. Convert the financial data to US$ using 1.82 N Fl = US$ 1.

From the balance sheet for 1994:

    Total assets less current liabilities = 8919 - 2226 = 6693 N Fl m = 3677 US$m

From the profit and loss account for 1994:

    Net profits less dividends = 662 - 140 = 522 N Fl m = 473 US$m

3. Does Heineken have any problems financing such strategies?

Heineken needs around US$46.4 million per annum to fund such strategies. This can be compared with its net worth of around US$3.7 billion and annual retained profits of around US$473 million. Conclusion: the company should have no significant problem.

Comment: the above calculation is crude. For example, it adds together capital and revenue items and it makes no attempt to estimate accurately the likely cost of a company acquisition. However, it is not meant to be an *accurate* calculation but rather to show that the company is within its normal financing limits if:

- it only undertakes the activities shown above; and
- it continues to make profits at the levels of 1994.

One problem identified in more recent data is that Heineken has had some difficulty holding its levels of profits. In these circumstances, the funds required for new strategies become a much larger burden and such ventures may not be affordable.

The financing of brewers' growth

1. If you were Heineken, would you raise more finance through long-term debt and expand faster?

The main issue here is one of *company policy* beyond finance itself. As explained in the case, the company has limited the amount of long-term debt that it was willing to raise from banks and other institutions. As long as such a policy remains, the decision will not change. Nevertherless, the question invites the *reader* to form a judgement on the matter and, to this extent, the reader is entitled to take a different view on such policy matters.

It could be argued that the real key here is to understand the extent to which growth opportunities have been missed from following such a policy. This is not clear from the case: it would need an assessment that even Heineken might have difficulty preparing since it would involve examining opportunities that had been rejected over the last few years through lack of funds. The evidence shows that the profit record of the company has shown real and steady growth over the last ten years. On this basis, it could be argued that the company has accepted most of its challenges and that finance has not been the constraining factor.

2. If you were Carlsberg, what arguments would you wish to consider about how you raised new finance? From whom would you seek advice?

The method of raising finance cannot really be separated from the *purpose* for which new finance is being sought. For example, if the new finance were being sought for another brewery at its home base in Copenhagen, then this would probably entail low risk and European banks might find it attractive. Alternatively, if the new finance were being raised for a joint venture in fish farming in the South Atlantic, then the risks would be rather greater, not least because it would involve a totally new and untried strategy for the brewers. In these latter circumstances, the method of raising the finance might need to be substantially different, perhaps involving retained earnings which is not subject to outside scrutiny in the short term.

Beyond the issue of purpose, there is also the matter of the impact on the company *ownership structure*. Carlsberg is controlled by a Danish trust, whose authority might be compromised if outside shares were issued or if some forms of long-term loans were obtained. Sources of funds would need to be assessed against this background. Effectively, this might rule out some sources of finance.

Having explored these two issues, the various options that remained would then need to be assessed against two main criteria:

- The costs of the funds from each source: cost of capital is explored in Chapter 9.
- The risks associated with raising funds from that source: these are also covered briefly in Chapter 9.

Corporate Strategy Lecturer's Guide, Pitman Publishing
© Aldersgate Consultancy Limited 1997

3. If you were Danône/Kronenbourg and had observed the increased segmentation in the beer market and global trends, what strategy would you follow to extend the company's beer sales beyond France? Where would you go? Why? What factors would you consider in the financing of any such expansion?

The lowest risk strategy might be to extend into the immediate neighbours of France: the risk would be low because it might not be necessary to build totally new plant with all its consequent problems and it would be easy to withdraw if the venture was unsuccessful. However, many such markets are difficult because of various barriers to entry: the UK market has some strongly entrenched brewers, the German market also has some powerful brewers on a regional basis. As a result, there might be a case for moving beyond Europe. However, this would entail more substantial funds and greater risk as new plant is set up or an existing brewer is acquired through a takeover.

The method of expansion would clearly be related to the level of funds required and the type of finance that would need to be raised. For example, an acquisition in an Asia-Pacific country might require local currency, local bank expertise and possibly government approval from that country. These matters would also need to be related back to the home country and its ability to raise funds from various sources. There would also be a need to consider the *alternative uses* within such a large group to which such funds might be employed: for example, it might be more profitable to invest in dairy plant rather than brewing. The result of such considerations is therefore many-faceted and complex.

Interbrew: the Stella Artois strategy

1. What are the benefits for Interbrew of its strategy of building specialist beers? What are the problems?

Benefits included:
- higher prices and profit margins;
- satisfying customer demand for higher priced premium drinks;
- obtaining growth without competing head-on against the big brands;
- satisfying ownership view of a cautious approach to growth.

Problems included:
- conflict with other brands distributed by their partners;
- difficulty in building global brands;
- lack of cost savings from economies of scale;
- long-term proposition.

2. What are the reasons for the restrained financial resources of the last few years? How do these relate to the culture of the company?

The company has relied almost entirely on retained profits to finance growth. It has almost no long-term debt and has been unwilling to raise funds through share issues. The reasons related back to the difficult merger that formed the company in 1988: the families that formed the company each desire to retain considerable control over its actions and need to approve all major initiatives. The family culture of the company has therefore a considerable influence over its approach to financial issues. In one sense, this has probably been expensive for the family shareholdings:

- Their wealth may have grown at a slower pace because they were unwilling to employ outside additional funds;
- Cheap outside debt finance was not employed by the company.

However, as owners, the shareholders are arguably entitled to act in this way, especially if they protect other stakeholders in the enterprise such as the workers and management. There is no obligation to seek headlong growth. If the culture of the company is to be cautious, then this may well be reflected in its approach to raising finance for new ventures.

3. Should Interbrew abandon its strategy of a series of small specialist beers and back at least one larger brand, say Stella Artois? What are the financial implications of whatever strategy you recommend? What are the human resource implications?

- The *advantages* of one larger brand might include: economies of scale, easier international entry, global brand building.

- The *disadvantages* of such a strategy might include: the falling away in support for the other Interbrew brands with some decline as a result, the abandonment of a

Corporate Strategy Lecturer's Guide, Pitman Publishing
© Aldersgate Consultancy Limited 1997

successful strategy that avoids clashing with larger brewers, the possibility that such a policy would be beyond its financial and physical resources.

It is important to understand that such changes in strategy offer no simple solutions and often involve difficult choices. Among the important considerations, there is usually a need to consider the financial and human resource aspects.

If the larger brand route were to be chosen, this is likely to involve raising much greater funds. In turn, this would entail either a new share issue or a loan issue funded from the banks. In the first case, there might be a loss of shareholder control and, in the second case, an increase in indebtedness that the existing shareholders might find unacceptable.

From a human resource perspective, the larger brand route might have signficant implications. It would clearly involve skills that the company does not necessarily possess at the time of the case: large brand management, economies of scale considerations in plant management, etc. Importantly, it might have other implications that are more difficult to assess but are also important: for example, the managers of the remaining smaller brands might feel left out of the new, major strategy development and become demotivated. All these areas deserve consideration along with the direct opportunity presented by the strategic route itself.

Financing growth at MorphoSys

MorphoSys is a company without sales and profits. Its business is to develop drugs that are at the forefront of medicine. When they have been developed, the rights to exploit them commercially will probably be sold to other pharmaceutical companies that have much larger resources in such areas: companies like Glaxo from Chapter 7.

Any funds invested in the MorphSys venture are therefore risky but the rewards are high. Companies investing in such companies want to assess the potential of the likely returns against the much greater likelihood of failure than would apply to larger, more traditional ventures such as the brewers explored earlier in the chapter.

1. What elements of the strategy of MorphSys justified the share investments made by companies and the Bavarian and federal government in the company?

Essentially, the promise of totally new drugs based on unique technology associated with antibody variants. In a sense, the *precise* technology matters less than the concept that it is new, unique and has large sales potential if successful.

2. How would you estimate the cost of capital for MorphSys? Do you think that such a calculation would provide a useful guide for shareholders?

The cost of capital cannot usefully be estimated by a consideration of the widespread trading of the company's shares, because there is no public offering at all. It therefore needs to be considered in the context of the actual funds raised and the interest that such funds could earn by being invested into other projects coupled with some risk element for the considerable likelihood of failure. Essentially, this amounts to the method described in Section 9.2.3.

It would certainly provide some guide for shareholders and *must* be employed, if they are to take a rational decision on whether to invest in the company.

3. Would you have invested in the company's DM 8 million financing programme in 1995? Give reasons for your views.

It is important to start by considering the expectations and risk profile of the person or company making the investment. If it is the only sum possessed by the investor, then some would consider such a high-risk investment in MorphoSys to be most unwise. However, if this were only one of a number of investments and one that could easily be afforded by the investor, then the potentially high returns might be considered to be worth the risk.

These are complex issues that rely heavily on personal judgements and expectations. They also rely on the alternative uses to which such funds might be put and on the risk profile of the person making the investment.

Corporate Strategy Lecturer's Guide, Pitman Publishing
© Aldersgate Consultancy Limited 1997

Chapter 10
Analysing operations resources

Synopsis of chapter

Operations are not always considered as part of corporate strategy, and so the chapter begins by considering the *importance* of operations strategy. It then considers the operations *environment*, how operations *add value* and sustainable competitive advantage, the *main areas* of operations and technology strategy and the role of operations strategy in *service industries*.

Summary

- Operations includes raw material sourcing, purchasing, production and manufacturing, distribution and logistics. Its coverage of the organisation's resources is therefore wide and comprehensive The importance of operations in the strategic process is first in delivering competitive advantage and second in providing co-ordinated support for products - that is, every aspect of order handling, delivery and service to the customer - so that sales orders can be won by the organisation.

- There are two major constraints on operations:

  1. They take time to plan and build.
  2. Once installed, they are expensive to change.

- These constraints mean that great care needs to be taken in arriving at the optimal strategy. The analytical process that accompanies such considerations will need to examine *where* and *how value is added* in the operations process from raw materials arriving at the factory gate through to finished goods being shipped to the final customer.

- It is evident from any analysis of the operations environment that the pace of technological change has clearly increased. Major changes in technology, often called *discontinuities*, also deserve careful analysis, as does global activity, particularly where it is aimed at cost reduction through the use of low-cost labour.

- Value added is an important part of the analytical process. It is likely to occur in the following areas:

  1. Adapting products to meet customer needs.
  2. Delivering better products than competitors.
  3. Adding value through enhanced performance or quality.
  4. Cutting the costs of manufacture.

- The methods of achieving operations strategy also involve human resource considerations and also the link between manufacturing and marketing.

- In any detailed analysis of operations strategies, part of the problem is the size and complexity of the resources under consideration. Tests can be applied to identify the major factors affecting the achievement of corporate objectives, adding value and the key factors for success identified for an industry. In addition to these basic procedures, operations strategy needs to examine seven strategy areas:

  - make or buy decisions
  - supplier relationships
  - manufacturing strategy
  - product design prior to manufacture
  - factory layout and procedures
  - logistics and transport
  - human resources implications

- When analysing organisations involved primarily in services, such as banking or travel, some special considerations apply. Services are different in five areas: intangibility, inseparability, heterogeneity, perishability and ownership. However, they still cover areas that have much in common with manufacturing: for example, raw materials, supplier relationships, stocks and work in progress.

- In practice, service has become an increasingly strong element in manufacturing strategy. Service usually needs to be delivered locally, and as a result this has provided some protection against increased globalisation of manufacturing. More generally, service is heavily reliant on human resources and investment in training and education.

Possible lecture structure

- Explore Toyota for the relationship between operations and corporate strategy: highlight design, plant efficiencies, team motivation and the way these and other elements run through the *whole* of the company's strategy.
- Examine the contribution of operations strategy to the corporate strategy process: use Figure 10.1 and the overhead chart that follows.
- Explore the operations environment for relevant trends, especially major changes in technology and global issues: use the chart that follows.
- Identify how and where operations strategies contribute to value added: use Figure 10.3 and the chart that follows.
- Analyse operations in organisations for the specific areas that are most likely to contribute to corporate strategy: use Table 10.2 and the chart that follows.
- Explore and explain the differences that exist between manufacturing and service industries in operations: use Table 10.4 to show differences and Figure 10.4 to draw out conclusions for services. Use the chart that follows for a summary of main areas.

Corporate Strategy Lecturer's Guide, Pitman Publishing
© Aldersgate Consultancy Limited 1997

Strategic project

International engineering companies have had mixed fortunes over the last twenty years. The German companies such as Siemens, Mannesmann, Thyssen and MAN have probably been more successful, but competition has been fierce from the Far East in technology, low costs and links with suppliers.

Why operations matters in corporate strategy

Three main reasons:

- Delivers competitive advantage and supports sales orders

- Often concerned with major *investments* inside the organisation and *new technology* outside the organisation that impact on its future

- Concerned with fundamental change in the organisation

Traditionally, operations has adopted a prescriptive approach to strategy planning, e.g. work analysis and planning.

Recently, operations has recognised that emergent perspectives are also required, e.g. empowerment.

Corporate Strategy Lecturer's Guide, Pitman Publishing
© Aldersgate Consultancy Limited 1997

Analysis of the operations environment

New technology: can shape future strategy.

Discontinuities: sharp, sudden changes in technology that can have a dramatic impact on the organisation. Typically after a discontinuity, organisations go through two phases:

- *Divergence*: development phase

  followed by

- *Convergence*: cost reduction or consolidation phase

Global production: low labour cost countries have a significant impact in some industries.

How and where operations strategies contribute to competitive advantage and value added

Two structural constraints:

- *Length of time to build some plant and factories*

- *Difficulty of altering them once they are installed*

Main elements of contribution from operations strategies:

- *Market adaptability*

- *Winning against competition*

- *Added value through enhanced performance or service*

- *Cutting the costs of manufacture*

- *Improved quality*

- *Human resource objectives in terms of worker satisfaction and job performance*

Corporate Strategy Lecturer's Guide, Pitman Publishing
© Aldersgate Consultancy Limited 1997

Analysis of the operations contribution to corporate strategy

Difficulty: size and complexity of the resources under consideration.

Tests can be applied to identify the major factors. These will include:

- *achievement of corporate objectives*
- *ability to add value*
- *key factors for success identified for an industry*

Operations contribution may come in seven strategy areas:

- *make or buy decisions*

- *supplier relationships*

- *manufacturing strategy*

- *product design prior to manufacture: could be the largest contributor*

- *factory layout and procedures*

- *logistics and transport*

- *human resources implications*

Case notes

Kvaerner's strategy to improve productivity at Govan Shipyard

1. Given the background of worldwide production over-capacity, what strategies are needed for individual shipyards to survive?

With excess capacity, shipyards were having to compete on price and delivery time for new vessels. All new yards need to compete on such matters through:
- cutting costs in design and technology;
- reducing the time taken to make new ships;
- using fewer workers to produce the same output.

2. How did Govan match up to this?

There were two important areas: production efficiency and labour relations.

Production efficiency involved such matters as:
- design and planning;
- production and production services;
- sub-contracting, i.e. producing some items outside the yard when this could be done more cheaply than inside.

Labour relations were taken at a slow pace in the early years for reasons associated with the long traditions at the yard. However, this approach was unsuccessful because it did not break down the previous non-commercial attitudes of the workforce. Hence, new procedures were introduced:

- Empowerment
- Information on work progress and co-ordination of work
- Co-operation between management and trade unions

3. Would you have acquired Govan if you had been Kvaerner in 1988?

Potentially, the shipyard had all the basic skills to survive and make adequate profits. However, it needed substantial modernisation with its associated investment costs. These needed to be added on to the low price that the company paid the goverment to purchase the yard. Informed opinion would be able to assess this reasonably accurately.

The other part of the cost was the culture that went with the skills which was not suited to a commercial operation. There was a cost associated with achieving change, which Kvaerner had to pay. This cost was much more difficult to assess accurately. In addition, the company made only limited attempts to begin the change process for several years, which effectively raised the cost. This was probably a mistake, though some would argue that it was better to be gentle in the beginning. For all these reasons, it was difficult to make an accurate assessment of the costs and benefits to Kvaerner back in 1988.

Corporate Strategy Lecturer's Guide, Pitman Publishing
© Aldersgate Consultancy Limited 1997

Toyota: taking out costs and adding value

1. Using the definition of corporate strategy in Chapter 1, identify which of the operations strategies undertaken by Toyota have a corporate strategy perspective and which are mainly the concern of operations management alone.

Design: corporate strategy perspective.
Kaizen: continuous improvement as a principle is close to the strategic concept of emergent strategy.
Kanban: the detail of this area is operations only, but the general principle might be seen as having a strategic dimension.
Layout: the detail is definitely operations only, but the principle might be strategic.
Supplier relationships: at a fundamental level, this certainly has strategic implications.
Just-in-time systems: much of this is operations, but a decision to invest in this area has strategic implications.

2. Examining the Toyota Manufacturing System (TMS) overall, to what extent do you judge this to be critical to the company's strategic success?

This question involves an element of judgement based on the best available evidence. This is acceptable in those areas of corporate strategy that have no simple solutions. In each case, such a judgement needs to be made on the basis of the evidence and the logic that flows from this. In the case of Toyota, the evidence from the company itself is that the TMS has made a substantial difference to the performance of the company over the last thirty years: sales growth, profits, product performance and quality have all been enhanced by such a system.

If you believe it to be critical, then how does this fit with strategy theories that lay stress on the market aspects of corporate strategy, such as Porter's Five Forces Model? If you believe operations to be relatively unimportant, then how do you explain the remarkable success of Toyota globally since the 1950s?

As the chapter discusses, operations can deliver competitive advantage and added value. If the TMS is examined in these areas, it will be evident that it has provided Toyota with substantial advantages. The implication is not that Toyota has made a mistake but rather that theories that lay stress on the market aspects of corporate strategy are only a *partial explanation* of corporate success.

3. Some commentators argue that it is relatively easy for market leaders such as Toyota to undertake the investment in machinery and training programmes to achieve strategic success but more difficult for smaller organisations. Do small companies have anything to learn from Toyota? If so, what?

Toyota started small: in the 1950s, it was only producing 18,000 vehicles per annum. It certainly had the protection of tariff barriers against fierce US competition at that time. However, with or without this help, it still had to make the necessary strategic changes. Thus all the lessons of the company's development may have some significance for small companies around the world involved in repetitive mass-manufacturing processes. The continuous improvement and attention to detail are probably among the most important considerations, coupled with the emphasis on quality and the involvement of many workers in the development process.

4. The case describes how Toyota became complacent in the 1980s. Do you believe that this was the company's main strategic problem in the 1990s or does it lie elsewhere?

There are a number of strategic problems in the car industry:

- production over-capacity on a global scale;
- the threat of low labour-cost countries;
- the increased expenditure needed for developing a new model;
- the investment involved in branding a car;
- the relative movement of currencies such as the Japanese yen, making models produced in countries such as Japan more expensive.

The complacency of Toyota needs to be set against these issues. Their relative importance will vary both with the company and with the country in which it is primarily located. Given the relative sophistication of Toyota on many of the above, it is probable that the most difficult area for the company to resolve is not complacency but currency movements. The company needs to build more cars in cheaper currency areas if it is to survive: hence the importance of European production.

Corporate Strategy Lecturer's Guide, Pitman Publishing
© Aldersgate Consultancy Limited 1997

Cutting costs and increasing customer satisfaction at SKF

1. What were the principle objectives of SKF in introducing the changes it proposed? How do they compare with the list of possible objectives in Section 10.3?

The main objectives were: to increase the flow of work, reduce inventories, increase quality, be more customer-responsive.

Possible objectives from Section 10.3:
- Market adaptability: SKF yes.
- Winning against competition: SKF possibly, but little stress laid here.
- Adding value through performance and service: SKF yes.
- Cutting costs through manufacturing: SKF yes.
- Delivering human resource objectives: SKF changes increased stress short term as teams were built.
- Link between manufacturing and marketing: SKF yes.

2. The case describes a number of detailed procedures adopted by the company to improve productivity at its main factiories: to what extent do you regard such processes as being part of corporate strategy? And, in contrast, detailed manufacturing strategy?

Many of the processes were manufacturing strategy in terms of their detail, but the underlying principles are rooted in corporate strategy in five areas:
- The emphasis on customer-driven responsiveness.
- The drive for quality.
- The shift from scientific-based work analysis (Taylorism) to team-based continuous improvement.
- Empowerment of teams
- Design, layout and other operations principles that increase efficiency and value added.

3. SKF described the impact on workers of the changes it had implemented. Would the impact have been less if the company had discussed the procedures further before they were introduced? What would have been the problems of such discussion?

According to the company, the problems were quite severe for some workers: the whole style of the way work was undertaken would be changed. It is difficult to see how further discussion could have significantly reduced the impact for two reasons:

1. It is often difficult to foresee the advantages and difficulties before they emerge on the factory floor: this certainly seemed to be the situation at SKF. In consequence, it is unclear what purpose would have been served by discussion of difficulties that could not be identified in advance.
2. Even if the difficulties could have been foreseen, further discussion might have only served to allow those opposed to such changes to slow down the inevitable. This would not have been desirable, given that the changes ultimately had a positive outcome.

ISS cleans up against its European competitors

1. In what way does the case indicate that ISS undertakes to ensure that its services are of the same high standard across Europe?

- By operating a pan-European business so that comparisons can be made.
- By training its operatives.
- By offering incentives and promotion.

2. What are the similarities between a manufacturing and a service business in terms of operations strategy? And what are the differences?

Similarities will include:
- Customer satisfaction
- Emphasis on quality
- Winning against competition
- Cutting costs of service at the same time as increasing quality
- Adding value through performance and service.

Differences will include:
- More localised than some manufacturing which can operate on a global scale
- Intangible product
- Inseparable from the person delivering the service
- Services cannot be stored or kept in inventory
- More difficult to standardise services since they depend on the person delivering them at the time.

3. Can service companies learn lessons from manufacturing companies' experience in operating pan-European businesses?

Yes, to some extent. The issues outlined above in Question 1 have been lessons learnt in manufacturing that could easily be applied in services.

In addition, there are some more general areas that might be applied:

- *Design*: investment in researching how the service is offered might prove highly productive.
- *Use of teamwork and empowerment*: services can benefit from these areas originally developed in companies such as Toyota.
- *Careful study of procedures for conducting the service*: low costs are important but not the only criterion in manufacturing. The same will certainly be true in some types of service for some customers: reliability and quality of delivery may be much more important in cleaning hospitals, for example.
- *Logistics*: it may be vital for service to have an exceptionally fast response to customer need. Logistics and transport systems may well provide guidance here.

Corporate Strategy Lecturer's Guide, Pitman Publishing
© Aldersgate Consultancy Limited 1997

Chapter 11
Background issues:
the purpose of the organisation

Synopsis of chapter

Before considering the possible mission and objectives for an organisation, this chapter examines four topics: developing the organisation's *vision* for the future; the implications of *technology* on strategy; the importance of *innovation processes* on strategic development; policy on *quality issues*. The chapter then draws some brief conclusions on competitive advantage and the purpose of the organisation.

Summary

- When developing corporate strategy, it is necessary to develop a *vision* of the future within which the organisation will operate. The main reason is to ensure that every opportunity is examined. There are five criteria that may assist in developing the vision: foresight, breadth, uniqueness, consensus and actionability.

- An internal and external scan of *technologies* is vital to the development of corporate strategy. It may alter the purpose of the organisation over time. Technologies need to be classified into base, core and peripheral. It is the core area that is most likely to deliver sustainable competitive advantage. Each technology then needs to be assessed against its competitors and for the time and costs of development.

- New *information technology* (IT) has opened up the possibility of greater strategic control in organisations. The control that can be exercised needs to go beyond basic financial data into people aspects of the organisation. At the same time, IT has presented new opportunities to develop sustainable competitive advantage. This can be done through concentration on specific areas - the impact approach - or through a wider spread of IT - the align approach. Technology developments are probably prescriptive in their approach overall but emergent in the detailed processes.

- *Innovation* contributes growth, competitive advantage and the possibility of leapfrogging competition. However, it can also be risky and result in major losses to the organisation. There are two major drivers for innovation: customer needs analysis - market pull - and technology development analysis - technology push. The innovation process can be both prescriptive and emergent.

- *Quality* is vital for most organisations but needs to be defined in the context of the expectations of its customers. Total Quality Managment (TQM) is the modern approach to quality delivery. It involves the whole organisation and emphasises the role of quality in meeting the needs and expectations of its customers. Not every organisation operates TQM but every organisation needs to give quality high priority in corporate strategy. This means providing the appropriate emphasis as strategy is developed. Although there are benefits from TQM, there are many costs. It often takes years for the full benefits to emerge, but the costs are often obvious from an early stage.

- Overall, purpose needs to be linked to *sustainable competitive advantage*. Such a process needs to be undertaken at the *business* level, rather than the *corporate* level, in most organisations.

Possible lecture structure

- As the four main areas of the chapter have no obvious close links, it is probably better to begin by referring back to two models that underpin the book, i.e. the prescriptive and emergent.
- It might then be appropriate to refer to *vision* as a starting point: many educational institutions now have statements in this area that might form the basis of critical comment, whatever view is taken of the models. The lecturer may care to explore the statement of her/his own institution.
- Alternatively, the vision of Daimler-Benz or another company (from Chapter 12) could form the basis of an early discussion in this area.
- The structure of the lecture can then be laid out: use the overhead of Figure 11.1.
- Explore the organisation's vision for the future and its strategic implications: use the chart that follows and the overhead of Table 11.1.
- Examine the implications of developments in technology for the organisation's strategy: use the chart that follows and Figure 11.2.
- Explore the contribution of IT in developing the organisation's purpose: use the chart that follows.
- Identify the main innovation processes relevant to strategy development: use Figure 11.4, Exhibit 11.1 and the chart that follows.
- Understand and develop the organisation's policy on quality issues: use Figure 11.5 and the chart that follows.
- Comment on the areas where the organisation is likely to have competitive advantage and consider the implications for the purpose of the organisation.

Strategic project

Daimler-Benz continues to attract attention in the press. At the time of writing (late 1996), it is engaged in restructuring its operations to bring them back to the focus described in the case. Students will find plenty of references to the progress of the company and could extend this into study of contrasting strategies between this company and its traditional rival, BMW. The latter company is engaged in reviving its UK acquisition, Rover Group, with substantial investment and major changes in working practices - a totally different strategy with significant risks.

Corporate Strategy Lecturer's Guide, Pitman Publishing
© Aldersgate Consultancy Limited 1997

Vision for the future

'... A vision articulates a view of a realistic, credible, attractive future for the organisation, a condition that is better in some important ways than what now exists.'

Bennis and Nanus

Reasons for developing a vision:

- In competing for business and resources, most organisations will benefit from a vision that articulates where they wish to be.

- It stimulates the development of the mission and objectives of the organisation.

- To explore new strategic opportunities.

- Extrapolating the current picture is unlikely to be sufficient for strategy development.

- It can provide a challenge for management at all levels.

Implications for corporate strategy of developments in technology

Main elements:

Scan technologies internally and externally

Classify technologies into:

- *Base*: common to many companies

- *Core*: most likely to deliver sustainable competitive advantage along with patents and special skills

- *Peripheral*: not mainstream to organisation

Taking each technology separately, it can then be assessed against competition and the costs of further development.

Two further considerations deserve careful exploration:

- *Speed of imitation*
- *Possible global exploitation*

Corporate Strategy Lecturer's Guide, Pitman Publishing
© Aldersgate Consultancy Limited 1997

Contribution of IT to developing the organisation's purpose

Information technology (IT) has opened up the possibility of greater strategic control in organisations.

IT may also influence the competitive situation in three ways:

- *Change to balance of power in industries*

- *Creation of competitive advantage*

- *Ability to reach new customers*

Analysis of IT can be conducted in two main ways:

- *The impact approach*: concentration on specific information projects designed to build competitive advantage

- *The align approach*: IT support is spread throughout the organisation to support a wider range of strategy developments

Innovation processes relevant to strategy development

Two major drivers for innovation:

- *Technology push*: the development of new initiatives in technology
- *Market pull*: the analysis of customer needs

Processes can be:

- *Emergent*: ideas freely available from many sources
- *Prescriptive*: more analytical and directed approach to innovation
- *Comment*: probably a need for both depending on the circumstances

Some guidelines in the search for innovation:

- Question the present business strategies and market definitions
- Consider carefully the purpose served by the current products
- Explore external timing and market opportunities
- Seek out competitors' weaknesses
- Deliver new and better value for money
- Search far and wide
- Seek to challenge conventional wisdom

Corporate Strategy Lecturer's Guide, Pitman Publishing
© Aldersgate Consultancy Limited 1997

Policy on quality issues

Total Quality Management (TQM) is the modern strategic approach to quality delivery.

Characteristics of TQM:

- *Works throughout the organisation*
- *Lays emphasis on workers being responsible for quality*
- *Tries to 'get things right first time', rather than rectify defects later*

Competitive advantage may follow from the adoption of TQM, if it is not successfully undertaken by competitors.

TQM has many costs, such as:

- *Training schemes for workers*
- *Cost of empowering workers*
- *Cost of a steering group to monitor quality programmes*

TQM often takes years to implement fully, whereas the costs are often obvious from an early stage.

Case notes

Imperfect vision at Daimler-Benz

1. With the future so uncertain, was there any point in Daimler-Benz developing a vision as the basis of its strategy?

Clearly if the future is likely to change substantially, there are real difficulties in developing a vision associated with it: by definition, the only vision will be cloudy and unclear. However, vision is not concerned with predicting the future. It may accept that the future is unclear and use this to set challenging and rewarding targets that can be flexible as the future changes.

In the case of Daimler-Benz, the root of the problem in developing a vision for the company does not lie in its uncertain future. It rests with an excessively broad definition of its vision and purpose. Back in 1985, it was focussed on cars and trucks and highly profitable. Setting the vision as 'integrated technology' is therefore about as vague as possible. It led the group into its wide range of acquisitions that had no unifying logic beyond satisfying the vision statement.

The vision statement could have been used to justify almost any acquisition that had a vague technology background. By the standards of the criteria set up in Table 11.1, it would have failed on its lack of clarity in uniqueness and foresight about an industry. It is just a generalised wish statement. No wonder the centre was accused of waffle in the graphic phrase quoted in the case of one of its managing directors.

2. Can a future vision be essentially very broad, as it was at Daimler-Benz? Or should vision be more focussed by constraints such as the existing core skills of the group?

If the company had been more focussed, it would certainly have been easier to develop a statement about its vision. If the areas are too broad, the vision becomes so vague as to be meaningless. If these broad generalisations are then acted upon, they can lead to the mess in which Daimler-Benz has found itself in the late 1990s. However, in fairness it should be said that a flawed vision was not the only reason for the company's difficulties.

Vision needs to build on the core skills and resources of the group. It may well develop out of these into new areas. However, it will essentially have somewhere to focus its perspective.

It follows that vision is difficult for holding companies, such as Daimler-Benz. The vision can be either defined at the business level, e.g. transport, or possibly in the context of the role of the holding company, e.g. to be a better parent for the whole of the group, though this is also vague. Parenting strategy is explored in Chapter 19.

Corporate Strategy Lecturer's Guide, Pitman Publishing
© Aldersgate Consultancy Limited 1997

Motorola provides a competitive advantage

1. Can you name business situations where such a system might provide competitive advantage?

Clearly, the case concentrated on a sporting occasion rather than a business opportunity. However, there are likely to be many opportunities when rapid and accurate communications can lead to major competitive advantage. For example:

- Commodity market trading where the latest price information is crucial to profit.
- Hospital emergencies where call-out procedures rely on such technology.
- Sales people taking an urgent sales order that can be actioned much more quickly as a result of such procedures.

2. What is the main long-term competitive strategy problem with such a technical advance?

It can be copied by competitors.

Such technical advantages rarely deliver long-term advantage in themselves. It is usually possible for the competition to replicate them over time. It is often the case that the competitive advantage represents between six months' and two years' worth of benefit.

Patenting represents the main strategic circumstance where there may be some protection. However, even here, there are technical difficulties in holding patents and vast expense is required in pursuing patent infringements. Moreover, any such battle represents time and resources taken from further enhancement of the basic development route. Scientists have to spend time preparing a defence for the area already developed, rather than exploring the next generation of advances.

3. What other elements of competitive strategy should the Motorola team pursue to ensure success?

- Bicycle design and performance.
- Team selection to obtain the best members.
- Team strategy to ensure that mobile information is used to best advantage.

In addition, the team should examine its rivals carefully to see what developments are being pursued by them. They should also examine innovative solutions outside the cycling industry. For example, many aspects of new cycle design and performance in the last five years have come from technologies completely outside traditional cycle development: better aerodynamics, new light-weight materials and so on.

Innovation at Corning

1. The case implies that innovation arises primarily as a result of a strong research and development (R&D) team. Is this all that is required for innovation? How would you judge the amount of funds to be made available for R&D in the first place and how would you assess the results? Based on your answer, what is your assessment of innovation at Corning?

The case concentrates on three major research initiatives successfully undertaken by Corning since the company was set up in the 1880s: the light bulb, mass-produced TV glass tubes and optical fibres for carrying telecommunications signals. The company also has a successful record in other areas such as catalytic converters and blood testing equipment. Many companies would be delighted with such a record of innovative new products.

However, the case does not record some aspects of the Corning culture that will be important in the development of innovation: for example, the links between R&D and marketing, the organisation structure needed to support and not stifle the technical skills at Corning.

Importantly, all the Corning innovations are *products*, yet innovation can occur *anywhere* in an organisation. For example, it might occur in stock holding or administration. The Corning concept of innovation is narrow and restrictive. It may well miss important and highly productive areas of development in the company. Case study 10.1 on Toyota shows how innovation was used to produce a whole series of ideas in technology processes that saved that company US$1.5 billion per annum. Corning is missing important areas of activity.

On the question of R&D funds for innovation, there is no easy answer. Many companies decide on such funds by taking them as a percentage of sales. However, Case study 10.3 on MorphSys shows how a company can raise this ratio to 100 per cent if the circumstances justify this.

2. Do customers have a role in the innovation process beyond passively examining the ideas produced by the R&D boffins? If so, what is that role and how does it relate to corporate strategy?

A possible weakness of the Corning approach was its apparent heavy reliance on technology push, rather than customer pull (see the text for explanation of these terms). In one sense, it is not possible to ask customers to speculate on what they do not know. However, there was little evidence beyond the solar energy example that customers were the driving force behind R&D development. Perhaps Corning was missing an opportunity here. However, their record is so good that it would not be fair to be over-critical on this matter.

The role of customer-pull innovation relies on the concept that surveying the wants of customers may lead to new and innovative products. The resulting areas of innovation

Corporate Strategy Lecturer's Guide, Pitman Publishing
© Aldersgate Consultancy Limited 1997

may rely less on technical developments and more on service or line extension developments. They are no less useful for all that, however.

3. Comment is made in the case study that the company is seeking to find another major innovation to match the three it claims to have pioneered already. Is this really the process of innovation or are there more modest ways that require smaller, incremental steps but still achieve competitive advantage?

There is some disagreement in the literature on the methods of attaining innovation: some favour the major step forward, e.g. Gluck, while others favour the incremental small step approach, e.g. J B Quinn. Although in practice most organisations would be prepared to accept whatever route leads to genuine innovation, the *method* by which it is achieved is important because it shapes the approach of the organisation to the task.

Corning apparently favours the big bang approach, but there are other ways forward that may be appropriate for other companies.

How Perrier Water lost its sparkle and its independence

1. Given that the purity of the product was so important, what two explanations did Perrier offer for its contamination? What does this imply about the company's procedures at that time with regard to quality?

The two explanations offered were: (a) that the North American production line had been contaminated by the benzene used to clean the machinery filling the bottles; (b) that the filters used to remove benzene, as the product was extracted from the ground, had not been changed sufficiently frequently.

This clearly implies that the company's quality procedures were poor. It should be noted that this was not just a matter of some minor improvement: the purity of the product is the essence of appeal for such mineral waters.

2. Once the situation was clear, Perrier decided to scrap all its product stock world-wide at a cost of US$200 million. Was this the total cost of failure? If not, what other costs might have been involved?

With commendable responsibility, Perrier acted fast to ensure that its difficulties were clearly publicised and acted upon. It was not the total cost of failure.

- Sales, and therefore profits, were then lost over the succeeding weeks as the product was no longer available.
- Sales were lost in the longer term as it was unable to recover its market share.
- The cost of cleaning up the factory and introducing new procedures was also significant.

Arguably, the biggest cost of failure was the loss of drive and energy by the company. The credibility of the main family owners was also affected. Ultimately, this led to the break-up of the Perrier group and part at least of this was related to the quality problem. In terms of the cost of quality failure, it could therefore be argued that the group would have obtained a higher value from Nestlé if Perrier sales had been higher and there had been no quality problem.

3. With hindsight, how would you assess the cost of preventing such a quality breakdown in the company? Could such a cost be set against a new quality improvement programme? What items might be included in the programme?

For most food products, the cost of contamination is very high: for example, salmonella contamination can cause a food factory to be completely closed immediately. Although the traces of benzene were very small and could not be equated to the problems of salmonella, Perrier failed to realise the impact of such a problem on its brand and customers. The cost was high and could clearly be set against the cost of a new quality improvement programme. Items to be included might have covered quality testing, the organisation of the production line, training programmes and the time taken to empower workers to take more responsibility for quality.

Corporate Strategy Lecturer's Guide, Pitman Publishing
© Aldersgate Consultancy Limited 1997

Chapter 12
Mission and objectives

Synopsis of chapter

The chapter explores the appropriateness and implications of developing the mission and objectives of the organisation. Four background issues that may influence such matters are explored: stakeholders, culture, leadership and ethics. The issues involved in developing the mission and objectives of the organisation are then considered.

Summary

- The *mission* of an organisation outlines the broad directions that it should follow in the future and outlines the reasoning and values that lie behind it.The *objectives* are a more detailed commitment consistent with the organisation's mission and specify a particular time period. They may be quantified in some cases; this may be inappropriate in others. Prescriptive approaches emphasise the need to set out a mission and objectives for the next few years for the organisation.

- Some emergent approaches doubt the usefulness of a mission and objectives because the future is so uncertain. Other emergent approaches accept the need for a mission and objectives but place great emphasis on the need to include the managers and employees in its development.

- Stakeholders are the individuals and groups who have an interest in the organisation and as a result may wish to have a say in its mission and objectives. The organisation needs to take stakeholders into account in formulating its mission and objectives.

- Problems arise because stakeholder interests may conflict. Consequently, it is necessary for the organisation to determine which stakeholders have priority. Stakeholder power needs to be analysed and this can be done in five stages: identification of stakeholders, establishment of their interests and claims, estimation of their degree of power, prioritised mission development, negotiation with key groups.

- The culture of the organisation will also influence and be reflected in the mission and objectives. Typically, attitudes to risk and the ability to undertake change will form and guide the development of such areas.

- Leaders can have a profound influence on mission and objectives. They may be particularly important in moving the organisation forward to new challenges. There is no agreement on how to analyse leadership. The best-fit analytical approach can be used. It is useful in strategy because it allows each situation to be treated differently. Leadership style can vary from shared vision to dominance. The style needs to be modified to suit the strategic situation.

- Business ethics are the standards and conduct that an organisation sets itself in its dealings within the organisation and with its external environment. These need to be reflected in the mission statement. There are three prime considerations in developing business ethics: the extent of ethical considerations, their cost and the recipient of the responsibility. There are differing views among organisations over what should be covered under ethics, reflecting fundamentally different approaches to doing business.

- The mission statement outlines the broad directions that the organisation will follow and briefly summarises the reasoning and values that lie behind it. The purpose of the mission statement is to *communicate* to all the stakeholders inside and outside the organisation what the company stands for and where it is headed.

- There are six elements in formulating a mission statement: nature of the organisation, customer perspective, values and beliefs, competitive advantage or distinctiveness, main reasons for the approach. Mission statements rely on business judgement but criteria can be developed to assess the results.

- Objectives translate the generalities of the mission statement into more specific commitments usually covering what is to be done and when the objective is to be completed. Different kinds of objectives are possible - some quantified and some not. There may be conflict between objectives, particularly between the long- and short-term interests of the organisation. Shareholding structures will impact on objectives. UK and USA companies are under greater pressure for short-term performance. Objectives need to be challenging but achievable.

- There is a danger in being too rational in the development of mission and objectives. Mission statements need to reflect the *values* of the organisation as well as a statement of its purpose.

Possible lecture structure

- Comment briefly on the Ford global objective in the Minicase and use this to introduce the different elements of the lecture: use Figure 12.1.
- Contrast prescriptive and emergent approaches to mission and objectives: use the chart that follows.
- Identify the main stakeholders and conduct a stakeholder power analysis: use Table 12.1 to explain possible conflict of interest, Figure 12.2 and the chart that follows on the five discrete steps.
- Explore the roles of organisational culture and leadership: use the chart that follows and refer back to Chapter 8. Explain the best-fit approach to analysing leadership using Figure 12.3.
- Identify the main issues involved in business ethics and their influence on the development of the organisation's mission: use the chart that follows.
- Develop a mission statement for the organisation: use the chart that follows and Exhibit 12.3.
- Develop the objectives: use the chart that follows.
- Distinguish between corporate, functional and business unit objectives.

Corporate Strategy Lecturer's Guide, Pitman Publishing
© Aldersgate Consultancy Limited 1997

Strategic project

The key to this project is to be critical of the statements and their underlying assumptions. Either business libraries or the companies themselves will supply a copy of their Annual Report and Accounts. Many of these will contain the research material that can then be analysed. Alternatively, most universities and colleges have developed such statements over the last ten years and they make a rich source of critical reading and comment for those so inclined.

Prescriptive and emergent approaches to mission and objectives

Mission of an organisation

- outlines the broad general directions that an organisation should and will follow;
- briefly summarises the reasoning and values that lie behind such directions.

Objectives

- represent a more specific commitment over a specified time period consistent with the mission;
- may be quantified but inappropriate in some circumstances.

Prescriptive approaches emphasise the need to set out the mission and objectives for the next few years.

Emergent approaches take divergent views:

- One approach doubts the usefulness of a mission and objectives because the future is so uncertain

- Another approach accepts the need for a mission and objectives but places greater emphasis on the need to include managers and employees in its development

Corporate Strategy Lecturer's Guide, Pitman Publishing
© Aldersgate Consultancy Limited 1997

Five discrete steps to analysing stakeholder power

1   Identify the major stakeholders.

2   Establish their interests and claims on the organisation, especially as new strategy initiatives are developed.

3   Determine the degree of power that each group holds through its ability to force or influence change as new strategies are developed.

4   Develop mission, objectives and strategy, possibly prioritising to minimise power clashes.

5   Consider how to divert trouble before it starts, possibly by negotiating with key groups.

The roles of culture and leadership in developing mission and objectives

Role of culture:

'The way we do things around here.'

Assess particularly:

- Attitudes to risk
- Ability to undertake strategic change

Role of leadership:

'The art or process of influencing people so that they will strive willingly and enthusiastically toward the achievement of the group's mission.'

Assess particularly:

- Need to inspire organisation
- Need to reflect and support employees
- Strategic need in some cases to take hard decisions, e.g. in failing business
- Leadership style: will vary from *shared vision* to *dominant*

Corporate Strategy Lecturer's Guide, Pitman Publishing
© Aldersgate Consultancy Limited 1997

Business ethics in corporate strategy

Business ethics are the standards and conduct that an organisation sets itself in its dealings within the organisation and with its external environment: need to be reflected in the mission statement.

Three prime considerations in developing business ethics:

- ***the extent of ethical considerations***

- ***their cost***

- ***the recipient of the responsibility***

There are numerous differences of view between organisations over what should be covered under ethics, reflecting fundamentally different approaches to doing business.

How to formulate a mission statement

Six main elements:

- *Consider the nature of the business. What business are we in? What business should we be in?*

- *Examine the customer perspective: customer benefits are more useful than descriptive comments.*

- *Reflect the values and beliefs of the organisation.*

- *Statements need to comment either on sustainable competitive advantage or on the distinctiveness of the organisation.*

- *The mission needs to summarise the main reasons for its choice of approach.*

Typically, the whole approach will take time and involve wide consultation throughout the organisation.

Corporate Strategy Lecturer's Guide, Pitman Publishing
© Aldersgate Consultancy Limited 1997

Developing the objectives

Objectives take the generalities of the mission statement and turn them into more specific commitments: usually, this will cover what is to be done and the timing.

Different kinds of objectives are possible: some will be quantified, some not.

There may be conflict between objectives, particularly between the long-term and short-term interests of the organisation.

Shareholding structures will also influence objectives. UK and USA companies are often under greater pressure for short-term performance.

Typically, objectives need to be challenging but achievable.

Case notes

The Ford Motor Company objective - to develop a global organisation

1. Who should be involved in devising the mission and objectives of the company?

This apparently simple question does not necessarily have a simple answer. Many would initially argue that a wide range of managers and employees should be involved in the process. However, there are two complications:

- *Why not involve a wider range of stakeholders?* There is no theoretical reason why shareholders, the government and so on should not be consulted. However, it would be most unusual to undertake this on a formal basis because of the complexity of handling the inputs and the culture surrounding such a wider consultation process: some might think that the company cannot make up its mind.

How to handle the situation where a radical new route based on judgement is proposed? In the case of Ford, the idea of developing a global organisation requires a radical repositioning of the company which may need a few centrally placed managers to carry it forward. It might not be appropriate in such circumstances to engage in open-ended consultation. Radical vision may demand a form of dominant leadership.

2. Should they stress the global issue or is globalisation a strategy to achieve the objective and therefore inappropriate for this [mission] *statement?*

This is primarily a matter of judgement with no simple rules. If the purpose of the organisation is to make and sell cars and other commercial vehicles, globalisation is not necessarily part of this mission. Certainly the way that Ford presented its new global strategy in 1994 would suggest that the aims of globalisation were to make cost savings through global sourcing of components, global R&D and so on. These are *strategies* to achieve the underlying objective of increasing sales and profits.

If this argument is correct, then the headline above the case is wrong: it should read, 'The Ford Motor Company *strategy* - to develop a global organisation.'

3. What should happen to such a statement when it has been prepared? Does it need to be circulated beyond senior managers? If so, to whom?

Unless there are some special reasons for confidentiality, such as survival for a near-bankrupt enterprise, there is an overwhelming case for its wide circulation within and outside the organisation. Stakeholders are entitled to know its purposes. There can be little to be lost by a public debate about the purpose as summarised in such statements.

Corporate Strategy Lecturer's Guide, Pitman Publishing
© Aldersgate Consultancy Limited 1997

Mission and objectives at Business in the Community

1. In what ways does this statement and contents differ from those of a commercial organisation?

The statement:

- Reflects values and judgemental issues rather more than would a commercial organisation.

- Makes no comparison with other competing institutions, but emphasises its distinctiveness.

- Contains a clear statement concerned primarily with the good of parts of society as a whole, rather than with the sectional interests of a business.

2. Are there any areas that you think would benefit from greater clarity or other developments? Can you improve on it?

In the original statement, the objectives are called 'strategic objectives'. Arguably, this muddles two quite separate strategic concepts, i.e. the objectives and the strategies to achieve those objectives.

None of the objectives are quantified: for example, what does 'measurably improve' actually mean? Is it possible to measure such concepts as 'quality, impact and sustainability'? How will they be measured? How will the improvement be defined and measured?

The objectives are addressed to the *charitable organisation* itself, but they appear to reflect what it wishes *business* to undertake. Arguably, this distinction should be clearer in that the charitable activities are within the control of the organisation, whereas business activity is not.

Pink Elephant Company

The case traces the history of the computer company with the above name and that of its parent, RCC or Roccade.

1. Do you think the company is wise to set an objective of boosting sales two- to three-fold in the long term? What are the problems with this approach?

Given the growth already achieved in recent years, the company can justify such high rates of sales increase in coming years. There is evidence to support what may be a challenging target.

The problems with the approach stem from its demanding nature and the extent to which it was discussed and agreed with those who have to carry it out. Clearly, with the market growing fast, it may be reasonable to set such an objective but if there were to be a downturn in the market, then it might become impossible. In turn, this might be demotivating for those who are still tasked with reaching such an objective.

The problem is more acute if the objective has been *imposed* upon those who have to execute it. In such circumstances, there may be little commitment to its achievement and considerable resentment. By contrast, if the objective has been discussed and agreed with those who have to achieve it, there will be a greater degree of willingness.

2. RCC has kept the identities and names of the companies it has acquired in order to preserve the entrepreneurial spirit of each company. Do you think that in these circumstances RCC itself can have any useful 'mission'? If so, what should this be?

If the companies that it has acquired have very different businesses, it is difficult to see how RCC can achieve sufficient focus to make a mission and objectives of value. In this situation, it may be better to adopt the parenting objectives of a holding company as outlined in Chapters 13 and 20.

3. Do you think that the privatisation of RCC should be reflected in its mission and objectives? If so, in what way?

Yes, because it will fundamentally alter the style and operation of the company. If it is not stated, then the purpose will have been unstated in an important area.

It is difficult to be precise without a statement of what is now being employed. However, the essence of the statement would be the purpose of striving to ensure that the business remains profitable and provides a reasonable return to those who owned shares in the company. It might also reflect the need to deliver profits as a means for survival and growth.

Corporate Strategy Lecturer's Guide, Pitman Publishing
© Aldersgate Consultancy Limited 1997

Chapter 13
Resource-based strategic options

Synopsis of chapter

In the context of the wide range of options that could easily be generated, the chapter first considers how they could be prioritised. It then explores four main option areas: the *value chain*, *resource-based capabilities*, *core competences* and *cost reduction* options. Finally, the chapter examines the resource options in some special types of organisation: small business, not-for-profit and diversified multi-product groups.

Summary

- It can be difficult to cope with the number of options that can quickly arise. There are three ways in which the process might be focussed.

  1. *Leadership*: can provide the guidance and vision to direct the search process.

  2. *Key factors for success*: can be identified to focus the options search into relevant areas.

  3. *Value added, competitive advantage* and *the organisation's mission and objectives* will provide strategic purpose to the process. These need to be considered early in options development.

- Resource options can be developed by considering the value chain of the organisation, which will help to identify competitive advantage. Value can be added early in the value chain, *upstream*, or later in the value chain, *downstream*. The choice of where and how value can be added will generate strategic resource options.

  - *Upstream* activities add value by processing raw materials into *standardised* products: such options concentrate on lower costs.

  - *Downstream* activities add value by marketing, service and other activities designed to produce *differentiated* products.

- Resource options can be developed from three main areas of the organisation. First, the *resource-based capabilities*: the resource assets of the organisation such as machinery and finance. Second, the *core competences*: the skills and knowledge accumulated over many years. Third, *cost reduction options*: the opportunities that exist in many organisations to reduce the costs incurred by the resources of the organisation.

- It is important to understand the distinction between two of the above areas:
  - *Resource-based capabilities*: the options that can be generated by the functional assets of the organisation.

- *Core competences*: the options deriving from such areas as the basic skills, knowledge and technology of the organisation.

- When related to market opportunities, *core competences* may lead to options for the organisation in four main areas: they range from small opportunities using current skills to major new areas that will deliver real scope for the future. New core competences may be needed to meet such important major options.

- There is also the possibility of *cost-cutting* as a resource-based strategy. It is possible to develop a model which examines this in a structured and cross-functional way.

- Some specific types of organisation present special resource-based opportunities and problems:

  - *Small businesses* have a limited range of resources. However, they can overcome this by employing outside advisers and concentrating resources. A more flexible service may provide a real competitive advantage.

  - *Charitable organisations* benefit from exceptional resources: their beliefs that drive the society and the use of voluntary workers. However, they may need to provide such people extra freedom to keep them motivated.

  - *Government institutions* have highly professional resources but may be bureaucratic in their approach, unwieldy and slow to respond to events.

  - *Diversified multi-product groups* can gain from the special resource of their corporate headquarters, the *parent* of the subsidiaries.

- *Parenting* may provide special functions, new initiatives, additional finance for growing areas, and formal linkages between the subsidiaries. The key issue is whether the parental resource adds extra value beyond those of the individual businesses.

- Parenting is more likely to add extra value when two conditions are fulfilled. First, the parent needs to understand the key factors for success of all the industries in which its subsidiaries are involved. Second, the parent itself needs to contribute or arrange some service or resource that is beyond that of its subsidiaries.

Possible lecture structure

- Explore the resources employed at Matra-Hachette/Lagardère Group and the lack of any real logic to the merger, including the different resources of the two parts.
- Comment on the large number of potential options and the consequent need for three priority guidelines: use Figure 13.1.
- Consider the *value chain* in the development of resource options, explaining the implications of upstream and downstream functions in generating options: use Figure 13.2, Table 13.1 and Exhibit 13.1.

- Explore the concept of *resource-based strategy options*: use Figure 13.3 and link back with earlier parts of the analytical process. Highlight on this Figure resource-based capabilities, core competences and cost reduction options.
- Explain resource-based capability options: use the chart that follows.
- Explain core competence options: use Figure 13.4.
- Explain cost reduction options: use Figure13.5.
- Examine resource options in some special types of organisation - how small businesses, not-for-profit organisations and diversified multi-product groups: use the chart that follows.
- Comment especially on the contribution made by the *headquarters* of multi-product organisations - the concept of *parenting*: use the chart that follows.

Strategic project

The activities of the main media companies in Europe centre on strategies related to the use of resources. There are plenty of sources: see *Financial Times*, 25 April 1996, p13; 23 September 1996, p15. There are equally important developments in other parts of the world which readers might like to investigate: for example, see *Financial Times*, 21 February 1996, p17 for US; see 10 October 1996, p13 for Japanese developments. In my opinion, this is an area where strategy is developing and changing radically as the book was going to press: technology, core competences, innovation, globalisation, personality clashes and good old-fashioned naked competition could deliver an interesting project.

Resource-based capability options

Resource-based options need to offer some *distinctiveness* over competitors.

One method of generating options would be to measure the resource-based capabilities of the organisation against three criteria and examine the implications:

- *Architecture*: the network of relationships and contracts both within and outside the organisation

- *Reputation*: the favourable impression generated by the organisation

- *Innovation*: the organisation's capacity to develop new products or services

New options in these areas may take lengthy periods to develop.

Corporate Strategy Lecturer's Guide, Pitman Publishing
© Aldersgate Consultancy Limited 1997

Resource-based options in some special types of organisation

Small business: unlikely to have at their disposal the resource range of larger companies.

- Employ outside advisers to act as consultants.
- Concentrate resources on particular tasks likely to yield added value and competitive advantage.
- Offer superior service.

Not-for-profit organisations: charities have two unique resources:

- Beliefs that drive the organisation forward.
- Voluntary workers who often devote exceptional effort to the organisation.

Not-for-profit organisations: government-funded institutions:

- Often highly professional resources.
- But may be exceptionally bureaucratic.
- Culture important in devising options.

Diversified multi-product groups: totally different resources in unrelated markets

- Each subsidiary has its own resources.
- Corporate headquarters - the *parent* - will also provide a resource: needs careful consideration.

Parenting

The parenting resource of corporate headquarters can offer:

- **Central functions and services**, e.g. international treasury management.

- **Corporate development initiatives**, e.g. centralised R&D or new acquisitions.

- **Additional finance for growth areas**: principle of product portfolio/growth share matrix.

- **Formal linkages between businesses**, e.g. the transfer of technology or core competences.

The purpose of parenting is to *add value* to the subsidiaries that are served. Otherwise, the extra cost of parenting cannot be justified.

For parenting to add value, the *role* of headquarters needs careful scrutiny. Specifically, the parent needs two skills:

- **Understanding of the *key factors for success* in all the industries of its subsidiaries.**

- **Ability to contribute *something extra*, perhaps in one or more of the areas outline above.**

Corporate Strategy Lecturer's Guide, Pitman Publishing
© Aldersgate Consultancy Limited 1997

Case notes

Hachette Media rescued, but what was the strategic logic?

*1. Why would bankruptcy at Hachette have been particularly unattractive to
M Lagardère? And to the banks?*

It would have meant that the assets of Hachette would have had to be sold at what
they would have fetched under the pressure of a rapid sale. It is quite likely that the
sale of such assets would have been significantly less than their value if they were
sold in other circumstances. To purchase assets in the earlier years and to help the
company survive in the later years, the banks had lent it substantial sums. It is
therefore possible that the banks would have been unable to recover the funds they
had invested. For these reasons, a solution that involved the company merging with
another, essentially without the use of cash, was preferable to one that involved the
sale under pressure of assets for cash, i.e. bankruptcy.

Strategic logic was therefore sacrificed in the face of a greater need to survive.
However, it could be argued that survival is the first objective of strategy so the
solution was not so unacceptable.

*2. What are the advantages of merging with another company that has similar
strategic interests?*

Possible advantages would depend on the specific circumstances, but might include:

• Development of joint core competences.
• Cross-fertilisation of skills and resources.
• Economies of scale in some areas, e.g. purchasing of common raw materials.
• Economies of scope, e.g. the use of a joint headquarters or salesforce.

None of these advantages were available to Matra-Hachette because of the wide
differences between the markets, resources and skills of the two companies.

3. If you were M Lagardère, what other options might you have considered?

The main problem was the media group, Hachette, so options would need to have
addressed this area. The obvious solution would have been to have considered a
merger with another media group. There was considerable consolidation taking place
in the world-wide media market at that time and Hachette was significant enough to
be attractive to another media partner, in spite of its profit problems in one area. Thus
a merger with Bertelsmann (Germany), News International (Australia) or one of the
medium-size UK groups was a possibility. The problems of such an arrangement
were: M Lagardère would have lost control and an important part of French media
would have passed partly outside French control.

Another more problematic option might have been to have closed *La Cinq* completely after negotiating further funds from the French banks. The original Hachette empire would then have continued as before.

A further option would have been to sell off part of Hachette to the highest bidder: for example, the distribution part of the media group's resources. The funds from such a sale might then have been used to resolve its difficulties elsewhere.

Corporate Strategy Lecturer's Guide, Pitman Publishing
© Aldersgate Consultancy Limited 1997

News Corporation builds a global television network - 1

1. How and where does News Corporation add value to its services? Where does it obtain its competitive advantage? What strategies has it adopted on barriers to entry?

News Corporation adds value through the wide range of activities conducted by its various companies, both in TV *and* in newspapers. Taking the value chain as a checklist, the company is involved in both upstream and downstream functions:

- *Inbound logistics*: purchasing news items, especially those where it can have exclusivity.
- *Operations*: making films for TV, writing stories for newspapers.
- *Outbound logistics*: satellite channels, encoders and encryption
- *Marketing and sales*: heavy promotion of its media offerings on its own media and rival media.
- *Service*: setting up telephone answering and other means of handling TV activity.

Competitive advantage comes from at least three areas:

- Some of its films, such as the *X-Files*, and purchase of TV Sporting rights, such as the Rugby SuperLeague.
- Its TV channels, encoders and encryption technology.
- Its cross-promotion of media through its ownership of various media channels.

2. How has the company's vision of its future been translated into reality over the last ten years?

- Development of a UK-based TV network
- Development of US-based TV network
- Beginnings of TV channels in China and the Far East
- Joint ventures and other links around the world.

3. If you were a competitor of News Corporation, what strategies would you investigate to counter any possible threat posed by encryption?

- Careful and thorough investigation of the News Corporation patent protection to estimate if and how it could be broken.
- Investigation of alternative encryption technologies *coupled with* the investigation of interest by other competitors to set up a rival method. This latter point is vital because any alternative might be too expensive for one operator and it would need to gain widespread acceptance if it was to become the standard.
- Set up a formal agreement with News Corporation.
- Invest in cable TV as an alternative channel to customers.

4. If you were developing the corporate strategy of a smaller company amid these industry giants, what strategy options would you investigate?

- Gaps in the markets served by the leaders: see Chapter 14, especially services.
- Resources that support or supply the main companies.
- New technology initiatives that go beyond what is currently available and undermine existing media: the obvious area is the Internet.

More formally, it would be helpful to review the strategy options suggested by core competences as the basis of development: see Figure 13.4.

Corporate Strategy Lecturer's Guide, Pitman Publishing
© Aldersgate Consultancy Limited 1997

Developing resource options at Eastman Kodak

1. How would you advise Mr Fisher to analyse his resources? What should he examine first? How should he approach the task?

It would appear that Mr Fisher has begun by establishing his priorities: the need to examine costs, the need to generate growth and so on.

Beyond this, the analysis of resource capabilities and competences will yield significant options for the future. At the time of writing the case, it would appear that some areas had been identified but significant areas of study remained. This is entirely correct: it may take some time to establish all the main factors in such a resource analysis, especially when they formed the foundation for future growth.

As far as a cost analysis is concerned, he might find it appropriate to use the cost structure outlined in Figure 13.5. It should be said that this is a generalised model that would need to be adapted to the specific needs of the Eastman Kodak company but it has the great benefit of providing a structured route forward.

2. What are the core resources, competences and skills of Kodak?

Core resources:

Architecture: Links with suppliers, distributors and customers in the photographic and media businesses.
World-wide network of companies and affiliated organisations.
Ability to develop film fast and cheaply: organisational skills required

Reputation: Brand name
Quality products and services

Innovation: Some recent innovations such as digital imaging, but weaker here.

Core competences and skills: silver halide technology, photographic film, digital imaging, photographic services including developing.

3. Do you agree that there is still plenty of scope for development in the traditional film and photographic business?

The *evidence* in the case does not provide a convincing picture, but this may simply arise from the brevity of the case study. Ideally, it would be useful to know more about when film is used, by whom, on what occasions, etc. Conclusions could then be drawn on whether there were very few additional occasions for its use or plenty of opportunities.

Judging from the material presented in the case, it would appear that there are *some* opportunities, but nothing really convincing. One issue may be the extent to which people will switch to alternative forms of recording their images, e.g. video recording.

However, even this is not convincing: people may choose to own both a still and a video camera.

Another method of approaching the question would be to examine the market share of Eastman Kodak: it may be large in some countries, indicating little scope for further growth. However, in other countries such as Japan, the market share is much smaller than one of its world rivals - *Fuji Film* - indicating some growth is still possible.

4. Is Mr Fisher following the correct strategy?

If the market is mature, then strategy may need to take place upstream and cutting costs while improving service may represent excellent strategy. However, it is not clear that this is the only strategy.

For example, Fuji has attempted with some success to gain market share by direct links with major film processors, by setting up fast developing laboratories and other attacks on parts of the Kodak franchise.

Other companies have launched specialist products and services that do not compete directly against Kodak but segment the market and compete on a flank: see Chapter 5.

All this suggests that Mr Fisher was correct in refocussing the company on film and associated skills and products, its area of real core strength. But the company also needs to experiment and become more *innovative* in its approaches to these areas. For example, exploring whether there is any other service that could use its extensive distribution contacts with photographic suppliers.

Corporate Strategy Lecturer's Guide, Pitman Publishing
© Aldersgate Consultancy Limited 1997

Chapter 14
Market-based strategic options

Synopsis of chapter

The chapter covers three main areas of strategic opportunity that are primarily market based: generic strategies, market options and expansion methods within the context of market options. It provides not only a description of the options but also a critical evaluation of their contribution to the strategy development process.

Summary

- Generic strategies are a means of generating basic strategy options in an organisation. They are based on seeking competitive advantage in the market place. There are three main generic options: cost leadership, differentiation and focus.

  1. *Cost leadership* aims to make the organisation among the lowest cost producers in the market. It does not necessarily mean having low prices. Higher than average profits come from charging average prices.

  2. *Differentiation* is aimed at developing and targetting a product against a major market segment, enabling it to be priced at a small premium. The cost of differentiation should be more than compensated for in the higher price charged.

  3. *Focus* involves targetting a small segment of the market by using a low cost focus or a differentiated focus approach.

- Some theorists consider it is important to select between the options and not to be 'stuck in the middle' but a number of influential strategists have produced evidence that has cast doubt on this point. Criticisms of the approach, based on logic and empirical evidence of actual industry practice undoubtedly have validity, but generic strategies still represent a useful starting point in developing strategy options.

- *The Market Options Matrix.* By examining the market place and the products available, it is possible to structure options that an organisation may be able to adopt. Such options may include moving to new customers and new products. Developing these options may involve the organisation in diversifying away from its original markets. Synergy is the main reason behind such diversification: the whole being more than the sum of the parts. This concept is associated with linkages in the value chain. The Market Options Matrix is a method of generating options, but provides no guidance on choosing between them. The main strategic insights come from the possibilities that are raised to challenge the current thinking by opening up the debate.

- The *Expansion Method Matrix* explores in a structured way the methods by which market options might be achieved. By examining the organisation's internal and external expansion opportunities and its geographical spread of activity, it is possible to structure the various methods that are available. Within the home country, the four main methods of expansion are: acquisition, joint venture, alliance and franchise. Each has its advantages and problems. Beyond the home country, there are additional means of international expansion, including exporting, setting up overseas offices and undertaking full manufacturing. The greatest risk associated with international expansion is probably currency fluctuation.

Possible lecture structure

- Explore briefly the market options available to the Dutch company Alcas and its joint venture Muzak Europe.
- Explain the concept of *market-based strategy options*: use Figure 14.1 and link back with earlier parts of the analytical process. Highlight on this Figure generic strategies, market options matrix and expansion method matrix.
- Explore generic strategy options and evaluate their potential: use Figures 14.2, 14.3 and 14.4. To provide an example, use Figure 14.5.
- Outline the Market Options Matrix and its contribution to developing market-based options: use Figure 14.8.
- Demonstrate the options prompted by the Expansion Method Matrix and their implications for market-based options: use Figure 14.9.
- Comment on the contributions of all three routes to the strategic development process: use the two-page chart that follows.

Strategic project

The mobile telecommunications market is fast-growing with major changes in technology still to emerge. Against such a background, companies are attempting to develop viable strategies. There are two types of company: those supplying equipment and those supplying services. It is the latter that seems to have the greatest potential for uncertain strategic developments. Equipment relies on economies of scale, branding and technologies that are well-known, if still to be fully exploited. By contrast, voice services are still forming alliances to take advantage of many new country opportunities, e.g. liberalisation in Europe, satellite services around the world. There are major strategic moves still to be made in this area based on market opportunities that deserve careful investigation.

Corporate Strategy Lecturer's Guide, Pitman Publishing
© Aldersgate Consultancy Limited 1997

Some comments on market-based strategic options - 1

Generic strategies

Low-cost leadership:

- How can it be an *option* for more than one company to be the sole leader?
- Radical technological change may undermine cost leadership.
- Cost leaders may also need to lead on price if they are to stay ahead: permanent price reduction by the cost leader may damage its market positioning.

Differentiation:

- Some forms of market differentiation are not based on price: the option is therefore over-simplistic.
- Identifying the need for differentiation solves nothing: it is the precise *form* that matters.
- Differentiation is not necessarily accompanied by higher prices: it may be used to build market share and lower profits.

continued ...

Some comments on market-based
strategic options - 2

Generic strategies *(continued)*

Focus:

- The distinction between broad and narrow targets is unclear, making the benefit difficult to evaluate.
- Although the *need* for a market niche strategy may have been identified, there is no guidance on the more difficult aspect of identifying *which* niche will be useful.

Stuck in the middle:

- Empirical evidence that some companies pursue *both* low-cost leadership *and* differentiation.

Market Options Matrix

- Useful in structuring the problem, but little value in identifying which option to choose.
- Many options require significant funds: only suitable for those with substantial resources.

Expansion Method Matrix

Useful at structuring the options but offers only limited guidance on choosing between them.

Corporate Strategy Lecturer's Guide, Pitman Publishing
© Aldersgate Consultancy Limited 1997

Case notes

Market opportunities at Muzak Europe

Before answering the questions, it is useful to undertake a brief analysis of the nature of the more fully-developed business in the USA. The purpose of such an analysis would be to explore its implications for the embryonic European business.

In the USA, each individual link earns on average US$ 652 per annum: US$ 150 million divided by 230,000 links. This is really quite a small sum per outlet. It suggests that, once the basic fixed costs of developing the music has been funded, the key business task is to gain as many links as possible at as low costs as possible. Each link will only earn a limited sum, but with many together the rewards are substantial.

It is also worth noting that the Dutch company had not selected distributors in each country prior to its new US contract. One of its first tasks and difficulties was to recruit them.

1. Undertake a SWOT analysis for the Muzak Europe company.

The SWOT analysis might include the following:

- *Strengths*: Major US backing, both technically and financially; low-cost method of distribution via satellite link; well-known name in Muzak.
- *Weaknesses*: No substantial existing distributors outside the Netherlands; low revenue per link.
- *Opportunities*: Fragmented market; large potential demand.
- *Threats*: No major individual threats but might easily be undercut on price from low-cost local producers; possibly dubious assumption that 'European' music existed.

Conclusion. It was not at all clear whether the company would be successful since it still had to sign up an important element of its business: its distributors. Even when the distributors were contracted, there would still be a lengthy period of build-up because each link only earned limited funds.

2. What market strategies did Muzak Europe adopt? What were the reasons?

It adopted the strategy of seeking distributors in countries outside Holland. It phased this process over several years: Germany, Britain and Scandinavia in 1996, Italy and Spain in 1997.

The reasoning appeared to be its limited resources outside Holland and the need to phase its expansion plans to suit its resources. Such a process is well accepted and entirely justified. The company may also have felt that it needed to use local distributors who would have a better knowledge of local market conditions, though this is not stated in the case.

3. What strategy options does Muzak Europe have for the future? What strategies would you recommend?

Beyond the brand name, the *competitive advantage* of the US Muzak link is unclear from the case. It may well be that the US company has communications experience with satellites that can usefully be applied in Europe, though such technology is hardly new. It may be that the new company will have a better resource base in terms of finance and technology: for example, the use of pre-prepared US tapes that would be cheaper to prepare than starting afresh in Europe.

Because the company is relatively small and is working in a fragmented market, it is important to establish the basis of its advantage. In reality, it will probably lie in its ability to supply music at prices lower than its rivals. However, to undertake this task, it will need economies of scale that go beyond US material and satellite links. The starting point is probably its partner distributors coupled with low prices to attract substantial business quickly. However, it should not expect to make a substantial profit for some years.

Corporate Strategy Lecturer's Guide, Pitman Publishing
© Aldersgate Consultancy Limited 1997

Two examples of generic strategy options analysis: the European ice cream industry and the global TV industry in the mid-1990s

1. If you were Nestlé in the European ice cream market, what strategy options would you pursue?

Nestlé has substantial market share in some countries, e.g. Italy and the UK, but very limited presence in others. It follows that the company should alter its marketing to suit its strengths in individual markets. Where it does not have such strengths, it may need to consider a different approach, e.g. a takeover of an existing company. Using this argument, strategy options would therefore be primarily national-based rather than pan-European.

In addition, it might attempt to operate a limited number of pan-European products based on its strong brand name and range of confectionery products. These might be distributed throughout Europe in a similar fashion to Mars Ice Creams, which has one main factory in France.

For Nestlé, generic strategies do not therefore adequately represent the range of options open to the company which split into at least three:

- Market share where it already has significant presence.
- Acquisition or some other means of entry in low-share countries.
- Pan-European activity for a limited number of selected brands.

It should be noted that the above does not pretend to represent all the options available to the company.

2. If you were News Corporation and someone recommended a low-cost option, what would your reaction be?

To some extent, the company has been following such an option in some of its TV channels for years, e.g. the early years of Sky-1 in the UK. However, the real problems with such an option are:

1. Technology.
2. Customer need for differentiation.

Technology is changing so fast in television that it is still not possible to fix on the lowest cost route: cable channels, digital television, new satellite channels, stereo sound, new forms of encryption, new joint ventures make it difficult to employ the simple economies of scale inherent in low-cost routes: they could simply be overtaken by technology.

Customers need differentiated products in media: everything from world sport to minority lifestyle cookery channels. Many customers are prepared to pay extra for their differentiation: e.g. pay-per-view for a World Boxing match. Low cost options may well come in global TV but they do not appear to represent the route forward at present.

3. Can Porter's generic strategies be used with equal confidence in both the European ice cream market and the global TV market?

In a fairly stable market such as ice cream, they may have a place as a starting point in assessing strategy options. However, as the answer above demonstrates, there can be problems: e.g. it was concluded that Nestlé should follow different strategies in different countries.

In the fast moving environment of global TV, the market opportunities, new technology and new deals currently being negotiated suggest that generic strategies have only limited usefulness. The competitive situation is changing too fast for the rather static model to be used with confidence.

Corporate Strategy Lecturer's Guide, Pitman Publishing
© Aldersgate Consultancy Limited 1997

News Corporation builds a global television network - 2

*1. Among the media companies, there is disagreement on the best route forward for corporate strategy: the **software** route versus the **hardware** route. Where does News Corporation stand in this debate? Do you judge that News Corporation has chosen the most successful long-term strategies?*

The *software* route relies largely on the use of television programming as the way to develop competitive advantage: this may also include the purchase of exclusive rights to films, TV programmes and books.

The *hardware* route is mainly concentrated on the equipment that delivers the television signal to the final customer: satellite and cable TV, plus TV stations in some countries.

News Corporation has interests in both strategies: it has negotiated some exclusive sports channel deals, while at the same time investing heavily in TV stations, satellite and encryption technology.

It is difficult to judge whether News Corporation has chosen well at this stage, because the whole business situation is changing so rapidly. As the case points out, the company nearly collapsed due to the costs of the UK satellite competition in 1990 but has subsequently made a major recovery. The potential for further significant losses is present but the company is protected to some extent by its involvement in newspaper publishing which has different strategies and is more mature. In its markets, News Corporation has a major market share which provides the group with a positive cash flow and a 'cash cow' for its more uncertain TV ventures.

The risks are significant but should all be containable, including the competitive threat. Probably the most uncertain area is that concerning Star TV and its relationship with the Chinese government. The significant losses being made on that channel at the time of writing will need some resolution over the next few years.

2. In such a fast changing market, is it possible to select a range of strategies and follow these through as the market changes? Or would a company such as News Corporation be better advised to have a general vision and then grab individual business opportunities as they arise?

From the published evidence, it would seem that News Corporation and other media companies do have a range of selected strategies. Given the large scale of investment required, this is probably essential if there is to be consistency in their policies.

However, this has not stopped companies also grabbing individual opportunities as they arise. The market is probably most unusual in the number of such ventures that are currently being developed. Any company that ignored such moves would be missing the essential opportunism that is still present in this rapidly-changing market. However, such opportunities need to be set against a background of their ability to contribute to an overall vision of the company: hence, vision is also important.

Corporate Strategy Lecturer's Guide, Pitman Publishing
© Aldersgate Consultancy Limited 1997

The question is therefore misleading: it is not a question of *either* one route *or* the other. Many companies are following *both* methods of strategy development.

3. What arguments and evidence would you investigate to judge whether Mr Murdoch was right about economies of scale?

Mr Murdoch is quoted in the case as indicating that there may be diminishing returns to being bigger. The argument is not entirely clear, but probably relates to:

- the costs of the complexity of trying to combine too many different media elements together;
- the costs of stifling the creativity, entrepreneurship and individuality of parts of an enterprise;
- the different customer needs in different countries and regions around the world.

To explore this area, it would be necessary to investigate precisely which parts of the above summarised the main arguments against economies of scale.

It would also be useful to explore the cost savings that were regularly being achieved as a result of the main economies of scale: e.g. joint programming, world-wide purchase of TV sports rights and the common use of satellite and encryption technology. From this, it should be possible to estimate whether the costs outweighed the benefits.

Corporate Strategy Lecturer's Guide, Pitman Publishing
© Aldersgate Consultancy Limited 1997

Strategic choice at British Aerospace

1. Examine the three options in the case in the context of the guidelines for core competences and decide what extra information would be needed for the company to pursue this resource area further.

Using Exhibit 13.2, it is possible to explore further the implications of core competences. For reasons of space, the extra information is only summarised below.

Criteria from Exhibit 13.2	Extra information to be explored		
	Option 1: Link with US partner	Option 2: link with GEC UK	Option 3: Seek alliances with Dasa and Aerospatiale
Technology	Unimportant	Important: unknown	Important: unknown
Links between products	Useful	Vital to clarify but little real scope to cut costs	Vital to clarify: room for real cost savings
Value added	Only parts supplier, so value added not high	Some potential but economies of scale limited	Real potential: needs exploring and will take time to negotiate
People skills	Important to handle US relations	BAe/GEC totally different cultures	Real differences in culture and style: learn from Airbus?
Financial resources	Medium	Medium	Large financial resources needed
Customers	Anglo-US large market	UK monopoly supplier: problematic?	New European base
Other skills	Unknown	Unclear	Unclear
New resources, skills and competences	Competences will decline over years	Unknown: need to be developed	Potential for real growth
Environment changes	Need to consider survival of US/UK alliance	Need to consider how US and Europe will change	Need to consider how US and Europe will change
Competitor resources	European competitors behind new US/UK alliance	Explore both US and European developments	Explore both US and European developments

2. Use the criteria for generating innovation to produce some additional options for BAe.

The options listed below come from the seven guidelines for generating innovation on pages 406 and 407. It may be that none will ultimately be successful, but those listed deserve careful analysis. The list is also not complete, nor definitive: many other options are possible.

Question the present business strategies and market definitions. Why are no Japanese or Far Eastern companies included in a possible deal? Admittedly, they have little expertise in these markets but this might allow BAe to remain the lead partner while accessing growing markets.

Explore external timing and market opportunities. An even more radical solution would be to build a Russian partnership, but the timing would have to be chosen carefully. The potential for technology exchange would be quite challenging.

Deliver new and better value for money. The case concentrates on external alliances and joint ventures. It ignores options that are *internally* generated within BAe. The Market Options Matrix could well generate some radical internal solutions. Perhaps, new products using new technology and new markets for its existing aircraft. Perhaps even backward or forward integration: for example, into airline instrument manufacturers. In turn, this might lead to new areas of cost saving.

3. Taking the three options identified in the case, where would you place them in Porter's generic strategies? Does such an analysis add significantly to the strategy considerations in this case? If so, in what way? If not, why not?

Option 1: Link with US partner. BAe would be likely to become the junior partner in such an arrangement in the long term. Nevertheless, it could expect to be operating with low costs and advanced technology by virtue of its heavy involvement in the world's largest market for aerospace. The new joint venture could therefore expect to be a low-cost leader.

Option 2: link with GEC UK. Linking with its rival UK competitor may lead to some economies of scale but they are unlikely to be a major source of competitive advantage because there is only limited overlap between the two companies. It might therefore become a product differentiator. However, such a categorisation means little when this option is primarily concerned with establishing a more broadly-based UK aerospace contractor.

Option 3: Seek alliances with Dasa and Aerospatiale. There would be little point in such alliances unless they were to lead to lower costs and increased product development, possibly producing differentiated products from new technologies. This might lead in broad target markets to low-cost leadership or differentiation or both, which Professor Porter would find unacceptable.

Corporate Strategy Lecturer's Guide, Pitman Publishing
© Aldersgate Consultancy Limited 1997

It would appear from the above that generic strategies do not always produce new insights: for example, alliances and joint ventures are not really explored in this concept. If anything, generic strategies somtimes appear to produce contradictions that cannot easily be resolved.

4. Use the Expansion Method Matrix to analyse the advantages and disadvantages of the three options in the case. What conclusions can you draw on the opportunities and problems identified above?

Option 1: Link with US partner. The advantages and disadvantages will depend on precisely what arrangement is made. However, it is likely that BAe will be the junior partner in any new enterprise. Although scale can be built quickly and no acquisition is needed, there might be significant problems over each party being able to contribute to such a deal and gain sufficiently from the arrangement to make it attractive.

Option 2: link with GEC UK. It is likely that this option would be the one to involve a full-scale merger in the long term with both companies forming a totally new company in the market. However, it is unlikely to build real economies of scale since the companies have little overlap in their product ranges. Moreover, the cultures of the two companies are so different that it is questionable whether such a business arrangement could be successful in the short to medium term.

Option 3: Seek alliances with Dasa and Aerospatiale. Such an alliance has been shown to work with Airbus but is also the most problematical in terms of the slow and plodding approach, the need to build partnership arrangements and so on. Yet, if this arrangement could *form the basis of a subsequent merger*, it might hold the best long-term potential to build a company of sufficient size to rival the largest US aerospace companies.

Comment: the above demonstrates that the *Expansion Methods Matrix* needs to be seen not as a mutually exclusive set of boxes, but areas that can lead from one to another and areas that can exist alongside each other in different parts of a business.

Chapter 15
Strategy evaluation and selection - 1

Synopsis of chapter

Once the options have been identified, according to classical prescriptive corporate strategy, the next task is to select from them. This chapter gives an *overview* of the entire process with Chapter 16 exploring some aspects of the selection process in more detail.

Chapter 15 examines the *main criteria* used in the selection process and suggests ways of prioritising them to make the selection process more manageable. The *initial evaluation* of the options using such criteria is then considered.

Summary

* This chapter provides an initial overview of the evaluation process. Such a process relies on developing criteria as a starting point for selection. These need to be developed bearing in mind the nature of the organisation: for example, commercial organisations will clearly require different criteria from non-profit-making ventures.

* There are six main criteria usually employed in commercial organisations: *consistency*, especially with the organisation's mission and objectives, *suitability*, *validity*, *feasibility*, *business risk* and *attractiveness* to stakeholders.

  * *Consistency* with the purpose of the organisation.
  * *Suitability* to the organisation's environment.
  * *Validity* of the projections and data used in developing the option.
  * *Feasibility* bearing in mind internal and external constraints on the organisation, such as technical skills and finance, competition, and the commitment of management and employees.
  * *Business risk* which must be at a level acceptable to the organisation.
  * *Attractiveness* to stakeholders, including shareholders and employees.
  * Internationally, evaluation of these criteria may be affected by national characteristics and by differences in the interests of stakeholders and governments.

* It is important to clarify the basis on which the process is to be carried out. Evaluation against the mission and objectives is useful to find the best strategic option. However, non-quantified objectives may be just as important for some organisations.

* In not-for-profit organisations, the criteria also need to reflect the broader aspects of its service or contribution to the community and to take into account the different decision-making processes and beliefs that motivate many such

Corporate Strategy Lecturer's Guide, Pitman Publishing
© Aldersgate Consultancy Limited 1997

organisations. This may make strategy option evaluation more diffuse and open-ended.

- Additional criteria for evaluation include the ability to build on the strengths and core competences of the organisation and to avoid its weaknesses. Generally in evaluation, strengths are more important than weaknesses, but occasionally a weakness cannot be ignored. Different parts of an organisation such as the HQ, the Strategic Business Unit (SBU) and those involved in individual projects will have different perspectives on the evaluation process. It is important to recognise this in selection.

- Evaluation usually employs common criteria across the organisation, such as contribution to value added and profitability. The strengths and weaknesses of these criteria need to be understood.

- The Shareholder Value Approach takes a broader perspective on evaluation than that provided by the specific project. It seeks to determine the benefit of such developments in the context of the whole SBU in which the project rests. However, it still relies on the assumption that shareholders are always the prime beneficiaries.

- Cost/benefit analysis has been successfully employed in public sector evaluation where it is important to assess broader and less quantifiable benefits. The main difficulty is where to place the limit on such benefits and costs.

Possible lecture structure

- Lecturers might like to begin by using the Eurofreeze case. Alternatively, students often find that an interesting initial approach is to take the mission and objectives of *their own or a rival educational institution* as the basis of selecting strategies. Some comment on actions undertaken at the institution over the last few years against such a mission and objectives can be quite involving.
- Develop the criteria against which an organisation wishes to judge its strategies: use Figure 15.2 and the chart that follows.
- Explore any criteria that are particularly important: use Figure 15.3, Table 15.1 and Table 15.2 and the chart that follows.
- Examine the factors involved in making an initial selection of the best option: use Exhibit 15.1 and the chart that follows.
- Explore the initial evaluation of the organisation's strategies in more depth: use the chart that follows.

Strategic project

Two examples of regional strategy: Music Television (MTV) has three regional strategies for Europe, Asia-Pacific and North America because music tastes differ so much around the world; many car companies have regional strategies because driving conditions and customer wealth vary significantly in different parts of the world.

Developing the strategy selection criteria

Six main criteria:

Consistency with the purpose of the organisation: a prime test for evaluating and selecting strategies.

Suitability of the strategy for the environment within which the organisation operates.

Validity of the projections and data used in developing the option must be tested.

Feasibility will depend on three factors:

- constraints internal to the organisation such as technical skills and finance
- constraints external to the organisation such as the response of competitors
- commitment from management and employees

Business risk also needs to be assessed because it may be unacceptable to the organisation.

Attractiveness to stakeholders, such as shareholders and employees: some options may be more attractive to some stakeholders than others.

Corporate Strategy Lecturer's Guide, Pitman Publishing
© Aldersgate Consultancy Limited 1997

Exploring criteria that are particularly important

- Important to clarify the basis of any initial selection of criteria.

- Evaluation against mission and objectives.

- Non-quantified objectives may be important for some organisations.

- In not-for-profit organisations, criteria may need to reflect the broader aspects of its service or role in the community.

- Building on strengths and core competences often important.

- Strengths are usually more important than weaknesses, but sometimes a weakness cannot be ignored.

- Different parts of the organisation will have different perspectives on the evaluation process: HQ, Strategic Business Units and those involved in individual projects.

An initial evaluation of the best option

Because of the large number of potential options and the need to examine some in great detail, it is often useful to make an *initial evaluation* and selection.

Only those selected are then subjected to the more detailed evaluation.

It is important to establish what is meant by 'best'.

It is useful to establish the requirements of the stakeholders.

In the initial evaluation of the best option, it is usual to calculate for each option:

- *profitability*
- *breakeven*
- *cash flow*

From a strategic perspective, it may be useful to explore:

- *projected sales levels* for any exceptional market share implications

- *projected levels of any cost reductions* for their feasibility.

Corporate Strategy Lecturer's Guide, Pitman Publishing
© Aldersgate Consultancy Limited 1997

Exploring the initial evaluation in more depth

Evaluation usually employs common and agreed criteria across the organisation, e.g. contribution to value added and profitability.

The strengths and weaknesses of such criteria need to be understood.

The *Shareholder Value Approach* **(SVA)**
takes a broader perspective on evaluation than that provided by the specific project.

SVA seeks to determine the benefit of such developments in the context of the whole SBU in which the project rests. However, it still relies on the assumption that shareholders are always the prime beneficiaries.

Cost/benefit analysis has been successfully employed in public sector evaluation where it is important to assess broader and less quantifiable benefits. The main difficulty is where to place the limit on such benefits and costs.

Case notes

Eurofreeze evaluates its strategy options - 1

1. Are these objectives suitable for selecting from a range of strategic options?

In order to assess the objectives, it is useful to consider them in the context of the mission statement. The mission is typical of some companies: a desire to be a 'leading producer' in a specific market or market segment. It gives the company a sense of importance and purpose. The difficulty is that it might be meaningless or inappropriate. In this case, it could be argued that it is meaningless: page 532 explores this point.

There is a connection between the mission and objectives: for Eurofrecze to become a leading company in the market place, it needs to build its profitability - hence, its proposed objectives concerning return on capital and earnings per share. However, *suitability* has a specific meaning: the choice between options needs to be governed by the environment of the organisation and by the ability to deliver competitive advantage.

In this context, the *environment* is clearly becoming more competitive. It is likely in these circumstances that profit margins will be under pressure. Against this market trend, Eurofreeze has set an objective of increased return on capital over the next six years. No evidence is quoted in the case to justify such an objective. Choice based on such an objective may therefore be unsuitable for the company.

The development of *competitive advantage* is an important aspect of company strategy: most organisations are not immediately endowed with such attributes and need to grow them over time. The only clue in the objectives is to move from low-value added to higher value items, but this may be regarded as vague and incomplete. Hence, the objectives need some further development if the selection criteria of competitive advantage is to have more meaning for the strategies that follow from them.

2. Are they consistent with each other?

They have some consistency in the area of return on capital and earnings per share: these were clearly expected to move in unison. In addition, to hold its market share, the company had the objective of shifting from low to higher added value items. This is also consistent with its objectives.

However, there is a significant problem: competitive pressures will make it difficult to 'hold its overall market share'. This objective may only be achieved by further investment, for example in lower prices or advertising. The chances of *raising* its return on capital at the same time as undertaking such investment are therefore not high. In this sense, they may not be consistent.

Corporate Strategy Lecturer's Guide, Pitman Publishing

Eurofreeze evaluates its strategy options - 2

1. Now that you know more about the market trends and increased competition of the industry, what is your assessment of the mission and objectives of Eurofreeze?

To hold its market share and remain a leading company, the company needs to invest significantly in its resources. It is significant that its leading branded rival, Refrigor, has been investing at a rate in excess of Eurofreeze. This was undertaken at Refrigor by reducing profitability and it is likely that the approach will be needed at Eurofreeze.

It is therefore totally unrealistic for Eurofreeze to expect to keep its leading status, hold market share and raise profitability at the same time. The mission and objectives have an internal inconsistency that needs to be resolved. There needs to be a choice made between raising profitability and holding market share.

This also means that any selection of strategy options also needs to be delayed until such matters are resolved: the basis of assessment will change depending on which objective becomes the leading one. If profitability is chosen, this might suggest options such as cutting costs and reducing the product range; if market share is chosen, this might favour options such as holding low margin sales and investing in new products.

2. Should the objectives be expanded? What about branded and non-branded items, for example? Clearer on the competitive threat? Further reference to financial objectives such as dividend payout policy? Specific reference to other matters such as ecological issues and employee job satisfaction? If your answer is yes *to any of these questions, then what considerations should Eurofreeze have taken into account in making its decision? If your answer is* no, *then what are the implications for strategy selection?*

These issues are matters of judgement: what one company would regard as an item to be included in the objectives would be for another something not to be mentioned at all. Many answers to the questions therefore may be valid.

Perhaps the only one that might universally be regarded as important to clarify further is the objectives regarding the competitive threat. Even its customers now pose a competitive threat. This area impinges directly on the development of competitive advantage in a strongly competitive environment. Options that might present themselves include:

- Building high-value specific product areas, like McCain and Sarah Lee. This might be set as a separate objective.

- Strengthening its high-value branded ranges in total. This might also be identified as a separate objective.

- Developing its sales to supermarkets of their own branded products. Again this could be set as a target.

It could legitimately be argued that some of the above are really *strategies* to achieve the overall marketing *objective*. However, if such strategies are vital and fundamental to the future of the company, it could be argued that they need to be identified within the objectives of the company: 'Our objective over the next six years is to raise our sales of supermarket own brands from x per cent to y per cent of our total sales.' This would be a legitimate development of this objective.

3. What are the possible implications of the customer and competitive trends on the development of strategy options for Eurofreeze? You may wish to undertake some of the analyses contained in Chapters 13 and 14 in preparing your answer.

Customers here include the supermarkets, even though the products are subsequently sold again to the individual domestic customer. Competitors also include the supermarkets, Refrigor, smaller frozen food manufacturers with very low costs and the specialist branding operations such as McCain. All these appear to be offering significant pressure on Eurofreeze.

Against this background, it would be worth investigating the resources and market options of the company.

Resources: core capabilities such as architecture, reputation and innovation would all suggest options to develop these further. The core competences listed in the case will also form the basis of further options. In turn, they need to be coupled with the options generated by Figure 13.4 in order to bring some imagination and originality to the list.

Markets: market options in a relatively mature market may initially appear limited to some simple product introductions. However, this would be too restrictive a view of the Market Options Matrix: it raises other possibilities of vertical and horizontal integration, market development to new customers such as the restaurant and leisure trade and so on. In addition, the Expansion Method Matrix offers options that the company really needs to explore through joint ventures, alliances and possibly even takeovers. For example, why not explore a joint venture with the German company, Dr Oetker? Eurofreeze seems to be totally unaware of such possibilities, which might help to strengthen its position against the power of the supermarket chains.

Corporate Strategy Lecturer's Guide, Pitman Publishing
© Aldersgate Consultancy Limited 1997

European expansion in the central heating market

1. Identify the market growth and competitive position characteristics of the European market and use these to assess the strategies that were developed.

The overall market was relatively mature with growth largely in line with the economic cycles of the countries concerned. Within this, there were some hopes of higher growth for the condensing boiler segment because of its better environmental attributes. The strategy of growth by acquisition therefore makes sense in that this is a faster route to expansion in a mature market. However, it should be said that this strategy cost US$900 million which some might regard as a significant expenditure.

What is less clear is the route taken to expand in the condenser segment. Having acquired some major companies, Blue Circle then appears to have largely ignored the product ranges obtained by the company in favour of a totally new boiler range in the condenser segment. It is difficult to believe that this represented the best use of the funds invested in its European companies.

2. How did the company overcome the cultural problems involved in developing across countries? What lessons, if any, can be drawn from this for strategy development?

It developed a pan-European team approach with some managers being brought together in a 40-strong team. It appears to have been successful at overcoming one of the classic problems in any international development: how to combine what needs to be standardised with what has to be varied for each local market. However, this was used to develop the new condensing boiler *product* that would be sold on a pan-European basis. It was not used to develop corporate *strategy*, which might be regarded as broader and encompassing less tangible concepts.

The lessons for strategy suggest that the different parts of the enterprise benefited from the opportunities to explore aspects of each others' business. The team approach also broke down the cultural problems associated with concentrating on one country. However, the lessons may be more limited in that the strategy itself seems to have been largely derived from a survey by two people rather than the team developing the product.

3. The strategy process appeared to make only a limited attempt to develop a series of options and then select from them: it concentrated on a pan-European route. What are the problems and opportunities of taking such a single-minded approach? Would you have investigated other options? If so, what options and why?

The problems of such an approach include the lack of exploration of some routes before selecting the optimal way forward and the lack of consultation with many people who would have to work with the chosen route.

The opportunities include the single-minded focus that is presented: it can be driven forward at a faster pace and with more vision than a broader range of options. For a market segment, this might represent a useful approach.

The obvious option that was not explored was that of allowing the individual companies to develop ideas for their own markets in condensing boilers. This meant that the full acquisition potential of its range of acquisitions up to 1993 was not really exploited in this segment.

4. Do you judge that its strategy will be successful? Are there any areas that you would like to see developed further?

It is difficult to make such a judgement. The cost savings from the approach and the resulting benefits remain unstated in the case study.

We know that the company spent US$ 30 million putting the project together and we know the price at which the product was launched onto the market. However, we do not know the prices or costs of its competitors, nor the extent to which the Blue Circle product was cheaper than its competitors as a result of its pan-European approach to design and production.

While there were clear advantages from the project in terms of team working and project design, there was no clear evidence that this was translated into real benefits for the customer. This whole subject needs to be investigated and shown in much greater detail for there to be convincing evidence of success. Until that is done, the strategy remains unproven at best. If some part of the cost of acquisitions of US$ 900 million is included in the above estimates, then it is difficult to see how a strategy that largely ignores such an investment programme can ever repay its costs.

Corporate Strategy Lecturer's Guide, Pitman Publishing
© Aldersgate Consultancy Limited 1997

Chapter 16
Strategy evaluation and selection - 2

Synopsis of chapter

This chapter examines in greater depth some of the issues raised in Chapter 15. There are six topics: *business judgement* which covers the logic and evidence of strategies in particular types of market, such as emerging, maturing and so on; *empirical evidence* such as the PIMS databank; *feasibility issues* concerning internal and external constraints on solutions; the assessment of *business risk* using various techniques; the consideration of *stakeholder interests*; and the selection process in *international* corporate strategy.

Summary

- The chapter explores some aspects of strategy choice in greater depth. The outcomes of strategy proposals are uncertain so *business judgement* needs to be applied in the selection of strategy.

- Some guidance is provided on strategy evaluation by an analysis of generic industry environments giving two broad categories: the *stage of industry maturity* and the *competitive position* of the organisation involved. After identifying the organisation's position according to these two parameters, simple choices then suggest themselves.

- Beyond this general framework, further guidance on appropriate strategies has been identified for specific types of industry: fragmented industries, emerging industries, mature markets and declining markets.

- Empirical evidence based on the PIMS Databank relates strategic actions to their results in terms of profitability and other criteria. According to PIMS, high quality and strong market share can make a positive contribution to profitability. High capital intensity is less likely to do so. Some researchers doubt the cause and effect relationships here. Acquisitions and mergers have also been studied for their impact on profitability, suggesting that many are unsuccessful. In some circumstances, diversification may be a successful strategy.

The chapter then explores the *feasibility of options*. It considers the subject from three perspectives: internal, external and the need for management commitment. In examining whether an option is feasible internally, the four main areas to explore are people, technical skills, financial resources and marketing and sales resources. Feasibility external to the organisation is also an important issue: customer and competitor reactions to a proposed new strategy will be major constraints in the selection process. Where managment has not discussed a strategy in advance with employees, their degree of commitment may also become a constraint. The new strategy needs to be communicated clearly and in a way that challenges and motivates staff.

- *Business risk* assessment is also important in strategy selection. This usually includes an analysis of financial risks. Risks can be viewed by using:

  - Sensitivity analysis, which examines the impact of variations in the assumptions underlying the evaluation, usually in the form of optimistic and pessimistic assessments;

  - Scenarios, which can be built up to take a broad view of future change in qualitative and quantitative terms;

  - Simulation modelling, which uses computers and has been successful in some situations. However, it cannot yet replicate complex corporate strategy decision-making requirements.

- *Stakeholders* also need to be assessed for their reactions to major strategy initiatives and to ascertain whether or not some interests should be prioritised, e.g. shareholders may or may not be given priority. Stakeholder reactions need to be assessed under at least five headings: financial risks for shareholders, employment levels for employees, management opportunities or redundancies, broader community issues such as pollution, the government response to strategy initiatives.

- *International strategy selection* is more complex, and the objectives and reasons for international expansion must first be clarified. The difficulty in international strategy is to find some basic pattern and logic for such developments in order to facilitate their selection. There are three significant areas: the possible need for a global strategy, the responsiveness to national interests and the history and culture of the organisation.

  Even for many so-called global products, there is often a need to provide some degree of local variation. The history of an organisation and its cultural values will have a significant impact on the strategic choice.

Possible lecture structure

- Take an example of *business judgement* from a recent edition of a daily newspaper and explore the extent to which those involved had to go beyond the facts that were available. Alternatively, use *EuroTunnel* which underestimated the investment required and left itself with US$14 billion debts. Explore the impact on the consortium of international banks that funded the project: *Financial Times,* 8 October 1996, pages 19, 20 and 22 has a useful summary.

Corporate Strategy Lecturer's Guide, Pitman Publishing
© Aldersgate Consultancy Limited 1997

- Explain the structure of the lecture which has six quite distinct elements: use Figure 16.1.

- Explore business judgement with regard to the inevitable uncertainties that arise from the selection of strategies using two routes:

  - generic industry environments with Table 16.1: Lifecycle Portfolio Matrix;
  - specific industry strategies: emerging, mature and declining markets. Use Figures 16.2, 16.3, 16.4, 16.5.

  Lecturers may care to note that the ADL Matrix used in the book is the *latest version* from that company. It differs from those used and published in earlier texts.

- Examine the empirical evidence of successful strategies: use Tables 16.2 - 16.6. Comment, if appropriate to the course, on the important academic debate concerning the nature of the evidence and its validity.

- Explore the feasibility issues that will limit the selection of strategies: use Exhibits 16.1 and 16.2 and the chart that follows.

- Assess the risks of each major strategy and the implications for the organisation: use the chart that follows.

- Identify the main stakeholders and consider how their interests are best served by the strategy options available: use the chart that follows.

- Consider the implications of operating in an international environment on strategy selection: use Exhibit 16.3, Table 16.7 and chart that follows.

- Summarise the prescriptive process of undertaking a strategy evaluation and selection.

Strategic project

The strategies of small companies can be useful in exploring the industry structure that has encouraged their development. To begin the process, to consider two research papers:

- Porter, M E (1980) *Competitive Strategy,* Free Press, Harvard - Chapter 9 on Competitive Strategy in Fragmented Industries.
- Cooper, A, Willard, G and Woo, C (1986) 'A Re-examination of the niche concept', *Journal of Business Venturing.*

These two items were reprinted in Mintzberg, H and Quinn, J (1991) The Strategy *Process*, 2nd edn, Prentice-Hall, Upper Saddle River, NJ.

Feasibility and management commitment

Some strategic decisions may need to be made by a centralised group of senior managers.

Workers may not have been consulted in advance, yet may be set challenging targets in connection with the new strategy.

Two prime conditions are then needed to attempt to gain the commitment of workers:

- *The strategy must be communicable.*

- *The strategy must challenge and motivate important members of staff.*

Corporate Strategy Lecturer's Guide, Pitman Publishing
© Aldersgate Consultancy Limited 1997

Analysis of business risk

Financial risk analysis

- Cash flow
- Breakeven
- Company borrowing requirements
- Financial ratio analysis

Sensitivity analysis

- Optimistic assessment
- Pessimistic assessment

Scenario projections

- Broader view of future developments
- Can take qualitative as well as quantitative view
- Less concerned with most likely view of future; more interested in contrasting views

Simulation modelling

Assessing stakeholders' reactions

Likely to include:

Financial risks for shareholders

Employment levels for employees

Management opportunities or redundancies

Broader community issues such as environmental concerns

Government response to strategy initiatives

Some specific international strategies

Multicountry strategy:

- targets individual countries or regions of the world
- international co-ordination is secondary to a country-by-country expansion programme

International low-cost strategy:

- sources production where costs are lowest
- sells products globally

International niche strategy:

- same product sold in same market niche in all countries of world
- often applies to up-market products

International combination strategy:

- regions of the world have their own production
- some regional or national variation in products made and marketed
- but global underpinning of strategy is clear, e.g. through R&D or branding

Case notes

Swatch to the rescue

1. Do you have any sympathy for the Swiss bank investors in 1984?

Certainly, some sympathy: all the evidence pointed to real problems for the Swiss watch industry. The Japanese had been highly successful over the previous ten years.

In this context, Nicholas Hayek then appeared on the scene. He was a well-respected entrepreneur but with an attitude to risk that was considerably different from the banking viewpoint. Mr Hayak started to describe a totally new concept in global branding of watches and a complete change in the way that watch production was undertaken in Switzerland. Such entrepreneurial flair is not always suited to more traditional banking methods of raising funds.

However, it could be argued that the banks could afford to risk some finance on the new venture. Moreover, the contribution to the Swiss economy if the venture was to be successful would be considerable. In consequence, the sympathy is somewhat limited.

2. What elements of business judgement would have persuaded you to support Mr Hayek's strategy selection?

In the judgement of this writer only, the main elements were:

- Mr Hayek's track record and his willingness to put in some of his own funds.
- The innovative nature of the solution.
- The emphasis on quality and differentiation.
- The core competences of the Swiss watch industry in this area.
- The commitment of the whole industry to make it work.

For these reasons, the strategy deserved to be supported, but it would have been a risk. It should be noted that the Swiss industry has never been able to regain its previous and traditional dominance of much of the global production of watch movements.

Corporate Strategy Lecturer's Guide, Pitman Publishing
© Aldersgate Consultancy Limited 1997

Strategy transformation at Nokia

1. Why did Nokia only select two areas for development? What is the strategic risk involved in selecting two areas out of six?

At the time the choice was made, Nokia had significant profit problems and did not have the funds for heavy investment across the whole group. This situation was aggravated by the diverse nature of its range of products: from tyre making to mobile telephones. Moreover, the company was clear that if it was to maintain its presence in telecommunications then it needed to invest heavily: there was no possibility of a small-scale investment in this area because its competitors were already spending substantial sums on R&D.

The strategic risk of selecting two areas out of six is that the wrong two areas are chosen. Giving up some product areas and concentrating on others will concentrate resources, especially when they would otherwise be thinly spread. However, the choice of areas is a major risk that could easily be incorrect. For example, choosing telecommunications and then discovering that one of its rivals had achieved a major technical breakthrough would have ruined Nokia as it was now firmly committed to that area. However, the company was in the distinctive position that many of its product areas outside telecommunications were already loss-making so it was only concentrating resources into profitable ventures.

2. Nokia appeared to decide on its strategy first and then consider the constraints. Is this wise? What would have happened if the strategy had not been feasible?

There is no single 'formula' for developing strategy. Thus there is no rule that says it is essential to consider the constraints early or late in the process, as long as they are investigated at some stage. However, it is important to make a final decision on the strategy only after any relevant constraints have been considered. In this sense, it could be argued that Nokia needed to be careful not to pre-judge its own proposals.

If the strategy had not been feasible, it is likely that it would have failed. The issue of feasibility is one that cannot be left until the basic strategy has been decided, but needs to be considered as the strategy is developed. In the case of Nokia, it would appear that the decision to concentrate on telecommunications was accompanied by evidence of real problems in other product areas, so that the decisions were concurrent.

Nevertheless, the external feasibility issues in telecomms were essentially unpredictable: for example, its rivals knew the well-publicised Nokia difficulties and could easily have made the process at the company more difficult. It is possible that the reason that this did not happen is because of the very high market growth rates in mobile telephones around this time: all the main manufacturers needed all their resources to meet market demand and were concentrating the bulk of their marketing activity to growing the market rather than scoring points against Nokia. Occasionally, markets move in favour of those who take the risk, such as Nokia.

Eurofreeze evaluates its strategy options - 3

The material in this case is typical of the type of analysis that some companies would undertake in the process of evaluating their strategic options. It involves:

- Projections over a ten-year period with the resulting cash flow being discounted back to the first year, i.e. 1995 in this case.
- Major assumptions about *sales* increases on some options. Much of such analysis contains major guesses that may be wildly out.
- More limited assumptions on *cost* decreases on some options. These can usually be estimated with greater accuracy, but typically have lower net gains for the business.
- Some heroic assumptions about competition being willing to accept without retaliation a new, more aggressive Eurofreeze.
- A lack of real innovation: there were no *substantive* new strategic initiatives, just plans to react to events in the existing marketplace. The most radical plans, options 4 and 5, still took the existing market/competitor configuration as the starting point: for example, where was the takeover bid, joint venture or whatever?

Some commentators would argue that the whole exercise shows how self-deceiving such estimates can be. Others would point out that the alternative is to do nothing: they would suggest that, despite all its inaccuracies, useful conclusions can be drawn.

The main points for this question are given in the table which follows.

Corporate Strategy Lecturer's Guide, Pitman Publishing
© Aldersgate Consultancy Limited 1997

1. What are the relative merits and problems of each option?

Option	Merits	Problems
1. Stop selling branded and own label vegetables and fruit.	• Pulls out of increasingly low value added area.	• Appears to solve nothing: overheads still need to be covered. • Does not seem to make substantive contribution to company strategy.
2. Stop selling branded vegetables and fruit but continue own label.	• Partially pulls back from low value added area.	• Same weaknesses as Option 1.
3. Extend specialist branded food ranges, e.g. pizza and gateaux.	• Clear, relatively low-risk growth plan. • Builds on existing strengths and develops competitive advantage.	• Low-risk option does not move the company forward in a substantial way.
4. Major cutback of range in first two years, then rebuild specialist areas from Year 4 onwards.	• Clearly higher risk • Option may underestimate gains since allows nothing for possible sale of assets, including product range, to a rival.	• Crucial to success of this option are the high profit levels near the end of its ten-year projection. These are extremely dubious. But lower levels would immediately make the option unattractive.
5. Become lowest cost producer through major investment.	• Radical changes proposed that would transform the company over a ten-year period.	• Major risk: competition will surely respond. • Major capital investment required: does not seem to be justified from this evidence.

2. In what way does the use of the portfolio matrix help the strategic debate? And in what way might it mislead the strategic decisions?

It is helpful in showing the dominance of Refrigor in the main market segments: the visual representation in Figure 16.6 brings out this point. Moreover, it shows where Eurofreeze is strongest, i.e. meat and fish. This might prove a strength on which to build. The matrix is also helpful in illustrating that there are no fast-growth segments in the market: this means that the market is relatively mature and companies need to build their strategy by more genuine innovation. Arguably, the strategy options from Eurofreeze are not sufficiently innovative to gain success.

The matrix is potentially misleading in that it does not show the consequences of dropping part of the range: the overheads would still need to be covered. The more fundamental assumption that portfolios can simply be shuffled around to produce higher returns is also dubious. Moreover, it says nothing about value added, competitive advantage or a host of other important strategic issues.

3. Consider what other strategic analytical tools, if any, might provide useful insights into the strategic choice debate: you might wish to consider a PEST analysis, a Five Forces analysis, generic strategies, a Market Options Matrix, value chain, innovations checklist (in Chapter 11).

For reasons of space, these are not explored in depth here but could clearly be developed. In general terms, the value chain, Expansion Method Matrix and innovations checklist would all merit careful exploration. This is especially true if it is accepted that the options explored in the case need some more radical alternatives, such as takeover, to be explored.

4. Which option would you recommend to Eurofreeze? Give reasons for your choice and explain the strengths and weaknesses of your choice.

None: there is a need for more innovative solutions. The existing proposals are all too boring or too risky. Back to the drawing board!

Corporate Strategy Lecturer's Guide, Pitman Publishing
© Aldersgate Consultancy Limited 1997

Chapter 17
Finding the strategic route forward

Synopsis of chapter

After exploring the *prescriptive* process in the previous four chapters, this chapter examines its problems. It then investigates the *survival*, *uncertainty* and *negotiated* strategic approaches as alternative models of the strategy process. The chapter finally explores the *learning-based* strategic approach. It concludes that it is this latter process that needs to be added to prescriptive strategy in order to find the strategic route forward.

Each strategic approach is examined both descriptively and critically. The chapter has been especially written to take account of the lack of agreement among strategists on the optimal strategic route forward: it deliberately offers a number of routes. In consequence, *students may need to be guided by the lecturer* on the validity or otherwise of each of the approaches.

Ultimately, the chapter offers the conclusion of the author: there are at least two perspectives to the exploration of strategy processes: prescriptive and learning.

Summary

- The chapter reviews the main methods of developing the strategy process. It starts by examining and critiquing the prescriptive model. It then examines other models, especially those from the emergent strategy process.

- The *prescriptive model* of the strategic process is largely linear. It has feedback mechanisms at various points to ensure that objectives, options and strategy choice are consistent with each other. Problems with the prescriptive approach cover four main areas: environment unpredictability, planning procedures, top-down approaches driven by the centre and the culture of the organisation that will allow the model to operate. Specific criticisms include the need for more dialogue, a greater flow of ideas and more adaptation to the environment. It may be possible to solve these problems within the prescriptive process but some strategists take a more critical view.

- *Survival-based strategies* emphasise the importance of adapting strategies to meet changes in the environment. The ultimate objective is survival itself. The approach adopted is to develop options for use as the environment changes. Options that seek low costs are particularly useful. Beyond taking the precaution of developing options, there is little that the individual company can do. There is an element of chance in whether the company will survive or not.

- The *uncertainty-based approach* concentrates on the difficult and turbulent environment that it asserts now surrounds the development of corporate strategy. Renewal and transformation are vital aspects of such strategy. Inevitably, they will involve uncertainty. Such uncertainty can be modelled mathematically. However, the long-term consequences are unknown and cannot be foreseen or usefully predicted.

- Uncertainty approaches therefore involve taking small steps forward. Management needs to learn from such actions and adapt accordingly. Because of the uncertainty about the future, the approach argues that strategy options and selection between them suggested by the prescriptive approach are irrelevant.

- *Negotiation-based strategies* emphasise the need to persuade colleagues and outside stakeholders. Coalitions and groups play an important part in strategy development. Such a strategic approach also needs to be seen in the context of negotiations with powerful customers and suppliers where bargaining and trade-offs will take place. Game theory attempts to predict the outcomes of customer reactions or, in some cases, to show how the outcome of negotiations may well produce a sub-optimal solution unless both sides of the negotiations realise the consequences of their actions.

- *Learning-based strategy* emphasises the importance of flexibility in developing unique strategies. Learning is not concerned with memory work, but with active creativity in developing new strategic opportunities. It has real value as a concept but is vague and lacks operational guidance in practice. Nevertheless, its insights need to be added to the prescriptive approach in the development of strategy.

- *International considerations* may impact on the strategy process during every stage. The ability of stakeholders to influence the process will vary with the country for historic, political and cultural reasons. The mission and objectives are likely to be rooted in the social and cultural systems of the country in which the strategy is developed. The environment may be important in another aspect of strategy development: the *home country* of an organisation seeking international scope will influence the way that the strategy is developed and managed. Options and choice in the selection process will be governed by the culture and social systems of the people involved in the process.

Possible lecture structure

- Begin with a brief exposition or exploration of the well-known Pascale/Honda Motorcycle perspectives on strategy: see Minicase.
- Outline the arguments contained in the chapter: use Figure 17.1.
- Summarise the prescriptive process that has been developed in the previous four chapters: use Table 17.1.
- Explain the problems that some strategists see in prescriptive models of the strategy process: use the chart that follows and comment as appropriate.
- Explore the alternatives to prescriptive strategy: survival-based, uncertainty-based or negotiation-based processes. Use Exhibit 17.1, Tables 17.3, 17.4 and 17.5.
- Outline the learning-based strategic route forward: use Exhibit 17.3 and Table 17.6.
- Comment on the extent to which the learning-based approach is needed as part of an organisation's strategy process.

Corporate Strategy Lecturer's Guide, Pitman Publishing
© Aldersgate Consultancy Limited 1997

- If appropriate, outline the implications of an organisation operating internationally for the strategy process.

The chapter also contains a more detailed description of some negotiation-based strategies. For reasons of time and subject matter, lecturers may feel that the greater detail in this area would be better tackled by the student reading the chapter material rather than be covered during the lecture.

Strategic project

Telecommunications strategy will be developing on a global basis over the next ten years: the leading providers of telephone services (not equipment) are examining how they will survive and grow. The main transformation has come from three related events:

- technology change;
- privatisation of many well-known companies, e.g. BT in the UK, France Telecom, Deutsche Telekom, Singapore Telecom (partially);
- the introduction of competition across Europe and other parts of the world, as the previous cosy monopolies of the large national telephone companies are brought to an end.

In exploring projects in this area, the topic is so vast that it might be preferable to investigate the subject from the viewpoint of a particular company.

As a starting point only:

BT into Europe, *Financial Times*, 22 May 1995, p17.
Indian telecommunications growth, *Financial Times*, 9 December 1994, p17.
Chinese telecommunications, *Financial Times*, 22 August 1994, p13.
Singapore Telecom, *Financial Times*, 22 December 1994, p17.
Italian telecommunications into Russia, *Financial Times*, 14 December 1995, p19.
Privatisation of Deutsche Telekom, *Annual Report 1994 and 1995*, plus share offer document October 1996.

Some problems with the prescriptive process

Environment
- assumed to be predictable
- but numerous instances where this has proved to be incorrect

Planning procedure
- assumed that major strategic decisions are initiated by a clear planning procedure
- whereas decisions in practice are complex, multi-layered and subject to management whim

Top-down procedures
- assumed that top-down procedures from group HQ to individual strategic business units represent the most efficient method for allocating funds and gaining management commitment
- whereas some research evidence indicates that managers find the process demotivating and unwieldy

Culture
- assumed that the culture of the organisation will allow the prescriptive model to operate
- whereas some cultures are in practice more suited to a top-down prescriptive approach than others

Some commentators have identified several areas not covered adequately in this approach:

- more dialogue
- greater flow of ideas
- organisation more adaptable with respect to the environment

Corporate Strategy Lecturer's Guide, Pitman Publishing
© Aldersgate Consultancy Limited 1997

Case notes

How Honda came to dominate two major motorcycle markets

Does prescriptive strategy need to be modified or would it be better, as Pascale suggests, to redefine the strategic process completely?

In exploring this issue, it would be useful to study the work undertaken by Professor Pascale which has been highly influential in highlighting the problems of the prescriptive approach: the case is able to offer only a brief summary. It would also be worthwhile to explore the surveys undertaken by Professor Toyohiro Kono of Japanese practice in the development of strategy during the 1980s: they appear to be rather more prescriptive than Professor Pascale's study would suggest. Hence, the Pascale evidence is not conclusive.

The evidence of adaptive strategic development at Honda US can be explored for its applicability to the relatively static motorcycle market. In this context, the evidence is quite clear: Honda benefited from luck and experimentation in its processes. The issue posed by this evidence is the extent to which this *one example* has wider strategic lessons.

The evidence suggests that, in the case of Honda US and UK, the most successful approach was to operate an emerging strategy and try out various possible routes to find the most successful. However, the evidence is hardly conclusive because:

- Honda is likely to have used prescriptive approaches to develop the superior quality and performance of its machines that were crucial long-term.
- Honda itself never regarded its approach as anything more than an attempt to solve a major problem. It was Pascale who identified it as a new and separate approach.
- Honda was coming from behind in the marketplace against dominant players: many *prescriptive* approaches would have said that going head-on against such entrenched support was unlikely to prove successful, e.g. see Chapter 5 on competitive warfare. Hence, it does not take an emergent strategist to criticise Honda.

Nevertheless, Pascale does have a point: there is a need to be adaptive in strategy - in Mintzberg's phrase, to *craft the strategy* beyond the prescriptive formula. In this sense, there is a real problem with prescriptive strategy. However, it will be evident from the previous four chapters that many strategists have seen merit in aspects of the prescriptive process. There may be weaknesses, but there are also real insights. If this conclusion is correct, it would be wrong to reject prescriptive strategy completely.

Developing strategy in European telecommunications service companies

1. Given the market growth coupled with the restrictions on opportunity, what are the advantages and problems with adopting the classical strategy process to develop strategies in this market?

Advantages:

- Suitable for the long time horizons needed to invest in new telecommunications technology
- Promotes clarity of vision and purpose in a market place that will change radically.
- Encourages a wide search for options, including alliances and joint ventures and a rational choice between them.
- Identifies the importance of implementation as a significant activity.

Problems:

- May restrict the ability to take new market opportunities as they emerge from the profound changes taking place as the market opens up;
- Emphasis laid on bureaucratic procedures and rational analysis may stifle innovation and personal commitment from individual managers;
- The central top-down procedures for strategy selection may not be appropriate for the wide market variations and the lack of two-way dialogue between those at the top and those lower down the organisation: especially true in large telecomms companies.
- Although formal planning may be appropriate to the culture of large organisations, the radical changes in the environment demand a more flexible approach to planning and to culture.

2. Can smaller companies attempting to find opportunities in this market also employ the classical process? Or would they be better to use a process that was more radical and innovative to structure their approach? If so, do you have any suggestions on the process that could be employed?

The long lead times in investing in this market mean that smaller companies will probably benefit from adopting some aspects of the classical approach: the formal identification of the main environmental changes, the analysis of resources compared to larger companies and the preparation of options might all be useful procedures.

However, smaller companies risk never becoming established if all they do is to use the classical process: they need to be more innovative. They need to find the new opportunities, new alliances, new customers and so on. This all argues for an alternative approach to strategy formulation, perhaps based on much closer consultation and discussion in individual parts of the company. The *learning-based* approach coupled with an emphasis on crafting a new strategy may therefore be more appropriate.

Corporate Strategy Lecturer's Guide, Pitman Publishing
© Aldersgate Consultancy Limited 1997

3. Some strategists argue that it is useless to predict ahead in fast-growing markets because there are too many uncertainties. What would be the consequences, if any, of following this advice in the European telecommunications market and not making any predictions? What implications does your answer have for a strategy process that is built on the need to make predictions?

'Prediction' here means estimating the levels of future demand, future competitive activity and other environmental changes, such as government and EU legislation.

To install new equipment in the telecommunications market takes years of planning and implementation. New alliances and joint ventures may happen quickly but are also more likely to take several years to negotiate and even longer to make them work well. It is against this environmental background that the arguments about prediction need to be set.

If there were to be no prediction in telecommunications, then the companies would simply still continue to rely on their current levels of investment and competitive arrangements. Other companies entering the market would be able to pick off new market opportunities because those already in the marketplace would be prevented from forming any judgement about the benefits and problems of such events. This is clearly poor strategy and against the practicalities of business.

It might be argued that there is a signficant likelihood of making a serious strategic error, but this would be to misunderstand the point above. It is likely to be better to do something rather than nothing: doing something has at least a probability of success, whereas doing nothing is highly likely to fail.

4. Given that the existing companies are dominant and are likely to have a bureaucratic style, and also given the uncertainties associated with liberalisation, what are the implications for company culture in the large telephone companies? What are the implications for the strategies they are likely to propose?

Company culture in the larger telephone companies across Europe is likely to be dominated by solid development that avoids risk-taking, sound policies and a desire to remain dominant. This will be accompanied by strong hierarchies, bureaucracy and a lack of innovation and commercial instincts. These elements of culture are likely to lead to strategies that are solid, dependable, low-risk and evolutionary. They are unlikely to be innovatory or market-driven. The whole approach is likely to seek to preserve the existing competitive situation and give preference to the existing companies.

European mobile telephones and Hutchison Mobilfunk

1. Apply the prescriptive strategy process to this company and indicate what conclusions you would draw about strategy.

For reasons of space, the following is in outline only:

Mission and objectives: the company was now part of a Hong Kong-based Konzern, and so these remained unpublished to outsiders. However, it would not be unreasonable to assume that the company wished to grow its turnover at least at the same pace as the market, possibly 25 per cent annually.

Environment: growing rapidly with increased competition and market liberalisation.

Resources: a small company with special strengths in personalised service and rapid turnaround of faulty telephones. Resources also in providing a telephone service.

Options generation to include: further investment from the Hong Kong parent; acquisition of German competitors; link with well-placed German manufacturers or service providers; and increased links with its fellow UK and French subsidiaries.

Strategy selection: difficult without more information, but the company clearly needed to invest substantial resources in the German market. At the time of the case, it clearly had a market share that could be expanded. Selection might also include acquisitions or links with other service providers in order to increase scale in the market.

2. Apply the survival-based and uncertainty-based strategy processes to the company and indicate what conclusions you would draw about strategy. Does it matter that it is more difficult to draw specific recommendations?

Survival-based strategy. This would follow some of the same arguments in Answer 1 above. However, there would be no question of making a strategy selection. This would be left to the market place to determine, as events dictated.

Uncertainty-based strategy. The environmental analysis of Answer 1 above might well be rejected, but the resource analysis would still be conducted. Options generation and selection would not be undertaken. The main strategy would be to establish small groups to monitor developments and then accept opportunities as they emerge.

For those who believe that the function of management is to manage, it *does* matter that it is more difficult to draw specific conclusions. For those that judge the function of management to be more limited because of the difficulties of the environment, there is less need to be concerned.

Corporate Strategy Lecturer's Guide, Pitman Publishing
© Aldersgate Consultancy Limited 1997

3. Identify the main elements of the company's likely resources and market position and use these to advise the company on whether any of the above three processes provides a useful model for strategy development. You can assume that the company faces the strategic task mentioned at the end of the case and that it has a viable, but not strong share, of the German market.

The main elements are outlined briefly in response to question 1 above. They imply that all three of the processes provide only part of the strategic route forward.

The prescriptive model provides some useful pointers. However, for a small company with only a viable market share, it leaves much to alternative methods of analysis and growth. Possibly the resource-based approach of Chapters 2 and 14 would provide more clues: for example, a more detailed analysis of core competences and resource capabilities. Certainly, there is a strong need for the company to explore the ways in which it can differentiate itself from others in the market. It would also be worth considering the innovative approaches of Chapter 11 and the Expansion Method Matrix of Chapter 14.

The uncertainty-based and survival-based routes do not seem to have the same rich source of ideas associated with them. However, they might arguably associate themselves with some of the routes in the previous paragraph, especially the survival-based approach.

Beyond all of the above, the *learning-based route* later in Chapter 17 represents an important additional model for use in devising routes forward. It would be consistent with the culture and style of Hutchison - small and friendly - and would begin to distinguish it from the larger and more anonymous competitors. The reader is recommended to return to this case after considering Section 17.5.

Strategic choice at MCI

1. How useful do you judge the prescriptive strategy process to be in analysing the strategy options available to MCI? The joint venture costing US$1 billion with News Corporation seemed to be rather vague at the time it was announced. Is this compatible with prescriptive strategy?

With its clear analysis of the environment, resources, strategic options and choice, the prescriptive strategy process clearly has some areas of insight to offer MCI. For example, it would show the company that its strengths lay in long distance rather than local telephone calls and in international alliances with companies such as British Telecom and News Corporation.

However, in some respects, the prescriptive process has only limited value: it says little about one of MCI's key competitive strengths, i.e. its stong customer orientation in the USA and its buccaneering-style management around the world. This style is essentially opportunistic and does not really lend itself to careful analysis of strategic options and selection. Arguably, the company might gain from a more measured approach but it would lose some of its entrepreneurial benefits as a result.

Although the MCI/News Corporation was to some extent rather vague, it had the great merit of taking market opportunities as they emerged. In other words, its vagueness is particularly emphasised by the certainties of prescriptive strategy process, but in reality this is a fault of the prescriptive approach. In other words, the vague opportunism is arguably a *real strategic strength*, as long as the two partners trust each other.

2. In the context of the uncertainties surrounding telecommunications, would you consider employing either the uncertainty-based or survival-based strategy routes? What are the benefits and problems of applying these two routes?

Both the uncertainty-based and survival-based routes rely heavily on the difficulties that arise in turbulent environments. There is little doubt that global telecommunications is characterised by such a description. However, the solutions offered by both approaches rely on short-term flexibility and may not be suitable for an industry, such as telecommunications, that has long time horizons for investment. For reasons of space, the benefits and problems are not explored here in depth. Suffice to say, that it is doubtful whether these two routes offer sufficient insights to make them worth pursuing in depth.

Corporate Strategy Lecturer's Guide, Pitman Publishing
© Aldersgate Consultancy Limited 1997

3. What changes, if any, would MCI need to consider if it were to employ the learning-based strategy process? Does the company's policy of partnerships constitute a learning-based strategy?

The case does leave the impression of a company dominated by a few key individuals making the key strategic decisions at the top. This would be typical of an organisation that has grown by its entrepreneurial skills over the last twenty years. To employ the learning-based process, the company would need to consider developing further its employee feedback mechanisms, group work, empowerment and the other areas of activity outlined in the chapter. In fairness, it is possible that MCI has already adopted some of these practices: it may simply be that the case study material has failed to identify these existing aspects of the company management style and culture.

The company's policy of pursuing partnerships derives from a recognition that MCI is incapable of developing the necessary infrastructures and generating the appropriate resources from within its existing company base. It needs such links. Such relationships are a typical part of learning-based strategy and, in this sense, that strategy is being adopted.

However, learning-based strategy goes beyond partnerships into empowerment and other issues. In this sense, partnerships are only a small part of the total range of any company's learning-based approach to strategy.

4. In the context of its highly competitive style, to what extent does the company already employ the negotiating-based approach?

There is little doubt that the company already has elements of this approach. Its keen awareness of its strengths, its desire to become larger and its flexibility towards partners underlines its ability to negotiate hard where required.

Chapter 18
Strategy, structure and style

Synopsis of chapter

This chapter explores a major strategic debate that has taken place over the last thirty years regarding the relationship between the strategy and the structure of the organisation. It begins by examining the work of Chandler and Williamson, who both took the view that strategy was determined first and structure afterwards. It then examines the criticisms that have been made of this approach, principally those suggesting that the two areas are inter-related. Mintzberg's study of the relationships between strategy and structure are then explored. Finally, the relationship between strategy and the management style of the organisation is investigated.

Summary

- For the *prescriptive* strategist, the strategy is developed first and then the organisation structure is defined afterwards. Thus, organisation structure is a matter of how the strategy is *implemented* and does not influence the strategy itself. However, from an *emergent* strategy perspective, the relationship between strategy and structure is more complex. The organisation itself may restrict or enhance the strategies that it proposes to develop. The existing organisation may even make certain strategies highly unlikely.

- Two well-known writers on strategy explored these areas in the 1960s and 1970s. The strategist, *Alfred Chandler,* contended that it was first necessary to develop the strategy. After this task was completed, the organisation was then devised to deliver that strategy. His conclusion was based on his study of the way that US businesses were formed and organised in the early part of the twentieth century. He only studied businesses that had developed from small enterprises into larger, more diversified structures. The economist, *Oliver Williamson,* explored the role of the centre in diversified businesses. He concluded that the centre should stand back from divisions when it came to allocating resources among them and, subsequently, to monitoring and controlling them. He supported Chandler's view that strategy came first and organisation structure afterwards.

- According to the early strategists, formal structures, clear responsibilities, identified lines of reporting and, for strategy development, a central directorate are all important elements of organisational design. They are undertaken after the basic strategy has been agreed. As organisations become larger and more complex, it may be necessary to form Divisions and decentralise some power to them.

- The *centralisation versus decentralisation* issue may be particularly important in designing the organisation's structure. According to many strategists, this should

Corporate Strategy Lecturer's Guide, Pitman Publishing
© Aldersgate Consultancy Limited 1997

only be undertaken once the basic strategy has been decided. There are no simple rules to define where the *balance* needs to be struck between centralisation and decentralisation.

- According to some modern strategists, Chandler's concept - strategy first and then structure to deliver it - may over-simplify the situation. There have been five major criticisms. Changes in the business environment and social values of the late twentieth century suggest that others *beyond* top management may need to contribute to strategy. This is called *empowerment* of the middle and junior ranks of managers. This can best take place before the final organisation structure is finalised. New processes for developing strategy are adaptive and involve learning mechanisms. They also need open, fluid structures that may not be best served by simple functional structures.

- The two broad parts of the value chain, upstream and downstream, suggest two broad organisation routes, one more rigid and centralised than the other. The implication is that strategy and organisation structure are more inter-related than previously suggested.

- When strategic change is radical, it may not be possible to define clearly the final organisation structure. It may be necessary to let the structure emerge as strategy changes and develops. Leadership style and content are also key determinants of strategy, especially where they involve a more collegiate and less authoritarian approach. In these circumstances, new skills and roles will certainly alter the balance between organisation and the related strategy.

- In exploring strategy and structure, it is useful to explore the links between the two elements. It is useful to start with the basic *design* of organisation structures. This will be governed by four main criteria: simplicity, least cost solution, motivation of those involved, existing organisation culture.

- In designing organisation structure, it is also important to consider the *complex links* that exist between the structure and strategy. Mintzberg has provided a process for understanding this. There are *six parts* to every organisation and *six methods* by which they can be co-ordinated.

- The parts and methods can be combined to produce *six main types* of organisational strategy and structure. They can be linked with typical key elements of the environment and other mechanisms. By this process, the organisation's strategy and its likely structure can be inter-related. In this sense, strategy is linked to structure. Most organisations do not match the six different configurations precisely, but they do provide guidelines that link strategy to structure.

- The choice of strategy and organisational structure will be determined more broadly by the *strategic fit* between the two areas, i.e. the congruence between an organisation and its structure.

- Every organisation has the choice of changing its *culture and style* when it changes its strategy. In many cases, a change of style is essential when a fundamental change of strategy is proposed. The content of the culture and style depend on the strategies proposed. There needs to be a degree of strategic fit between the two areas. Importantly, culture and style take time to change and may move *more slowly* than the proposed strategy.

Possible lecture structure

- Comment on the relationship of strategy and structure: use Figure 18.1 and the Sony case to make the point that Sony would have needed to redevelop its structures and strategies as it expanded across Asia.
- Outline the two perspectives on strategy and structure: use Figure 18.3 (and comment that this over-simplifies the situation in a more advanced lecture).
- Review the historical reasons that prompted the development of organisational structures to match the chosen strategy: use the two charts that follow on Chandler and Williamson.
- Explore the implications of designing structures to fit the strategy: use the chart that follows and Exhibit 18.1.
- Critically evaluate the arguments that strategy and structure have a more complex relationship than that suggested by the early strategists: use Exhibits 18.2 and 18.3.
- Explore the benefits and problems associated with the newer, learning organisational structures in relation to strategy: use the chart that follows.
- Explore how strategy and structure are inter-related: use Figure 18.6 and Exhibit 18.5.
- Understand the concept of strategic fit between strategy and structure: use the chart that follows.
- Evaluate the importance of changing the management style of an organisation at the same time as changing its strategy: use Exhibit 18.6.

Strategic project

The car industry is usually a good project area to select, because of the large amount of data available. There is little point in recommending specific research material since so much is available. Most students can become overwhelmed by the amount of data, so the main advice might be to guide them towards selecting part of the market, e.g. sports cars, four-wheel drive vehicles, luxury cars. This both makes the project more manageable and investigates a strategic solution to the issue of over-capacity, i.e. to specialise in a segment that is still growing.

Corporate Strategy Lecturer's Guide, Pitman Publishing
© Aldersgate Consultancy Limited 1997

Strategy before structure: Chandler's contribution

Alfred Chandler studied a number of leading North American companies during the early part of the twentieth century.

His conclusions

- As companies grow in size and complexity, they need a *general office* to handle the planning and co-ordinating work of the various parts of the business.

- The general office was concerned with the long-term strategy of the company.

- Once the strategy was formulated, the general office then designed a suitable organisation structure to implement the agreed strategy.

Key points

- Chandler concluded that strategy came before organisation structure.

- His evidence for this conclusion came from a study of industrial development in the early part of the twentieth century.

Strategy before structure: Williamson's contribution

Writing in the 1970s, the economist, Oliver Williamson, explored the role of the centre as organisations became more diverse.

Unlike Chandler, his work was based on theoretical concepts and there was no new empirical research.

Conclusions

- The role of the central HQ of a diversified company was to allocate resources to between its various divisions and then to monitor and control them.
- The centre should undertake this task by standing back from its divisions.
- The strategy of the diversified company needed to be resolved first with the organisational structure to follow.

Key points

- According to Williamson, strategy came before structure in the diversified company.

- Conclusions based on a consideration of the management of a diversified holding company only.

Corporate Strategy Lecturer's Guide, Pitman Publishing
© Aldersgate Consultancy Limited 1997

Designing organisation structures to fit the strategy

Chandler identified four key parameters for strategy growth that would influence organisational structure:

- *Expansion of volume*
- *Geographical dispersion*
- *Vertical integration*
- *Product diversification*

There were two main consequences:

1 Increased bureaucracy

Larger companies may actually perform better with more formal systems, but there may also be lower job satisfaction, higher absenteeism and staff turnover.

2 Increased decentralisation

Organisations that become more diverse in products or markets, need to re-organise and probably to devolve power: the centre can no longer make the relevant decisions.

Strategic fit between strategy and structure

- For an organisation to be economically effective, there needs to be a matching process between the organisation's strategy and its structure: the concept of *strategic fit*.

- Organisations need to adopt an internally consistent set of practices in order to undertake a proposed strategy.

Such practices go beyond organisation structure into such areas as:

- *Strategic planning process*
- *Recruitment and training*
- *Reward systems for employees and managers*
- *Work to be undertaken*
- *Information systems and processes*

Key points

Strategic fit may not be fully resolved by considering only strategy and structure.

It may even be necessary to revisit strategy, even when the implementation process is formally under consideration.

Corporate Strategy Lecturer's Guide, Pitman Publishing
© Aldersgate Consultancy Limited 1997

Case notes

How Sony moved out across Asia

1. What were the main reasons for Sony's expansion into East Asia?

In 1967 and 1973, Sony acquired two factories in Taiwan and South Korea. These were used to assemble imported components before export to other countries. However, there was no real strategic drive for such activity: the reasons were largely a result of acquisitions by Sony of other Japanese companies that happened to own the factories. In 1982, Sony opened two further new factories in Malaysia and Taiwan.

However, the real strategic shift came in the mid-1980s as the Japanese yen rose significantly against the US dollar and made Japanese home production expensive. The move overseas was also assisted by the substantially lower wage costs in some Asian countries. It was also claimed to be motivated by a desire to bring employment to these countries, so raising their purchasing power and enabling them to become markets for its electronic goods. By the mid-1990s Sony had some 17 plants in Asia outside Japan.

2. How should Sony set up structures to manage such a range of manufacturing and marketing opportunities?

Sony decided to maintain most of its research and technical development in Japan. Only the production units were located outside the home country. The company also followed a policy of locating production employees roughly in proportion to the breakdown of the world consumer electronics market.

With such a wide spread of factories coupled with the components and finished goods that needed to be shipped between them, a sophisticated control structure based in Japan was required to manage the daily logistics. In addition, key elements of strategy were also decided at Sony headquarters in Japan: essentially, the organisation structure of its subsidiaries was designed to carry out the chosen Sony HQ strategy.

The issue that arises is whether this was the most appropriate structure, i.e. the structure that would lead to optimal performance by its operating units. Although in the short term Asian subsidiaries were given little local initiative, this was essential because of the need to co-ordinate activities from the centre. However, in the longer term such a policy may lead to lack of sensitivity to local market needs and, importantly, to a lower level of motivation among employees and managers because they simply have to take orders from Japan. Although not stated in the case, there were reports of such problems arising at Sony factories in the UK. However, moving to empower local companies would destroy the inter-connected nature of the Sony production system. Strategy and structure might need to operate in a more sophisticated way.

How General Motors organised its future

1. Since the 1920s, the organisation structure of GM does not appear to have changed fundamentally: separate divisions still report to the centre. So what has changed about the company and its environment? What implications if any might this have for a change in the relationship between the centre and the divisions?

Some aspects of relatively recent strategy appear to have been decided at senior level, e.g. the decision to move out of cars and into EDS computer systems and Hughes aerospace. Nevertheless, it would seem desirable that, with increasingly sophisticated middle management, they should be more involved in the strategy making process.

The difficulties partly involve the shift in the culture of the organisation to include wider consultation, but also the need to cope with increasingly complex global structures where many key decisions have still to be co-ordinated at the centre. The new Ford Motors global structure described in Chapter 20 shows one attempt to overcome these problems. In this context, GM has traditionally given some autonomy to its regional operations, GM Europe, GM Asia-Pacific and GM Latin America. North America is, however, still the dominant partner.

2. When a company grows as large as GM, what problems would you envisage in operating a divisional structure?

Divisional structures are designed to operate with large companies, but there are inevitably still problems:

- Deciding what remains at the centre, e.g. cash and currency management, some R&D.
- Divisions may become overly competitive.
- Duplication of staff and equipment.
- Inconsistent policies across divisions.
- Co-ordination difficulties.
- Cash management.
- Divisionalisation demands good financial controls, which may occasionally break down.

3. Are the learning strategy concepts of Senge relevant to GM's strategy and structure?

Senge argued that such concepts derive partly from changes in the environment. The environment in which the car companies operate has changed radically over the last twenty years. This aspect of learning strategy is certainly relevant to GM.

Senge also said that they arise from the need for an organisation to create and explore new ideas from within itself. Thus learning will come from experimentation, discussion and feedback within the organisation.

Corporate Strategy Lecturer's Guide, Pitman Publishing
© Aldersgate Consultancy Limited 1997

Large companies, such as GM, tend to have more formal and bureaucratic structures that may inhibit such learning strategy concepts. However, this does not mean that learning is irrelevant to GM, rather that it is more difficult to organise and encourage. The issue is not whether such concepts are relevant, but how they can be developed in large organisations.

4. Can strategy 'emerge' in such a large company? If so, why, where and how?

In exploring this question, it is useful to make a distinction between corporate strategy and strategy at the divisional or SBU level.

- *Corporate level strategy.* With large companies and lengthy investment programmes, it is difficult for strategy to emerge at the centre because of the need for the formal planning systems that allocate funds from the centre to the divisions. It may be very difficult for the centre to cope with strategies that are simply allowed to arise when the divisions feel it appropriate.

- *Divisional or SBU level.* Yet, it is the divisions that are the main determinants of strategy. The Rumelt evidence shows that it is the division or SBU that is critical to delivering profitability: see Table 16.2, page 555. There is every reason to encourage the division to adopt a strategy process that involves *crafting* unique strategies: in the sense that emergent strategy encompasses such an activity, then strategy at divisional level can be said to emerge.

There are other aspects of strategy under the general title of 'emergent' strategy: see Chapters 2 and 17 for a discussion of these. It is less clear whether such approaches are relevant to large companies such as GM.

ABB empowers its managers

1. How important to the strategy of empowerment is the sophisticated financial control system, Abacus? And how vital is the central monitoring (e.g. Lindahl)? What does this mean for empowerment?

In some respects, ABB has attempted to transform completely its company culture over the last ten years: its chief executive, Percy Barnevik, has become well known as a strong advocate of empowerment. The case examines how this has arisen and draws on evidence from various sources to show that, even in ABB, empowerment has its limitations. There are certain decisions in corporate strategy that still have to be taken at the centre and cannot be given to individual managers. One such area is that of cash and currency management, which is still highly centralised. Another aspect of empowerment is the need for the centre to ensure that matters do not get out of hand: hence the importance of the Abacus system.

Importantly, when introducing empowerment, the company has rightly recognised that a major culture change does not happen overnight. It may take years to change the attitudes of individual managers. In the intervening period, it is therefore important for senior managers, such as Lindahl, to monitor developments and ensure that the proposed changes are pursued.

For empowerment, this means that it is unlikely to be introduced without some opposition. It will be necessary to take time for the revised processes to become part of the company. During this period, there may be a lack of strategic fit between the strategies, the organisation structure and the culture of the company. This needs to be monitored and considered, but is a normal part of the process of adjustment and is to be expected.

2. If the world is becoming increasingly global, do you think that ABB's unit empowerment can continue? Or will it need to be more aggregated? If so, what does this mean for the empowerment strategy?

Unit empowerment means that each individual unit is given more decision making power in its area of operation around the world: the fragmentation may not be appropriate in the following circumstances:

- for global customers;
- for the development and sharing of global R&D and technology costs;
- for global sourcing of production, as described in Chapter 10.

This is a serious difficulty for empowerment that has not always been clearly recognised. The problems that can arise are shown at ABB with its announcement of changes in the empowerment strategy in 1994: see page 652 for details.

Corporate Strategy Lecturer's Guide, Pitman Publishing

3. If empowerment is so valuable strategically, why are there companies that might not have followed the lead of ABB?

There is no conclusive proof that empowerment is 'so valuable strategically'. It is certainly valuable in some circumstances, but there are areas of strategy that it does not address. Moreover, there are significant difficulties in operating empowerment as demonstrated above and in the Sony case earlier in this chapter.

Even if empowerment held some attractions, the case also shows quite why other companies might not have followed the lead of ABB. There are numerous problems:

- The long lead times and lengthy consultation procedures required all have a cost.
- The resources needed to tackle such a radical change in company culture may be required for more urgent events, e.g. major turbulence in the environment.
- Organisation culture is a function of a much wider range of influences - *see* Chapter 8 for a discussion - against which empowerment may be inappropriate, irrelevant or insignificant.
- Strategic change is complex: *see* Exhibit 18.4. To concentrate on one small aspect - empowerment - may be to ignore much more important aspects of the total process that will be more effective in producing results.
- It may not suit the dominant *national* culture of some companies: Hofstede demonstrated that some national cultures need more certainty and strong leadership (*see* Chapter 8).

All such areas are matters of judgement: senior figures, such as Mr Barnevik at ABB, have to make their choices. It is usually the case that it is impossible for organisations to undertake everything. Leaders in other companies may have made the choice to concentrate on other strategic issues.

In strategy, there is rarely one single answer to all problems and empowerment should be seen in this context.

Chapter 19
Resource allocation, strategic planning and control

Synopsis of chapter

The chapter covers the main elements of the implementation process, in particular the relationship with strategy itself, the implementation of objectives and the use of strategic planning. It also explores resource allocation and the main elements of the control and monitoring of strategy.

Summary

- Implementation covers the activities required to put strategies into practice. The basic elements of this process are: general objectives; specific plans; the necessary finances; and a monitoring and control system to ensure compliance.

- There are three major approaches to implementation: comprehensive, incremental and selective. Implementation in medium-sized and small businesses may be less elaborate but needs to follow the same general principles.

- According to Pettigrew and Whipp, implementation is best seen as a *continuous* process, rather than one that simply occurs after the formulation of the strategy. Hrebiniak and Joyce placed *boundaries* on implementation depending on the ability of managers to consider every choice rationally and to evaluate the impact of implementation on strategy itself. Emergent approaches to strategy imply that implementation needs to be considered not just as a single event but rather as a series of activities whose outcome may to some extent shape the strategy.

- When setting objectives and tasks, it is important first to establish who *developed* the strategy that is now to be implemented. This will influence the implementation process.

- Individual objectives and tasks follow from the agreed overall objectives. It may be necessary to experiment to find the optimal combination of events. In fast-changing environments, rigid objectives may be made redundant by outside events.

- Communication and co-ordination are vital to satisfactory implementation. These are especially important where the organisation is seeking benefits from synergies or value chain linkages.

- The resource allocation process provides the necessary funds for proposed strategies. Where resources are limited, the centre is usually responsible for allocating funds using various decision criteria. Criteria for allocation include the delivery of the organisation's mission and objectives, the support of key strategies and the organisation's risk-taking profile, together with special circumstances, such as unusual changes in the environment. There is a risk that the resource allocation process will ignore the need to use resources more effectively and strategically.

- Strategic planning makes the strategy process operational in some organisations, but it is no substitute for basic and innovative strategic thinking. The basic process of strategic planning may well cover background assumptions, long-term vision, medium-term plans and short-term plans. Importantly, the input of new ideas and revisions into the process are significant elements of its development. Strategic planning has been heavily criticised by some researchers as being too bureaucratic and rigid in its approach, but attitudes are beginning to mellow as long as the process is narrowly defined.

- There are a number of different styles for conducting the strategic planning process, including strategic planning, strategic control and financial control. The selection of a style depends on the circumstances of the company. Formal strategic planning in small companies may help, especially when external finance is being sought.

- Monitoring and control systems are important in assessing strategy implementation and how the environment is changing. The necessity of obtaining information in sufficient time to take the required action is crucial. There are a number of ways in which strategic controls can be improved. All rely on having simple, cost-effective and useful information about the organisation and its environment. It has been argued that strategy control and budgeting should be linked. This is not recommended because strategy monitoring is more concerned with exploration while budgeting is more focussed on achieving specific short-term targets.

- International aspects of strategy implementation follow the same principles but are complicated by culture, geographical diversity and other factors.

Possible lecture structure

- Begin by considering the Air France case which explores the difficult dividing line between strategy and implementation.
- Comment more generally on the subject matter of the complete implementation process: use Figure 19.1.
- Outline the nature and types of implementation: use Figure 19.2 and Table 19.1.
- Identify the inter-relationships between strategy and implementation: use the chart that follows and Exhibit 19.1.
- Understand the way that the objectives, tasks and timing are implemented: use Exhibit 19.3 and Figure 19.3. Also use the chart that follows. Then use Exhibit 19.4.
- Describe how resources are allocated between parts of the organisation: use the chart that follows.
- Explore how strategic planning can be conducted and critically evaluate its merits: use Exhibit 19.2 and Figure 19.4 as examples; then use Figure 19.5 for the process

and Exhibit 19.5 for the reasons for failure. Use the chart on planning styles that follows, if relevant to the lecture content.

- Outline the main elements of control and monitoring and investigate their importance for corporate strategy implementation: use the chart that follows.

Strategic project

The references at the end of Chapter 19 plus those at the end of Chapter 2 will provide an excellent starting point for a thorough and useful investigation of this important topic. The texts by Bob De Wit and Ron Meyer (1994) *Strategy: process, content and context,* West Publishing, Minn, USA, and Henry Mintzberg and J B Quinn (1991*) The Strategy Process,* Prentice-Hall, NJ, also have useful selections of readings for those without access to library-based material.

Inter-relationships between strategy and implementation

Empirical research of Pettigrew and Whipp

Implementation is best seen as a continuous process, rather than one that simply occurs after strategy has been formulated.

Intended rationality and minimum intervention: Hrebiniak and Joyce

There are boundaries on implementation because managers may need to:

- Simplify the situation and be unable to consider every choice rationally

- Change only what is necessary

Other emergent approaches to implementation

- Emphasise the need to consider implementation as a series of activities whose outcome may to some extent shape the strategy

- Stress the educational and political aspects of implementation

Objectives, task setting and communication

Handling objectives in fast-changing environments: three guidelines

1. Flexibility in objectives and tasks within an agreed vision.

2. Empowerment of those closest to the environment changes, so that they can respond quickly.

3. Careful and close monitoring by the centre of those reacting to events.

Communication and co-ordination of objectives in large organisations is necessary:

1. To ensure that everyone has understood.

2. To allow any confusion or ambiguity to be resolved.

3. To communicate clearly the judgements, assumpions, contingencies and possibly the choices made during the strategy decision phase.

4. To ensure that the organisation is properly co-ordinated.

Corporate Strategy Lecturer's Guide, Pitman Publishing
© Aldersgate Consultancy Limited 1997

How resources are allocated

There are three basic criteria when allocating resources:

1. The contribution of the proposed resources toward the fulfillment of the organisation's mission and objectives.

2. Its support of key strategies.

3. The level of risk associated with a specific proposal.

Note that 'resource allocation' may ignore the need to use the existing resources more effectively and strategically.

Planning strategies and styles

Reasons for the variation in the styles of strategic planning include:

- *Environment*
- *Product range*
- *Leadership and management style*

Campbell and Gould identified three main styles as being most common:

- **Strategic planning**: the centre is involved in formulating the plans of the various businesses.
Possible example: Canon.

- **Financial control**: the centre exercises short-term financial control but otherwise the businesses are highly decentralised and able to operate as they wish.
Possible example: Hanson.

- **Strategic control**: between the two above. Some involvement in planning and some monitoring of operations.
Possible example: Nestlé.

Corporate Strategy Lecturer's Guide, Pitman Publishing
© Aldersgate Consultancy Limited 1997

Information, monitoring and control

Important because information can be used to:

- Assess resource allocation choices.
- Monitor progress on implementation.
- Evaluate performance of individual managers.

Main elements of a control system:

- Information must be in time to take action.
- Need to distinguish between financial and strategic monitoring.
- Need careful thought and experimentation.

Improving strategic controls

- Concentrate on the key performance indicators and key factors for success.
- Distinguish between corporate, business and operating levels of information: monitor only what is relevant.
- Avoid over-reliance on quantitative data.
- As controls become established, consider relaxing them.
- Create realistic expectations of what the control system can do as it is being introduced.

Case notes

Implementing an unpopular strategy at Air France

What are the reasons for Air France's poor performance?

Both the administrative and salary costs of the airline were considerably in excess of its main competitors. There was also evidence of a lack of control in the operations of the airline, e.g. the introduction of 11 profit centres suggests that, prior to this time, it was unclear where and how profits were made. However, major problems still remained, such as the excessive bureaucracy and the large numbers employed. The unions had vigorously objected to the proposed cuts in employment.

The reasons for the poor performance were therefore:

- A failure of management to introduce commercial working practices and adequate and workable controls.
- A failure of management to recognise the power and influence of the trade unions.
- A failure of the unions themselves to face the reality of the increased competitive pressure of the new international environment.

Is this a problem of the correct strategy, but poor implementation? Or does the strategy itself need to be changed in the face of union opposition?

Major change is unlikely to be popular, especially when it involves a substantial reduction in the workforce. However, it is occasionally necessary for management to consider the survival of the company, which was at stake here. If this means reducing the workforce, then that is the strategic decision that has to be taken. In this sense, the strategy is correct for the medium term.

However, the issue of *how* to reduce the workforce also needed to be addressed. There was little point in provoking a crisis with the unions without the means to resolve it. The implication of this was that the strategy needed to be modified at least in the short term, for example by implementation in stages or by further government help.

Strategies that cannot be implemented are not worth the paper that they are written upon.

Corporate Strategy Lecturer's Guide, Pitman Publishing
© Aldersgate Consultancy Limited 1997

Strategic planning at Canon with a co-operative corporate style

1. What are the main problems of large companies such as Canon in managing the strategic planning process?

To some extent, the issues will vary with the environment, the products and the leadership and culture of the company. However, there are likely to be some common issues in larger companies:

Bureaucracy and systems
One consequence of larger size is the need to formalise communications and relationships. This may lead to an over-formal structure that will make it difficult to produce innovative solutions. Canon has introduced extensive formal planning procedures but has attempted to overcome the difficulties by encouraging open and challenging discussion.

Links across the company
In large enterprises, there is a tendency for individuals and groups to identify with the division that employs them rather than the company in general. This is quite natural but has the real disadvantage that synergies, core competences and other cross-company activities are difficult to identify and exploit. Canon has clearly had major success in exploiting its technologies beyond their initial products. It has undertaken this task by stimulating cross-company co-operation through cross-company teams working on specific projects. This latter point is not in the case description, but can be found in the Harvard Case, the reference for which is given in the note on the next page of this *Guide*.

Culture and change
With larger enterprises, the culture is likely to change more slowly and in smaller steps. This may be a problem if significant change is required because the environment itself is changing rapidly: Canon faces a specific problem here because it is heavily involved in such areas as computer printer technology, video and information systems. For years, it has advocated open discussion about such issues in the knowledge that this will influence the culture of co-operation. It is assisted by the Japanese national culture which supports discussion until agreement has been reached by all the major participants.

Rivalry between divisions
If there is competition for scarce funds from the centre, this may be a significant problem. It will depend on the management style and leadership set by the centre. In the case of Canon, it is unclear whether this is a signficant issue.

2. How has Canon succeeded in remaining innovative? Could it do even better? If so, how?

It has used two principal mechanisms:

1. *Open and friendly style*, in which people can make mistakes without feeling threatened.
2. *Well-focussed strategy,* either for a new technical development, e.g. video recorders, or against an identified competitor, e.g. Xerox.

Its growth record is such that it is difficult to see how it could have done better. It is really one of the success stories of the last thirty years.

Special note

The references for the Canon case are:

Harvard Business School Case (1983) *Canon Inc (B)*, reference number 9-384-151, and *Note on the World Copier Industry in 1983*, reference 9-386-106.

Kono, T (1992) *Long Range Planning of Japanese Corporations*, de Gruyter, Berlin.

Financial Times, 16 February 1996, p31.

Canon Inc, *Annual Report and Accounts 1994.*

Hamel, G and Prahalad, C K (1994) *Competing for the Future*, Harvard Business School Press, Boston, Mass.

Informal strategic controls at Nestlé

1. What characterises the Nestlé style of strategic planning? To what extent is this a function of its large size? Its product range? Its geographical spread?

The Nestlé style is characterised by two mutually supporting activities:

- Formal planning systems described in Figure 19.4 and the text.
- Informal checks and balances through direct discussions, conversations between colleagues and so on.

The formal planning systems are certainly a function of its large size: it is essential to have well developed mechanisms for monitoring and reviewing progress in large organisations. The Nestlé system is typical of such companies. The author (RL) recalls a similar system when he worked at what is now called Kraft Jacobs Suchard.

The system is also a function of its product ranges: coffee, dairy products and so on tend to be relatively mature markets without rapid change. Hence, they lend themselves to planning cycles that can look ahead three years with some certainty, unlike other markets such as computer software where this is unrealistic.

The Nestlé strategic planning style may also derive from its geographic spread: its global operations certainly place particular demands on resources and activities. The distinction between the SBUs at the *strategic* level and the zones and operating companies at the *operational* level is also typical of large multinational food companies needing to be responsive to global strategy and national variations.

2. What, if any, are the dangers of informal strategic controls such as those operating at Nestlé?

Informal strategic controls are only dangerous if they become the *major* means of communicating and monitoring organisations. In the nature of human relationships, there will always be informal contacts: they provide a useful means of communication between many parts of the organisation. Occasionally, the message is distorted so it needs to be complemented by more formal mechanisms, but this is not a problem.

If they become the prime means of monitoring, then there may be several dangers, for example:

- Missing out vital data or not supplying it in time for action.
- Distorting the message.
- Excessive dominance by the politics of the organisation: see Chapters 8 and 21 for a fuller discussion of this important area.
- Lack of clarity in strategic direction and action.
- Inability to respond rapidly to strategic change if the approval mechanisms are unclear or tortuous.

Informal controls are useful, so long as they are balanced by more formal procedures such as those described at Nestlé.

Financial planning at Hanson plc

1. How did Hanson achieve its results? What did the Hanson Group Headquarters contribute to the process?

Hanson achieved its results in two major ways:

- It bought companies cheaply and then broke them up for sale of some parts to other companies.
- It imposed strict financial disciplines on the parts it retained, especially with regard to the forms of investment it was prepared to accept: cost-cutting plant was acceptable but investment in research and development was not.

Hanson Group Headquarters contributed through its clarity of vision, entrepreneurial and acquisition skills, strong philosophy of company management, appointment of bright and talented managers to the divisions it retained, strict financial controls. It should be noted that some of these elements go beyond the Campbell and Gould description of Hanson's financial strategy.

2. To what extent could the Hanson style be considered as a form of empowerment of middle managers?

Hanson managers were certainly given substantial powers of decision-making for their subsidiaries. This is a form of empowerment that proved highly successful and is perhaps not fully recognised in some of the commentary on the Hanson group and its style of financial controls. It is entirely consistent with the view of Williamson as to how diverse conglomerates should operate: *see* Section 18.3, page 627.

However, it should be recognised that the Hanson empowerment was strictly limited. There was very little room for manoeuvre in many respects. Some managers may have found the heavy emphasis on short-term profitability, at the expense of any form of longer-term investment, partially demotivating.

3. What are the dangers, if any, of the Hanson strategic style?

Some commentators have been critical of the group's strategy of asset sales and low investment in the companies it retained: often called *short-termism* because of its emphasis on immediate results. However, it could equally be argued that the fault partly lay with the previous owners and managers of such assets. As the case points out, for certain types of industry with limited growth prospects, such strategies have real merit. Sometimes it is difficult to distinguish between a genuine concern about short-termism and a more general resentment that the senior managers at Hanson were exceptionally adept at spotting and exploiting under-valued assets.

More generally, the dangers of the Hanson style lay in the need to repeat the success on a larger scale with each new acquisition. Moreover, its emphasis on financial results inevitably led to short-term performance measures taking precedence over investment. These issues are reflected in the second case on Hanson in Chapter 22.

Corporate Strategy Lecturer's Guide, Pitman Publishing
© Aldersgate Consultancy Limited 1997

Special note

The references for the Hanson case are:

Hanson Annual Report and Accounts: 1985 onwards.

Financial Times:
9 June 1989
30 March 1990
18 September 1991, p15
18 May 1994, p22
4 June 1994, p1
17 August 1994, p15
2 December 1994, p19
23 February 1995, p31
25 April 1995, p21
2 August 1995, p9.

Chapter 20
Organisational structure and people issues

Synopsis of chapter

The chapter explores how organisational structures are designed in relation to strategy. It then explores the special structures that are particularly suited to stimulating innovation. Finally, it explores people-management issues in a strategic context.

Summary

- In building the organisation's structure, it is essential to start by reconsidering its purpose. This will often provide some basic guidance on the structure required. In addition, there are nine main elements of organisational design: age, size, centralisation/decentralisation, overall work, technical content, tasks in different parts of the organisation, culture and leadership. All these elements will be inter-related with the organisation's strategy.

- There are six main types of organisation structure, each having advantages and disadvantages. The *small organisation* structure is self-explanatory. The *functional organisation structure* has been mainly used in small to medium-sized organisations with one main product range. As organisations develop further ranges of products, it is often necessary to *divisionalise*. Each division then has its own functional structure - marketing, finance, production, etc. As organisations become more diverse in their product ranges, the headquarters may just become a *holding company*. An alternative form of structure for companies with several ranges of products is the *matrix organisation*, where joint responsibility is held between the product structure and another organisational format such as the geographical structure. This type of organisation has some advantages but is difficult to manage successfully.

- All organisations must be able to innovate as part of the strategic process, but such innovation needs to be commercially attractive if it is to be viable. An organisation structure tht integrates and co-ordinates all the functional areas of the business is desirable. As innovation is open-ended and flexible, the process needs to be experimental with flexible structures, close co-ordination and power distributed throughout the innovating group.

- In terms of innovative structures, a matrix organisation may be more effective because it is more integrative. In some circumstances, a separate, parallel organisation tasked with developing innovative solutions may be employed.

- In building the most appropriate structure, it is important to keep in sight the need for simple, cost-effective structures. Environmental factors, such as market change and complexity, will also impact on the proposed structure. In general, increased change and complexity suggest more flexible, less centralised structures.

- Traditionally, it has been argued that increased standardisation and mass production need a more centralised organisational structure. With modern technical systems, decentralisation is recommended, with decision making being handed back to groups of workers. Since each organisation is unique, issues of structure and staffing make it difficult to develop unambiguous rules to implement strategy. The impact of strategic change on employees and managers is a major consideration that deserves separate and detailed discussion.

- Measurement of achievement and the subsequent reward for good performance can be powerful methods of directing corporate strategy. However, it may be difficult to develop reward systems that coincide fully with the organisation's strategic objectives. Staffing issues, such as recruitment, appraisal and training, are essential to the implementation of strategy. Formal procedures need to be built into the consideration of new or revised human resource management procedures.

- Four different types of international organisation can be identified: global, transnational, nationally responsive and international subsidiary. Each will require a different form of organisation and relationship with the central part of the organisation. They derive from the twin strategic pressures for globalisation in some markets and responsiveness to national or local needs. These trends are not mutually exclusive, and so give rise to the four different types of international organisation.

Possible lecture structure

- Take an example of a strategy, such as profit recovery at Rolls Royce, and explore the implications in terms of organisational structure. Use Figure 20.1 to outline the main considerations.
- Understand the main principles involved in designing the structure of an organisation to meet its chosen strategy: use the chart that follows and Exhibit 20.1 to show links with strategy.
- Outline the six main types of organisation structure and assess their advantages and disadvantages in relation to particular strategy: use the chart that follows, and also Figures 20.2-20.5 and Exhibits 20.2-20.5.
- Develop the special organisation structures that are more likely to lead to innovative strategies: use the chart that follows and Exhibits 20.6 and 20.7.
- Make recommendations on the most appropriate organisation structure: use the chart that follows and Exhibits 20.8 and 20.9.
- Explore how senior managers can be selected and motivated to implement the chosen strategies: use the chart that follows.
- Outline the additional considerations that apply when developing structures for international organisations: use Figure 20.6.

Strategic project

A useful starting point from a strategic perspective might be to explore the strategies suggested by Professor Michael Porter for fragmented industries: Porter, M E (1980) *Competitive Advantage*, The Free Press, Harvard, Chapter 9. It will also be important to investigate the development of global strategies: the references at the end of Chapter 18 will provide a starting point. It will then be necessary to explore McDonald's Restaurants (US), probably using their *Annual Report and Accounts* which provides a useful amount of data. Some Burger King data is available from the *Annual Report and Accounts* of its parent, Grand Metropolitan (UK) but it has in the past lacked some of the detail of McDonald's material.

Corporate Strategy Lecturer's Guide, Pitman Publishing
© Aldersgate Consultancy Limited 1997

Main elements of organisational design

The elements are not in any particular order:

- Age

- Size

- Environment

- Centralisation/decentralisation decisions

- Overall work to be undertaken

- Technical content of the work

- Different tasks in different parts of the organisation

- Culture

- Leadership

The six main types of organisational structure

- Small organisation structure:

  flexible, informal, dependent on management style of leader or owner

- Functional organisation structure

- Multi-divisional structure

- Holding company structure

- Matrix organisation structure

- Innovative organisation structure

Corporate Strategy Lecturer's Guide, Pitman Publishing
© Aldersgate Consultancy Limited 1997

Organisational structures for innovative companies

From work of Kanter surveying US companies in the 1970s and 1980s:

- *Importance of matrix structures*: break down barriers and lead to more open reporting lines. Also useful in providing a network for individuals to move outside their own positions.

- *Need for parallel organisation*: separate group to run in tandem with the existing hierarchy. The new group was left to develop its own working relationships among its members.

- *Work of the parallel organisation*: such a group tasked with finding innovative solutions, acting independently and without day-to-day pressures. Work was integrative, cross-functional, flexible and with little hierarchy. Often empowered people lower in the organisation.

- *Participative/collaborative management style*: involved persuading rather than ordering and sharing favourable results of successful initiatives.

Building the most appropriate organisational structure

Basic considerations:

- Simplicity

- Least cost solution

- Motivation of those involved

- Existing organisation culture

Other factors:

- Environment

- Resources and technical systems

- The strategy to be implemented
  (or at least explored, if the strategy is
  essentially experimental)

- Strategic change: explored separately
  because of its importance

Corporate Strategy Lecturer's Guide, Pitman Publishing
© Aldersgate Consultancy Limited 1997

Motivation and staffing in strategy implementation

Reward systems can be designed to achieve strategic objectives:

- *One form of reward* is direct remuneration: promotion and career development are other examples.
- *Strategic objectives* may be longer-term than managers' desire for short-term recompense.
- *Rewards focussing* on individual performance may not be appropriate for strategy involving group effort.
- *Rewards encouraging innovation and risk-taking* may be difficult to measure quantitatively, so judgement may be involved.

Formal organisation structures and staffing procedures - new strategies may call for new recruitment or for existing staff to undergo training and development:

- *Appraisal:* an examination of existing skills and people represents the starting point.
- *Training:* for some new strategic directions, it may be possible to train existing staff
- *Recruitment:* it may be essential to move outside the existing organisation for some new strategies.
- *Leadership:* radical new strategies may call for a change of leadership.

Key point

These considerations are fundamental to new strategic directions, underlining the importance of human resource management at the highest levels of strategy development.

Case notes

Organising for survival at Rolls-Royce Motors

Can any useful lessons on organisation be drawn from Rolls-Royce cars for other companies whose survival is not in question? If so, what are they?

The case describes a car company that came close to collapse in the difficult economic period of the early 1990s. It was particularly badly hit because it was at the luxury end of the car market and because its breakeven was high compared to its total unit sales. It was also producing a car that had a unique reputation and extraordinarily strong branding. It employed craft processes that involved individual skills no longer used in the mass-production car companies. To an extent the company was unique and its strategic difficulties reflected this situation.

However, the solutions to its strategic problems - survival in the short term and growth in the longer term - were not unique to the company. They provide lessons for many other companies:

- *The signal of factory closure.* As the case points out, this is a powerful sign to those that remained that the survival of the company was in question. Strategic change often needs to be accompanied by signals, though they may not be as drastic as this. Chapter 21 explores strategic change in more depth.

- *Change of organisation structure:* The reorganisation of the remaining factory into 16 zones allowed the company to reduce costs, introduce new cheaper working practices and, at the same time, drive for higher quality. Many organisations might benefit from a new structure to accompany a new strategy, even if the structure change was not strictly necessary.

- *New working relationships:* The new organisation was accompanied by empowerment on the factory floor and by team working. Many organisations might wish to consider these as part of new strategies, where appropriate.

- *Integration of different functions and departments:* Design at the new model stage was radically improved by an integration process that involved actions in different areas being considered simultaneously. Innovative solutions often result when functions co-operate, rather than deal with each other from a distance. Such solutions may be particularly appropriate for the experimentation involved in a *design* stage: they may be less useful for ongoing activities.

Strategically, the company was in a powerful position in the medium term to exploit its unique brand name, but it needed to generate profits in the short term to make this possible.

Corporate Strategy Lecturer's Guide, Pitman Publishing
© Aldersgate Consultancy Limited 1997

Organisation structure at Telepizza

1. What organisational structure would you propose to match the strategy at Telepizza? In answering this question, you should consider that the company has recently undergone profound change with the shareholders pressing for greater returns on their investment.

At present, the company is operating a loose structure, rather than one where formal reporting plays a major role in the company. The case does not describe the detailed structure that currently exists but makes the point that much of the decision-making takes place at local level.

In many respects, the company still operates each of its pizza restaurants as a small company organisation described in Section 20.2.1. As a result, empowerment and local incentives have been major factors in the rapid sales growth of the company. There is absolutely no evidence in the case to suggest changing this arrangement.

The shareholders, difficulties derived from the rapid growth of sales rather than poor organisation. They would not be helped if the strong and lively entrepreneurial flair was lost as a result of re-organisation.

2. To what extent does the structure need to remain loose in order to encourage the dynamic entrepreneurial spirit that has characterised its growth? What are the problems with this approach?

It is desirable that the organisation remains loose as long as possible in order to continue to build growth. The problems with such an approach are:

- The company may experience poor profit and cash control because the systems are weak.
- The quality of the product which is so important to its success, according to the case, may suffer if central monitoring is ignored. There might be a temptation for individual outlets to sacrifice quality for quantity and the centre would never know.
- Entrepreneurs might compete with each other inside a restaurant outlet on price or service, which may not be advantageous for the company.

3. Is it inevitable that the company will begin to lose its entrepreneurial flair as it grows larger? How is it proposing to hold on to this approach?

The evidence of Greiner in Chapter 8 would suggest that it is likely that it will become more bureaucratic: age and size will probably make the company less dynamic. Hence, as the enterprise grows, there may be a need to define more precisely the geographical territories or face the possibility that restaurants will compete against each other. This will limit the loose nature of the structure.

The company is attempting to hold its growth by restricting franchises to existing holders and by funding much of its growth internally. It wanted to retain the loyalty of its existing people. However, it is highly likely that some of the initial zip will go out of the company.

4. What is your view of the company's international growth strategy - sensible expansion or a waste of scarce management resources, given the continued expansion possibilities in Spain and the resource difficulties of supervising foreign operations?

Although full details are not given in the case, it is likely that significant resources are devoted to the international growth in the 50 centres operating abroad. There will inevitably come a time when further growth in Spain will be difficult: international opportunities will then maintain the momentum of the group. Moreover, international growth would be one way of offering an incentive to those individual managers unable to find new outlets in Spain.

However, there is no evidence that growth has disappeared in Spain. Given its strengths in the home market, it is surprising that so much effort seems to have been devoted to international expansion with all its associated costs and pressures.

Given that international expansion has now taken place, one way forward is to find a *balance* between the home market expansion and foreign growth. At the time of the case, it would appear that international growth should take second place to completing national expansion in Spain. However, this does not mean that international growth should stop, rather that a judgement is required on the pace of such expansion.

Case note

Readers may be interested to know that the founder, Mr Leopoldo Fernandez Pujals, reduced his shareholding from 40 per cent to 22 per cent in June 1996. The well-known large Spanish bank, Banco Bilbao Vizcaya (BBV), bought 18 per cent of the company. This move was a prelude to the company seeking a listing on the stock market for its shares through a public offer of 40 per cent of its shares in September 1996: BBV was acting as co-ordinator of the share issue, with Merrill Lynch responsible for a placing of part of the shares internationally.

The company was beginning to mature: the founder was selling part of his initial interest and the shareholding was becoming more widely available and institutionalised.

Corporate Strategy Lecturer's Guide, Pitman Publishing
© Aldersgate Consultancy Limited 1997

How Ford Motors went global

1. What were the arguments in favour of the new global strategy?

The main argument was the substantial saving in development time and costs for new models: it was decided to build essentially the same model around the world under-the-skin, even though the surface design might look different. Savings were also expected to be made in the costs of purchasing materials from outside suppliers. The result would be annual savings of around US$3 billion.

2. What process was used to develop the global strategy? Did this help or hinder the decision making as Ford subsequently went global?

The precise evidence and logic for this important decision seems to have rested largely on the judgement of three senior directors. Their initial view was that the whole company needed to move to a global structure.

Once this had been established, two teams were set up:

- To see whether the *Zetec* powertrain could form the basis of the globalisation push. This team examined the different ways the item was used across the company and the different ways that Ford operated in different countries. Since each part of Ford was so different, it was rapidly concluded that there were only limited advantages from globalising just this element.

- To examine the global competitiveness of the Ford motor company. This team examined competition and their use of global activities to enhance profits: R&D, purchasing, branding, etc.

From their different perspectives, both teams concluded that Ford needed to be more global. A detailed study team was then set up and an announcement made to Ford employees in April 1994. A transition management team was then set up to carry forward the detailed planning to the launch date of the new structure in January 1995 in the USA and Europe with the rest of the world to follow one year later.

The above process helped the decision to go global because it clearly involved significant numbers of senior executives around the world. Moreover, the teams that developed the global concept approached the potential savings from different angles and reached the same conclusion. When the decision was reached, Ford made a deliberate policy of announcing its intentions to all its employees. During the transition phase, a special team was set up to progress developments. All these elements would have assisted the process.

3. Do you consider that the global decision was made at a point in time or was there a sense that the decision to go global emerged as the organisation changed?

With hindsight, it is evident that the company had been moving in this direction for some years, perhaps without realising it. The *Zetec* powertrain was one example of some increase in international co-operation. However, it has to be said that there seems to have been no clear drive towards globalisation from the regional operating companies and, in this sense, the decision did not emerge but was clearly prompted by a judgement at the centre in North America.

4. What are the advantages and problems of the matrix structure that has been set up to manage the global operations? How does Ford plan to overcome the difficulties that can arise? Are you convinced by Ford's arguments?

The advantages and problems of the new matrix structure are no different from those described in Chapter 20: it was expected to lead to real cost savings as global activities were undertaken, but it would be complex and slow in operation. Ford was planning to overcome the difficulty of lengthy and tortuous decision making by four arrangements:

- empowering those lower down the structure;
- delayering from fourteen down to seven in its larger groups;
- giving prime operational decisions to the VPCs, not the functions, so the matrix was biased in favour of the new global car groups;
- retaining key strategy decisions at the corporate centre.

It is not at all clear that these actions will be enough to overcome the difficulties of matrix management and, at the same time, achieve globalisation. Some of the confusion has arisen because the company decided to use this as a mechanism to change other aspects of the culture of the company: the 'wrecking ball' mentioned in the case may be useful but could possibly confuse those involved on the need for global co-operation. More generally, it could be argued that matrix management with its desire to *compromise* between different interests was not compatible with the basic *centralisation* necessary for the cost savings of global strategy.

5. It is possible to have employee empowerment yet retain a global strategy at the centre of the company?

Yes, as long as the empowerment is clearly understood to involve *operating* decisions only. Global *strategy* can still be decided at the centre in terms of its general direction and then employees empowered to make decisions within this global objective. It should be recognised that such a constraint might limit the scope for initiative in some respects, but the Ford company is so large that there would still be substantial initiative even within such a restriction.

Corporate Strategy Lecturer's Guide, Pitman Publishing
© Aldersgate Consultancy Limited 1997

Chapter 21
Managing strategic change

Synopsis of chapter

The chapter analyses the meaning and importance of strategic change. It investigates the causes of change, before exploring the prescriptive and emergent approaches to managing change. Finally, it analyses the elements of a strategic change programme, including resistance to change and the politics of change. The international section explores the issues of multi-cultural team working.

Summary

- In the management of strategic change, a distinction needs to be made between the *pace* of change, which can be fast or slow, and *strategic* change, which is the pro-active management of change in an organisation. Strategic change is the implementation of new strategies that involve substantive changes beyond the normal routines of the organisation.

- In managing strategic change, it is useful to draw a distinction between prescriptive and emergent approaches. Prescriptive approaches involve the planned action necessary to achieve the changes. The changes may be imposed on those who will implement them. Emergent approaches involve the whole process of developing the strategy, as well as the implementation phase. This approach will also involve consultation and discussion with those who will subsequently be implementing the change.

- Strategic change is concerned with people and their tasks. It is undertaken through the formal and informal structures of the organisation. Understanding the *pressure points* for influencing change is important if such change is to be effective. Strategic change is important because it may involve major disruption and people may resist its consequences. Even where change is readily accepted, it will take time and careful thought. Strategic change carries important hidden costs.

- To manage strategic change, it is important to understand what is driving the process. There are numerous classifications of the causes with two being explored in this text.

- Tichy identifies four main causes of strategic change: environment, business relationships, technology and new entrants to the organisation, especially a new leader. Kanter, Stein and Jick identify three dynamics for strategic change: environment, lifecycle differences across divisions of an organisation, political power changes. Precision on the causes of change is important in order to manage the change process effectively.

- There are a number of *prescriptive routes* for the management of change: two were examined in the chapter. Kanter *et al* recommend a three-stage approach involving three *forms* of change and three *categories of people* involved in the change.

Essentially, the route is a top-down guide to managing planned change and its consequences throughout the organisation.

- Lewin developed a three-stage model for the prescriptive change process: unfreezing current attitudes, moving to a new level and refreezing attitudes at the new level. This model has been widely used to analyse and manage change. Prescriptive models of change work best where it is possible to move clearly from one state to another: in times of rapid change, such clarity may be difficult to find and such models may be inappropriate.

- There are a number of *emergent approaches* to strategic change. The two explored in the chapter concentrated on the longer-term, learning culture routes to change. According to Senge, the learning organisation does not suddenly adopt strategic change but is perpetually seeking it. Hence, the organisation is using its learning, experimentation and communication to renew itself constantly. Strategic change is a constant process.

- According to Pettigrew and Whipp, their empirical study of strategic change identified five factors in the successful management of the process. They were environmental assessment, leadership of change, the link between strategic and operational change, human resource aspects and coherence in the management of the process. Emergent models of strategic change take a long-term approach and may have limited usefulness when the organisation faces short-term strategic crisis.

- The choice between prescriptive and emergent strategic change processes will depend on the situation at the time: ideally, emergent change should be chosen because it is less disruptive and cheaper. In reality, a prescriptive approach may be necessary.

- To develop a change programme, the Change Options Matrix sets out the main areas where change is possible: it is important within this to focus and select options. Selection from the matrix can best be undertaken by an understanding of the culture of the organisation: the Cultural Web can be useful here. A more detailed process to achieve change can then be planned out with six overlapping areas providing a starting point. Resistance to change is probably one of the chief obstacles to successful strategy implementation. It is likely to be lower if strategies are not imposed from the outside.

- The politics of strategic change needs to begin by attempting to persuade those involved to adopt the new strategy recommendations. Beyond this, a Macchiavellian approach may be necessary to ensure the desired changes are achieved. More generally, strategic change activities may include identifying supporters, attempting to change opposition views and building the maximum consensus for the new proposals. Preferably, this should be undertaken prior to any decision meeting.

- Once change has been agreed, it is necessary to move beyond any past disputes and pick up the new challenge in a positive fashion. This will happen more easily if the culture and style of the organisation have been well prepared in advance to *welcome* change and not regard it as a threat. Leadership has an important role to play in leading strategic change: vision, communication, trust and self-knowledge are all desirable competences in good change leaders. They also need to be

Corporate Strategy Lecturer's Guide, Pitman Publishing
© Aldersgate Consultancy Limited 1997

responsive to the situation of the time and to be creative so that innovative solutions can be found.

- Cultural differences between countries can make strategic change difficult to implement. There are special difficulties where *team working* is required because different cultures have different ways of working, different expectations of success and different time-scales. The most obvious problem in team-working is a lack of trust. The best solution is for the team to explore this topic in itself. Beyond this, the best solution is for team members to have the time to resolve their problems. There is also a need for an acceptance that team members are unlikely to be as confident, nor possibly as competent, as they are in their home environments.

Possible lecture structure

- Use the Hoesch case to explore some of the change issues: what are they? Why is change important? How does it impact on strategy? Use Figure 21.1 to summarise the issues.

- Explain the nature of strategic change and its implications for strategy development: use the chart that follows and Figures 21.2 and 21.3.

- Analyse the causes of change: use the chart that follows.

- Examine the *prescriptive* approaches to managing strategic change: use the two charts that follow.

- Examine the *emergent* approaches to managing strategic change: use the chart that follows plus Figures 21.5 and 21.6.

- Link a strategic change programme with the type of change required: use Figure 21.8 and the chart that follows.

- Draw up a programme of strategic change appropriate to the strategic task: use Exhibit 21.1, Table 21.2 and the chart that follows on culture, style and leadership.

Strategic project

The case references will provide a basis for further investigation of these companies.

Nature of strategic change

Strategic change is the pro-active management of change.

Its activities will include: *'The induction of new patterns of action, belief and attitudes among substantial segments of the population.'* E H Schein

Prescriptive approaches to strategic change

- The implementation actions that result from the decision to pursue a chosen strategy.

- Such change may possibly be imposed on those who have to implement it.

Emergent approaches to strategic change

- The whole process of developing the strategy, as well as the actions that result after strategy has been developed.

- Such change may involve experimentation, learning and consultation among those involved in the change.

Corporate Strategy Lecturer's Guide, Pitman Publishing
© Aldersgate Consultancy Limited 1997

Causes of strategic change

Four main causes of strategic change - Tichy

- *Environment*: economy, competition, etc.
- *Business relationships*: alliances, acquisitions, etc.
- *Technology*
- *People*: new leadership, new entrants to organisation, etc.

Three dynamics for strategic change - Kanter, Stein and Jick

- *Environment*
- *Lifecycle differences*: different parts of an organisation are at different stages of development and therefore have different size, shape and resource allocation needs.
- *Political power changes inside the organisation*: individuals, groups and stakeholders struggle for power.

Key point

Need to explore and define more precisely for the organisation concerned.

Prescriptive approaches to managing strategic change: the Kanter *et al* approach

Three-stage prescriptive approach from Kanter et al has two elements:

1 Three forms taken by the change process:

- The changing identity of the organisation.
- Co-ordination and transition issues as an organisation moves through its lifecycle.
- Controlling the political aspects of organisations.

2 Three major categories of people involved in the change process:

- Change strategists responsible for leading strategic change.
- Change implementers with direct responsibility for change management itself.
- Change recipients who receive the change programme with varying degrees of anxiety and challenge.

Corporate Strategy Lecturer's Guide, Pitman Publishing
© Aldersgate Consultancy Limited 1997

Prescriptive approaches to managing strategic change: the Lewin approach

Unfreezing and freezing attitudes from Lewin has three elements:

1 Unfreezing current attitudes

- Old behaviour must be seen to be unsatisfactory by the group concerned and therefore changed.
- This might be undertaken by leaking information on the need for change or confronting those involved.

2 Moving to a new level

- A period of searching for new solutions then follows.
- Includes information on new values, organisational culture and structure.

3 Refreezing attitudes at the new level

- Once a satisfactory solution has been found.
- May involve positive reinforcement and support for decisions taken.

Emergent approaches to managing strategic change: the learning theory approach

Starts from the position that the organisation does not suddenly adopt strategic change but is perpetually seeking it.

Process of learning is *continuous*: as one area is learnt, so new avenues of experimentation and communication open up.

The learning approach emphasises:

- *Team learning*
- *The sharing of views and visions for the future*
- *The exploration of ingrained company habits*
- *People skills as the most important asset of the organisation*
- *Systems thinking*: the integrative area that supports the four above and provides a basis for viewing the environment.

Corporate Strategy Lecturer's Guide, Pitman Publishing
© Aldersgate Consultancy Limited 1997

Choice of strategic change programme

This will depend on the organisation, its culture and leadership style.

For example:

- *Centrally-directed management style* might emphasise the organisation of work and formal distribution of power.
- *Open-learning, empowerment style* might emphasise team building, training and education.

No universal answers: examine the *culture* of the organisation for indicators on choice

An *example* of strategic change in the open-learning, empowerment style:

1. Mobilise commitment to change through joint diagnosis of business problems arising from the change objective.
2. Develop a shared vision of how to organise and manage for competitiveness.
3. Foster consensus for the new vision, competence to enact it and cohesion to move it along.
4. Spread revitalisation to all departments, pushing it from the top.
5. Institute revitalisation through formal policies, systems and structures.
6. Monitor and adjust strategies in response to problems in the revitalisation process.

Strategic change: culture, style and leadership

Four areas of competence for leaders -
from Bennis and Nanus:

- *Vision*

- *Communications*

- *Trust*

- *Self-knowledge*

Two other areas of competence:

- *Responsiveness to the situation*

- *Creativity*

Corporate Strategy Lecturer's Guide, Pitman Publishing
© Aldersgate Consultancy Limited 1997

Case notes

Strategic change at Hoesch

1. In acquiring Hoesch, what purpose was served by introducing the 4K programme? Why did such benefits outweigh the costs?

The purpose of the 4K programme was:

- To strip away the rigid and encrusted structures that had characterised the previous company philosophy;
- To release the energies of the workforce for the new opportunities available;
- To conduct a thorough review of all operations in the company;
- To emphasise the particular areas summarised by the four Ks: customers, costs, creativity and communication.
- To encourage ownership by the workers, rather than consultants brought in to advise the company.

The costs of the programme can be implied from the case study: the four years that it took to implement the changes, the effort by employees spent on protest rather than productive work, the cost of consultants to make recommendations for the re-organisation.

The benefits of the programme were improved productivity, lower operating costs, innovative ideas on working practices and improved communication throughout the company. These will outweigh the costs above because they represent real and continuing benefits that will continue long after the protests and other events have been consigned to history.

2. As a matter of implementation policy after a take-over, would you always attempt to introduce a new programme of that kind?

Not necessarily: implementation has to be sensitive to the *context* of the business and its specific strategic opportunities and problems.

There were some real benefits from the programme, such as the four elements of the 4Ks. These items would be reflected in many strategic programmes:

- Kunden: increased customer-driven emphasis is important.
- Kosten: lowering costs usually has a positive outcome.
- Kreativität: innovation has been a constant theme throughout the text.
- Kommunikation: a significant part of learning-based strategy.

However, such items cannot simply be accepted without question. For example, the pharmaceutical company Glaxo purchased the Affymax biotech group in 1995 (*see* page 235) for its *new product potential*, rather than lower costs or customer issues. Such programmes are context-sensitive.

Owens-Corning reveals its strategies for change

1. What were the main problems at the acquired company?

- Immediate worries about the American way of doing things, job security and the future of the company.
- Uncertainty of employees as their company moved from being outside the mainstream business of the previous parent to being an important part of a European enterprise.
- Declining productivity as attention focussed on the intentions of the new parent.
- Lack of customer focus and the need for repeat business.
- Need to integrate the business into both Owens-Corning and its European operations.

2. How would you categorise the strategic change analysis here?

From Tichy's triggers for change, the pressures were characterised by:

- *Business relationships*: uncertainty was caused through the acquisition by a new and foreign parent.
- *People*: the acquisition was coupled with a new leader, Mr Warren Knowles, and his requirements for success.
- *Environment*: competitive pressures for repeat business allowed little time for the company to adjust to the new situation.

In this case, the Kanter *et al* dynamics adds one important dimension only:

Political power changes inside the organisation: the increased emphasis on customer orientation would have caused a shift in the power balance away from production and towards marketing inside the company.

In both of the above cases, it should be noted that *only* those elements of the strategic change analysis that were *relevant to Owens-Corning* are listed. Other factors such as technology or lifecycle differences are deliberately not covered because they were not important for this analysis.

3. Do you think the approach would have been the same if a substantial number of employees were to be made redundant as part of the take-over?

Possibly: the company gave no promises in any event, so it did not reduce the uncertainty for employees: 'I cannot guarantee your jobs'.

However, if there had been redundancies, the Owens-Corning style using extensive discussion and informal access to its senior management might have needed to change. Some companies would argue that, if there were to be redundancies, it would be better to undertake this quickly and without a lengthy analysis of the emotional responses. This would have required a different approach from that taken.

Corporate Strategy Lecturer's Guide, Pitman Publishing
© Aldersgate Consultancy Limited 1997

United Biscuits pulls out of the USA

1. What would be the effect on employees of the major strategic switch between February and July 1995? What actions would you have taken in July/August 1995 in these circumstances, if any?

Clearly all employees would have been faced with a major period of uncertainty. In analysing the situation in July/August 1995, it is useful to begin by considering the *causes of change* and to distinguish between North America and rest of world.

North American employees: the sale announcement introduced major doubts. Who would own the company? Would employees keep their jobs? It was actually in the interests of UB to hold the Keebler company together because it would gain a higher price from the sale by this means. Hence, it was important that UB reassured its US employees as much as possible and tried to resolve the sale as quickly as possible.

Rest of the World employees: the sale was sudden and was accompanied by announcements that implied the senior management had been taken by surprise. To this extent, there was a lack of credibility in announcements from the centre. It was therefore important to reassure workers with messages of hope, coupled with positive moves to signal a new determination to succeed. This was difficult in the circumstances as limited finance was available for any major strategic moves. However, some inexpensive first steps could be taken, e.g. perhaps project teams could be set up tp address:

- new innovative initiatives in biscuits and snacks;
- the competitive threat from Pepsi;
- new European/Pacific product opportunities.

2. Given the successful sale of its US interests in November 1995, what strategic change programme would you be seeking for the late 1990s?

To provide the basis for new initiatives, it might be useful to use the *prescriptive* Lewin approach on the Rest of the World employees:

- *Unfreezing attitudes*: clear announcement of problems, etc.
- *Moving to new level*: involve employees in study groups, etc.
- *Refreeze*: dependent on outcome of the Keebler company sale in November 1995 and the reports of the project teams mentioned above.

After the traumatic events of the previous years and the increased competitive pressure from Pepsi, it was important to move ahead positively, confidently and with some real plans for investment. It would also be important to encourage a new attitude of change in the company that might have been best served by *a new learning and experimental approach to strategic change*. Hence, the emergent approach to strategic change might also make a contribution over the longer term: the *Five Factors* analysis would offer guidance here on possible approaches.

Culture and change at merchant bankers, S G Warburg

1. Undertake an analysis of the changes that have taken place in the culture and power balance across the company since the take-over. What conclusions can you draw for employees and management?

The culture and power balance have changed radically since the take-over by Swiss Bank Corporation (SBC). One of the major difficulties in the case is to make sense of the sheer *variety* of changes, but five major areas can be identified:

- *Take-over by SBC*: new company procedures on employee remuneration, approach to new business, new organisation structure, etc. Being part of a larger organisation would also represent a major change for a company that had previously taken all its decisions on its own premises in the City of London.
- *Departure of senior staff*: some 1000 apparently left, including some key players in important areas of the business. There was a threat that they would take their customers with them.
- *Replacement of the old guard by new, younger managers with a different approach to business methods*: sales increases from having the right city banking contacts were replaced by a new, younger and more analytical approach.
- *New culture*: based less on high rewards for the key individuals and more on equality and team-playing. This was coupled with an increasingly analytical approach to customer and product profitability.
- *Global developments*: Warburg was no longer a separate company but part of a new global network being built by SBC. There was already broking strength in Asia and there was talk of adding a US investment bank.

The main impact for employees and management was the large-scale nature of the changes that were being introduced all at once during this period. The resulting uncertainty was made worse because the bank had clearly gone through a period of turmoil even before the SBC take-over. In 1994, it had failed to merge with Morgan Stanley, thus signalling to employees that all was not well. The power balance had changed radically with the old managers moving out and the new being given positions of power, yet still relying on some of the old for advice and business contacts.

All employees and managers must have been concerned for their *individual* futures, even though SBC would ensure that the bank itself survived. They would also have been confused by the depth and breadth of the strategic change that appeared around them.

2. With hindsight, would you have managed the essential changes at the merchant bank differently from the senior managers who undertook them at the time?

Given that individual employees were a key factor for success to the overall profitability, it might seem surprising that so much was being attempted so quickly. However, SBC needed to make changes and clearly took the view that it was better to take some of the most painful steps quickly, e.g. redundancy and fundamental changes in working practices.

Corporate Strategy Lecturer's Guide, Pitman Publishing
© Aldersgate Consultancy Limited 1997

Since the *emergent* model of strategic change copes less well with such dramatic and sudden swings in fortune, it is probably not useful to use this method to analyse the changes that occurred. Taking the *prescriptive* approach and using the Lewin model:

- *Unfreezing current attitudes*: this was really conducted with a vigour and power that was probably in excess of what was required. After the failed merger turmoil of 1994 and the arrival of a new parent in 1995, it would have been evident that the situation would have to change.

- *Moving to a new level*: it could be argued that the case is an accurate description of the uncertainties that are present as such a new level was still being established. The company remained at this stage as the case was written. It is for this reason that the case is complex. However, others would also argue that this stage also showed the major faults in SBC's handling of the strategic change process:

    1. It was not entirely clear what SBC really wanted with regard to people, business and organisation structures: what vision for the future?

    2. SBC appeared to be unable to organise any useful debate or consultation with those involved on the solutions to its concerns about profitability, working practices and so on: what concerns do you have?

- *Refreezing attitudes at the new level:* the company appeared to think that it had now reached this stage. Mr Ospel is quoted as saying, 'There are a few areas where we are facing problems, but by and large we should be pleased at where we are.' In reality, it may well be that at the time of the case it was still trying to resolve significant areas of strategic change. Arugably, it was unlikely to resolve its difficulties until it had recognised the amount of work still to be done.

3. Is the company likely to come through the change period with success or will there be permanent problems?

Nothing is permanent in such fast-changing financial markets. All employees and managers were likely to put the past behind them and look to the future. In this particular industry, such a culture is deeply embedded so permanent problems are unlikely from an employee viewpoint.

The more fundamental issue is the environment itself: it is turbulent, unpredictable and reliant on talent, technology and substantial financial resources. The company and its employees will need to draw some important lessons from this situation. Arguably, there needs to be a more open attitude to the need for permanent change through:

- a greater reliance on experimentation,
- team cultures,
- shared vision on competitiveness,
- new competences in some financial markets through training and recruitment,
- new taskforces to tackle innovation and so on.

It will be evident that these suggestions are closer to the *emergent model* for strategic change and rely especially on the insights from turbulent markets.

Chapter 22
Building a cohesive corporate strategy

Synopsis of chapter

There are three main parts to the chapter: the *Seven S Framework* is used to bring the strategic elements together, including a discussion of its use into the 1990s; *short-term implementation* issues are then explored; finally, some *longer term strategic issues* related to the purpose of the organisation and the role of corporate strategy are addressed.

Summary

- The 'Seven S Framework' can be used to bring the elements of strategy together. Each element is equally important and all need to be considered in the development of corporate strategy: strategy, structure, systems, style, staff, skills, superordinate goals. However, the model does little to explain the logic and the methodology of developing the links between the elements.

- Peters and Waterman used the 'Seven S Framework' as the basis for an empirical study on the attributes of the excellent American companies in the 1980s. They emerged with eight qualities, some of which were very basic and some more demanding - the latter including an emphasis on innovation and on the devolution of power to individuals and groups.

- Pascale also used the 'Seven S Framework' when he investigated apparent tensions and conflicts between the various elements. His research established what he described as four factors that would drive stagnation or renewal in the strategic process: fit, split, contend and transcend. *Fit* relates to the coherence of strategy. *Split* describes the need to devolve responsibility in large organisations. More controversially, Pascale concluded that there would always be some tensions and contradictions in strategic development: he called this the *contend* factor. His research also suggested that the strategic challenge was to attempt to manage such difficulties: he called this the *transcend* factor.

- In implementing corporate strategy, it is useful to identify the immediate tasks that need to be undertaken: they will include setting *milestones* to measure the progress along the way and setting up *controls* to ensure that overall guidelines on finance and other resources are not breached as the implementation proceeds.

- The *strategic staircase* is a useful concept for plotting out the implementation process. It is based on the assumption that it is possible and relevant to identify the final *objective* of a strategy. The steps backwards from this objective to the current time are then specified, including resources, strategies and intermediate plans. As a first stage, the strategic staircase ignores such *softer strategic issues* as negotiation with workers, power blocks and culture. These are more difficult to build in as separate steps because they are less predictable, but they may, in practice, be crucial to the implementation process.

- Many organisations attempt to re-examine the future environment, but the most important elements may be difficult to predict. A useful route forward may be to adopt the scenario-building approach. However, part of the reasoning for scenario building is not *prediction* but rather *preparation* in the event of the unpredictable happening.

- Organisations rarely stand still: it may also therefore be appropriate to re-examine the vision, purpose and mission of the organisation and also its culture and style. The values and ethical standards also deserve to be reappraised, along with an examination of stakeholder relationships. There will always be an element of chance in corporate strategy. Luck will make a contribution to the development of workable proposals. Finally, it is the conclusion of this book that both prescriptive and emergent approaches should be used in the development of corporate strategy.

Possible lecture structure

- Use the Novartis merger to illustrate the many elements of strategic change that need to be brought together. Summarise the structure of the lecture using Figure 22.1.
- Understand how the organisation's various elements can combine together to form the organisation's corporate strategy using the 'Seven S Framework': use Figure 22.2.
- Consider whether there is one standard of excellence for all corporate strategy situations: use Exhibit 22.1.
- Examine the contention that contradictions and tensions assist the corporate strategy process and can lead to stagnation or renewal: use Exhibits 22.2 and 22.3.
- Identify the immediate elements and tasks that need to be undertaken to implement the strategy process: use Exhibit 22.4.
- Outline the strategy implementation concept of the strategic staircase: use Figure 22.3.
- Evaluate some of the main issues involved in the longer-term task of developing corporate strategy: use Exhibit 22.5 and the chart that follows. No chart is offered for an overall conclusion as most lecturers will wish to present their own comments.

Strategic project

The article accurately describes how the Hanson Group is being split into four different trading companies. At the time of preparation of the case material (late 1996), this had still not taken place so it is not possible to provide specific references to its progress. Students may wish to relate the changes at Hanson to the development of the holding company: some might say, 'The rise and fall of the holding company.' Chapter 18 will provide a useful starting point in investigating this strategic topic.

Re-examining the organisation

Organisations rarely stand still: some grow, some decline.

The environment itself may change rapidly.

The resulting changes inside the organisation raise fundamental questions about the purpose of the organisation.

Three areas deserve re-examination:

- *The purpose of the organisation.*
- *The culture and style of the organisation.*
- *The values and ethical standards of the organisation.*

In spite of all the attempts of corporate strategy to guide or just cope with the future, there are always unpredictable elements beyond corporate strategy.

In the words of the German chemical company, Henkel:

> *'To succeed in business, you need skill, patience, money ... and a bit of luck.'*

Corporate Strategy Lecturer's Guide, Pitman Publishing
© Aldersgate Consultancy Limited 1997

Case notes

The strategy implications of creating Novartis

1. Is personnel the main area to be tackled at this stage?

Certainly the case would suggest that the consequences of the merger were uppermost in the minds of employees immediately after the announcement. In this respect, the personnel implications represented an important area to be tackled in the early stages of its development. However, many personnel issues cannot be resolved without reaching conclusions in other areas. Several examples will make the point:

- The case does not provide the data, but it was necessary for the company to gain US regulatory approval before the merger could go ahead. This was not expected until November 1996, some eight months after the merger was announced.
- It had not been resolved whether some parts of the chemicals and agriculture businesses would remain in the new group or be sold. Clearly, this would affect the numbers of employees who would remain in the group after the merger.
- At the time of the announcement, the new combined headquarters administration had not yet been resolved. It was known that there were likely to be substantial savings in both Basel and New Jersey, but the extent of the savings and the number of employees remained to be estimated at the time of the case.

In practice, there were a series of related strategic issues that all needed to be resolved at the same time: the new *strategy* of the combined group, the organisation *structure* that would accompany this and the *systems* that would operate it. These are three elements of the 'Seven S Framework' discussed in the chapter.

2. How important. if at all, is it to build a new combined corporate culture? What steps might be involved?

Whatever happens, a new combined corporate culture will *emerge* even if Novartis does nothing: the 'way we do things around here' will arise as a consequence of the new merged company, its history, organisation, politics and products, even if no positive cultural moves are developed. The real question is whether Novartis should consider carefully how they might *build* a new combined corporate culture.

Building a new corporate culture should be an integral part of the strategy of the merged company because it represents an opportunity and because it will be needed if the core competences, value chain, synergies and new sustainable competitive advantages are to be exploited to the full. In order to build the new culture, the other elements of the 'Seven S Framework' - skills, staff and style - could be employed. However, it may be better developed as a more detailed model using material from Chapter 8: *see* Figure 8.3 for a summary. Each of the elements of that Figure could then be considered: some will be fixed, but some could be shaped to provide a completely new culture. Case study 18.2 - *ABB empowers its managers* - shows clearly how a merger can provide an opportunity for an entirely new culture to be developed.

Long-term purpose at TomTec Imaging Systems

1. Would you be willing to take such a fundamental decision? What about your colleagues and their families?

There can be no single 'right answer' to this question. This is where corporate strategy meets the preferences of the individual in terms of lifestyle, ambitions, personal preferences and related issues.

These are fundamental issues that deserve to be explored for their consequences for corporate strategy. Everyone is entitled to their views, though many will wish to consult with others who would be affected by any decision made. Once basic decisions have been made about the relative importance of the different choices, the consequences for corporate strategy can then be explored.

2. What is the purpose of such a business? To make increased wealth? To enjoy a comfortable lifestyle, even if the full potential cannot be obtained?

For TomTec, it is likely that the founder, Peter Klein, regarded growth as being more important than a comfortable lifestyle back in Germany. Conceivably, growth was the only way that he and his fellow investors could recover the funds that they had put into the company: two years after the move, the company was still only at breakeven.

The question of the purpose of the business does need to be explored by all those who are *stakeholders* in the enterprise. For this reason, it is not enough for Mr Klein to put forward his views: those of his colleagues and others affected by the move to the USA need to be heard. They will then shape the purpose of the business and its mission and objectives. The case shows that it is always important to explore thoroughly these questions and their implications for corporate strategy.

Corporate Strategy Lecturer's Guide, Pitman Publishing
© Aldersgate Consultancy Limited 1997

A fundamental shift in strategy at Hanson plc

The case presents a critical analysis of the Hanson demerger. Its technique appears to be wholly plausible but is, in my opinion, flawed. The first three questions are designed to take the reader on an evaluative journey through the arguments and evidence used in the case. The final question invites a more critical approach than the repetition of Professor Gary Hamel's opinions about strategy development.

1. What strategy did Hanson adopt so successfully until the early 1990s? Why did it suit the environment of that period?

There were three strands to the strategy:

- Increased shareholder value through tight financial controls and an emphasis on short-term financial performance. The environment reflected moves to deliver increased value to shareholders.
- Low capital investment with short payback, low risk and the sale of under-utilised assets. This was a period of high inflation when such policies had a much lower level of risk.
- Major cutbacks in numbers employed, which was supported by the UK's Thatcher government of the 1980s.

Some of these aspects are explored more fully in Case 19.3.

2. In what way has the environment changed subsequently? To what extent did Hanson use such changes to justify the demerger?

Several major trends have emerged:

- Shareholding has changed with the large institutions becoming even more dominant. They have not regarded diversified holding companies as attractive investments, but have preferred to diversify their own share portfolios.
- Inflation has reduced, making the low investment route above less attractive.
- Several commentators have argued that cutbacks in numbers employed, often through delayering and downsizing, have gone too far.
- Global competition from low labour cost countries has provided its own pressure on companies to reduce costs.

Hanson has responded to these trends by proposing to demerge its business. In addition, it has announced its intention to invest more heavily in its remaining operations and lengthen the period over which such investments have to pay back. Beyond this, Hanson did not appear to be responding specifically to the above trends.

3. What were the main doubts expressed about the demerger? How did they relate to a shift in strategic thinking over the last five years? What evidence does the case put forward to show that Hanson has recognised this strategic shift?

The main doubts expressed about the demerger concern the methods that Hanson has used to manage its companies over the last twenty years. According to the case, the company has concentrated on delivering shareholder value. Its relationships with other stakeholders such as customers, suppliers and employees have been *adversarial*. The case points out that some strategic thinking has moved to regard *closer* relationships with stakeholders as being more valuable. The case writer argues that closer relationships with stakeholders are usually reflected in longer-term investment practices. The case writer makes no attempt to justify this assertion, nor provide any evidence to back his claim that the most efficient supplier relationships have now become more co-operative.

As a result of this change in strategic thinking, the case writer argues that Hanson may face significant difficulties if it attempts to take a longer-term view of investment. For example, it would need to build improved relationships with other stakeholders besides its shareholders. It would not be enough for Hanson to lengthen its payback criteria and allow other aspects to remain the same: there would need to be a change of culture. According to the case, Hanson has not yet recognised this aspect of the strategic shift in thinking.

4. Do you think that the Hanson demerger will be successful? Give reasons for your views.

It should be noted that the description of the change in the environment and the shift in strategic thinking described in the case is probably an over-simplification in several respects. There is no evidence that delayering is completely finished, nor that all companies have now developed a new relationship with stakeholders based on mutual trust. These are generalisations made by the case writer that seem to rely on contact with Professor Gary Hamel, rather than some more general survey of strategic practice.

Moreover, demerger at Hanson does not rely solely on longer-term investment for success. There are a number of other sound policies related to greater focus in the individual businesses after demerger that may also prove effective. The implication of these comments is that the Hanson demerger may indeed be successful and the Hanson critics may be confounded. The conclusion of the case writer may therefore be gloomy and over-cautious.

Corporate Strategy Lecturer's Guide, Pitman Publishing
© Aldersgate Consultancy Limited 1997

Overhead transparency masters

Fig 1.1

Analysing corporate strategy

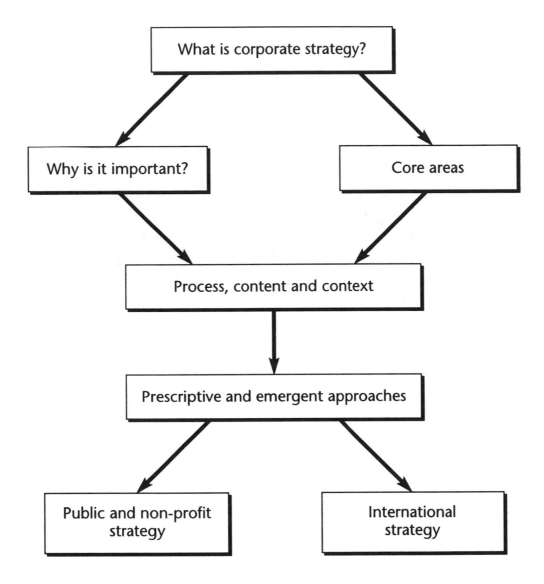

Fig 1.3

Some examples of how corporate strategy links the organisation's resources with its environment

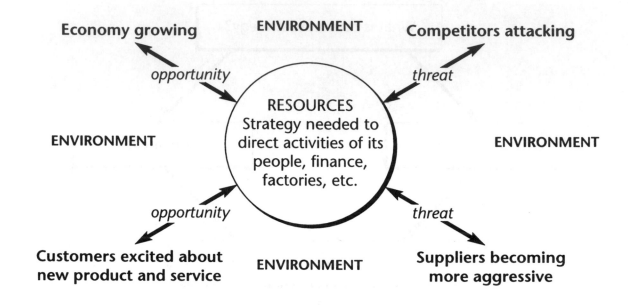

Economy growing

ENVIRONMENT

Competitors attacking

opportunity

threat

RESOURCES
Strategy needed to
direct activities of its
people, finance,
factories, etc.

ENVIRONMENT

ENVIRONMENT

opportunity

threat

Customers excited about
new product and service

ENVIRONMENT

Suppliers becoming
more aggressive

Fig 1.5

The three core areas of corporate strategy

(a) As they are usually set out for reasons of clarity and analysis ...

(b) As they are in reality ...

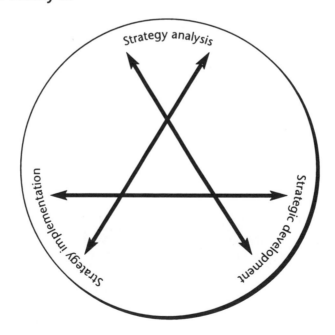

Fig 1.6

The three elements of the strategic decision

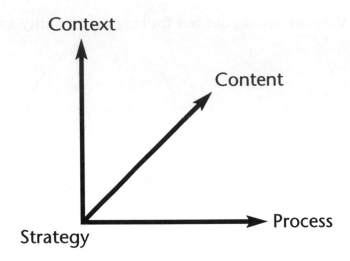

Source: Adapted from Pettigrew, A and Whipp, R (1991) *Managing Change for Competitive Success*, Blackwell Publishers, Oxford, p26. Reproduced with permission.

Fig 1.7

Prescriptive and emergent approaches to the three core elements

(a) The prescriptive approach

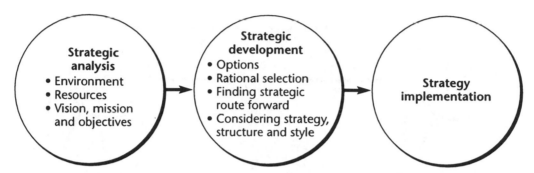

(b) The emergent approach

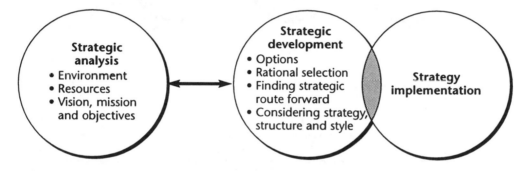

Fig 1.8

The prescriptive and emergent strategic processes

(a) The prescriptive strategic process

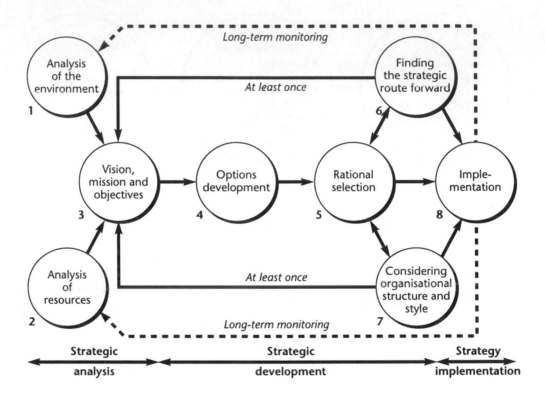

(b) The emergent strategic process

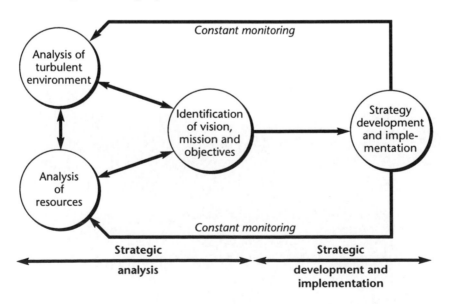

Fig 2.1

How the prescriptive corporate strategy process works

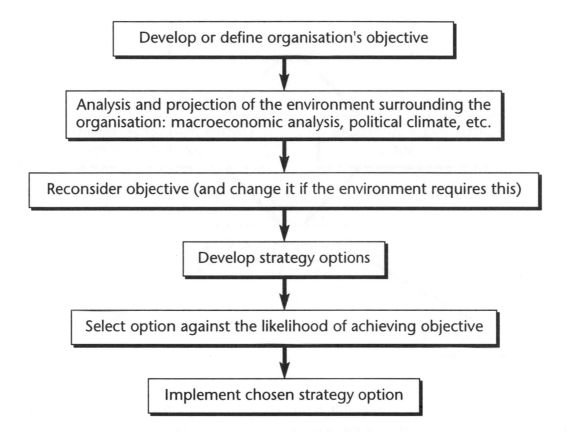

Develop or define organisation's objective

↓

Analysis and projection of the environment surrounding the organisation: macroeconomic analysis, political climate, etc.

↓

Reconsider objective (and change it if the environment requires this)

↓

Develop strategy options

↓

Select option against the likelihood of achieving objective

↓

Implement chosen strategy option

Corporate Strategy Overhead Transparency Masters Pitman Publishing © Aldersgate Consultancy Limited 1997

Fig 2.3

One view of how the emergent strategy process works

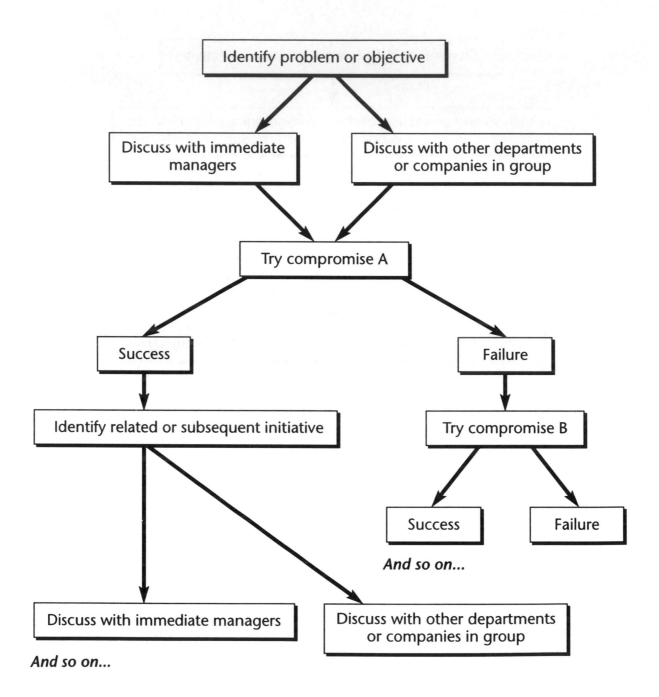

Fig 2.4

The prescriptive strategic process: the position of profit-maximising, competition-based theories

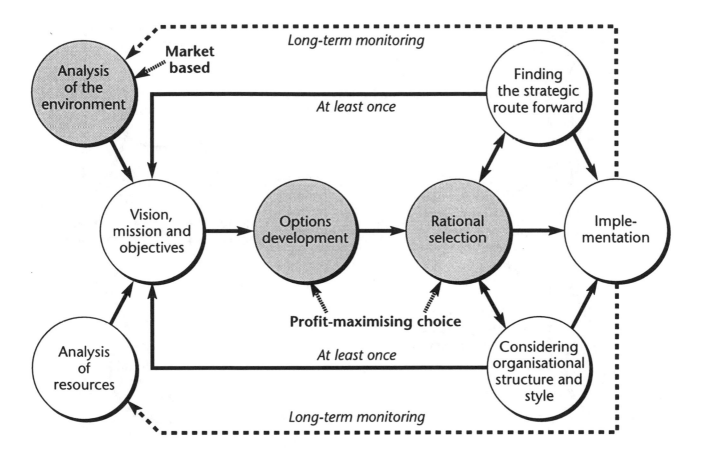

Corporate Strategy Overhead Transparency Masters Pitman Publishing © Aldersgate Consultancy Limited 1997

Fig 2.5

The prescriptive strategic process: the position of resource-based theories

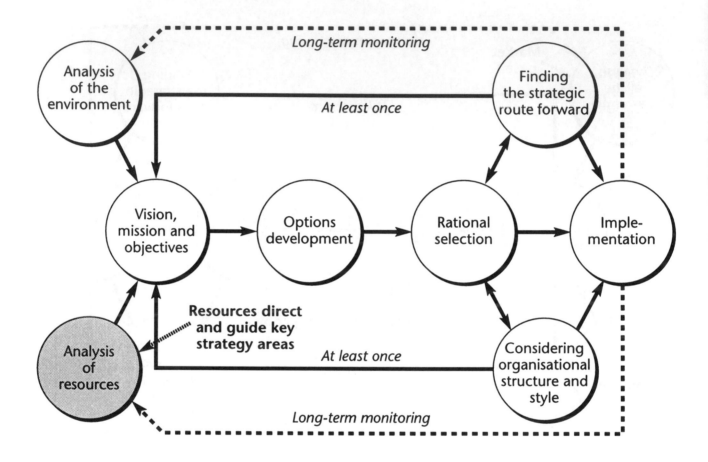

Corporate Strategy Overhead Transparency Masters Pitman Publishing © Aldersgate Consultancy Limited 1997

Fig 2.6

The prescriptive strategic process: the position of socio-cultural theories

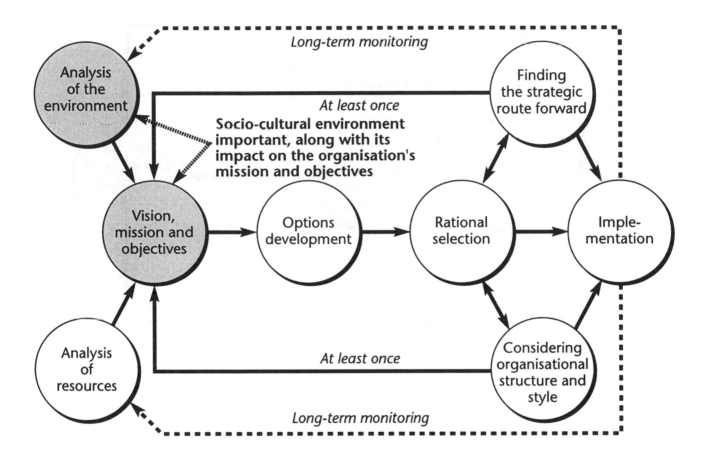

Fig 2.7

The emergent strategic process: the position of survival-based theories

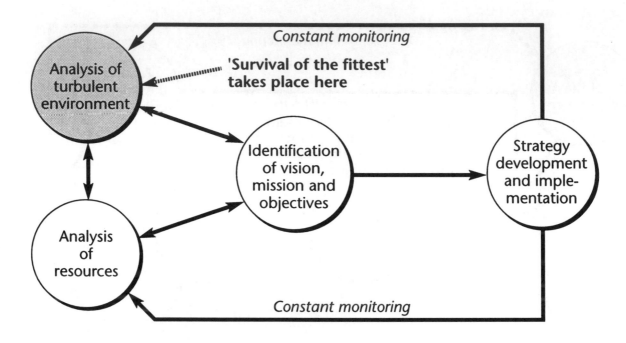

Fig 2.8

The emergent strategic process: the position of uncertainty-based theories

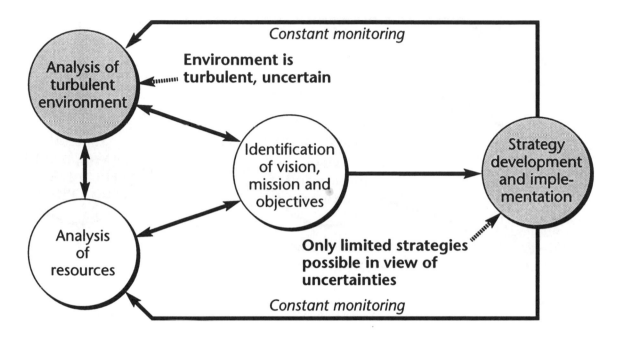

Fig 2.9

The emergent strategic process: the position of human-based theories

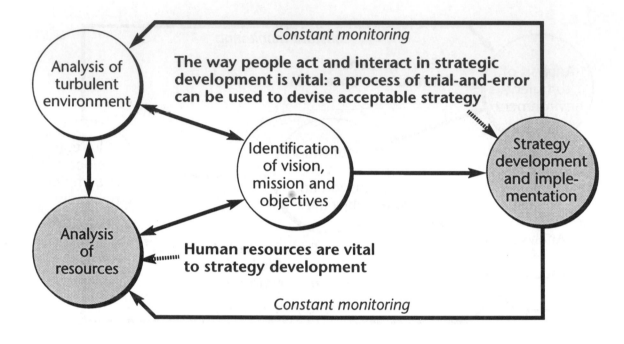

Fig 3.1

The six basic factors influencing the organisation

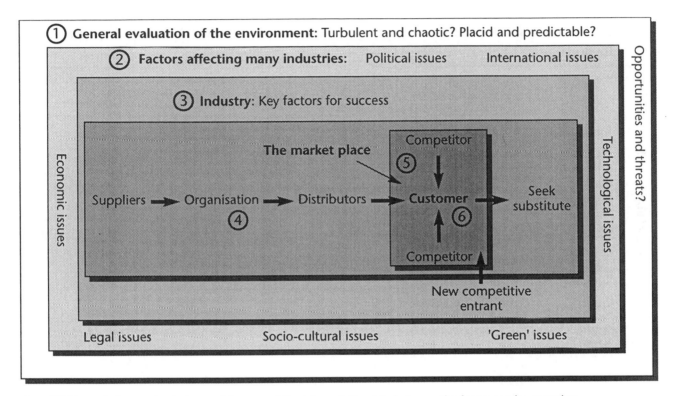

Note: Within an industry, the balance of forces and the inter-relationship between the forces can be complex. It is not fully shown above.

Table 3.2

Assessing the dynamics of the environment

Environmental turbulence		Repetitive	Expanding	Changing	Discontinuous	Surprising
Changeability	*Complexity*	National	National	Regional Technological	Regional Socio-political	Global Economic
	Familiarity of events	Familiar	Extrapolable		Discontinuous Familiar	Discontinuous Novel
Predictability	*Rapidity of change*	Slower than response		Comparable to response		Faster than response
	Visibility of future	Recurring	Forecastable	Predictable	Partially predictable	Unpredictable surprises
Turbulence level	Low	1	2	3	4	5 High

Source: *Implanting Strategic Management* by Ansoff, I and McDonnell, E, © 1990. Reprinted by permission of Prentice-Hall, Inc., Upper Saddle River, NJ.

Exhibit 3.1

Checklist for a PEST analysis

Political future

- Political parties and alignments at local, national and European or regional trading-block level

- Legislation, e.g. on taxation and employment law

- Relations between government and the organisation (possibly influencing the preceding items in a major way and forming a part of future corporate strategy)

- Government ownership of industry and attitude to monopolies and competition

Socio-cultural future

- Shifts in values and culture
- Change in lifestyle
- Attitudes to work and leisure
- 'Green' environmental issues
- Education and health
- Demographic changes
- Distribution of income

Economic future

- Total GDP and GDP per head
- Inflation
- Consumer expenditure and disposable income
- Interest rates
- Currency fluctuations and exchange rates
- Investment, by the state, private enterprise and foreign companies
- Cyclicality
- Unemployment
- Energy costs, transport costs, communications costs, raw materials costs

Technological future

- Government and European Union investment policy
- Identified new research initiatives
- New patents and products
- Speed of change and adoption of new technology
- Level of expenditure on R&D by organisation's rivals
- Developments in nominally unrelated industries that might be applicable

Exhibit 3.2

Some guidance on building scenarios

- Start from an *unusual viewpoint*. Examples might include the stance of a major competitor, a radical change of government or the outbreak of war.

- Develop a *qualitative description* of a group of possible events or a *narrative* that shows how events will unfold. It is unlikely that this will involve a quantitative projection.

- Explore the *outcomes* of this description or narrative of events by building two or three scenarios of what might happen. More than three scenarios is usually difficult to handle. Two scenarios often lend themselves to a 'most optimistic outcome' and a 'worst-possible outcome'.

- Include the inevitable *uncertainty* in each scenario and explore the *consequences* of this uncertainty to the organisation concerned – for example, 'What would happen if the most optimistic outcome was achieved?' The PEST factors may provide some clues here.

- Test the usefulness of the scenario by the extent to which it leads to *new strategic thinking* rather than merely the continuance of existing strategy.

Corporate Strategy Overhead Transparency Masters Pitman Publishing © Aldersgate Consultancy Limited 1997

Fig 3.3

Porter's Five Forces Model

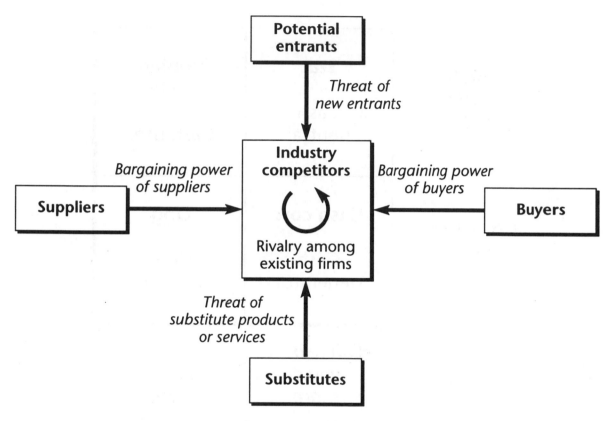

Source: Reprinted with the permission of The Free Press, a division of Simon & Schuster, from *Competitive Advantage*: *Creating and Sustaining Superior Performance* by Michael E Porter. Copyright © 1985 by Michael E Porter.

Fig 3.4

The product portfolio matrix – individual products or product groups categorised by market growth and share

	High relative market share	**Low relative market share**
High market growth rate	**Star** Cash neutral	**Problem child** Cash user
Low market growth rate	**Cash cow** Cash generator	**Dog** Cash neutral

Fig 4.1

Possible interconnections between the three main areas of market analysis

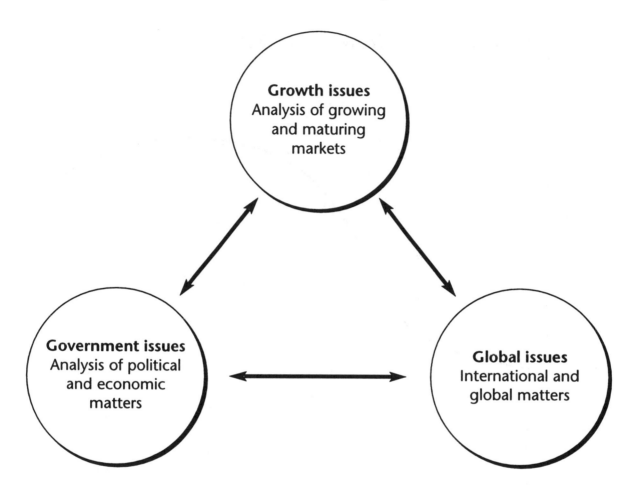

Fig 4.2

Stages of the industry life cycle

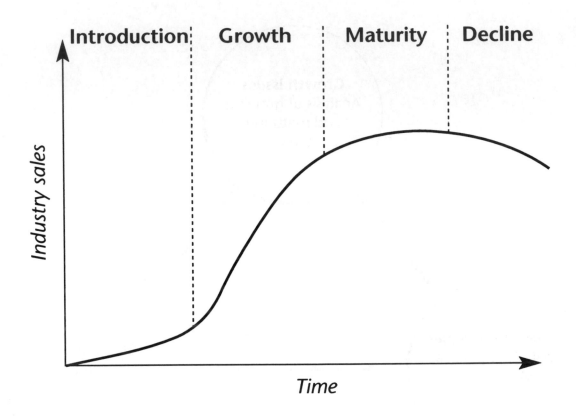

Fig 4.4

Industry life cycle and cyclicality

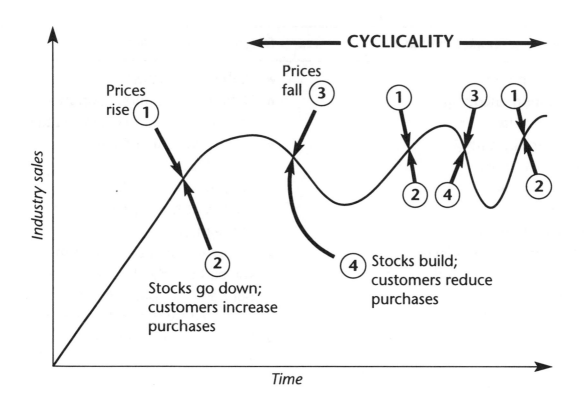

Table 4.3

Government and industrial policy

Laissez faire: free-market approach	*Dirigiste: centrally directed approach*
<ul><li>Low entry barriers</li><li>Competition encouraged</li><li>Little or no state support for industry</li><li>Self-interest leads to wealth creation</li><li>Belief in laws of supply and demand</li><li>High unemployment levels</li><li>Profit motive will provide basis for efficient production and high quality</li></ul>	<ul><li>High entry barriers</li><li>National companies supported against international competition</li><li>State ownership of some key industries</li><li>Profit motive benefits the few at the expense of the many</li><li>Failure in market mechanism will particularly affect the poor and can only be corrected by state intervention</li><li>Need to correct monopolies controlled by private companies</li></ul>

Exhibit 4.3

Seven criteria to establish whether an organisation needs to undertake a more extensive macroeonomic analysis

1 Does the external business environment influence capital allocations and the decision-making process?

2 Have the previous long-range plans been scrapped because of unexpected changes in the environment?

3 Have there been any unpleasant surprises in the external business environment?

4 Is competition growing in the industry?

5 Is the business more marketing oriented and more concerned about the ultimate customer?

6 Do more and different kinds of external forces seem to be influencing decisions, and does there seem to be more interplay among them?

7 Is management unhappy with past forecasting and planning efforts?

If any of the above is answered affirmatively, then further analysis may need to be undertaken; an increase in the number of positive answers means that the need may be greater.

Exhibit 4.4

Typical economic issues involving both government and industry

- Government tax and legislative activity.

- Specific impact of macroeconomic growth on an industry. (For example, house construction particularly relies on a buoyant economy in a way that food does not – we need to eat but may be able to delay moving house.)

- Cyclicality of demand and investment in an industry.

- The level of derived demand. Some companies, particularly in the industrial area, depend on their *customers'* economic prospects for their demand – for example, bricks and door frames depend partly on demand derived from the construction industry.

- Raw material supplies and costs.

- Industry negotiations on wages and conditions of work.

Table 4.4

Comparison of world exports and world manufacturing value added

	1960–70	1970–80	1980–90
Annual growth in world trade (%)	9.2	20.3	6.0
Annual growth in manufacturing value added (%)	N/A	3.1	2.1

Source: UNIDO

Fig 5.1

Computer analysis: the main considerations

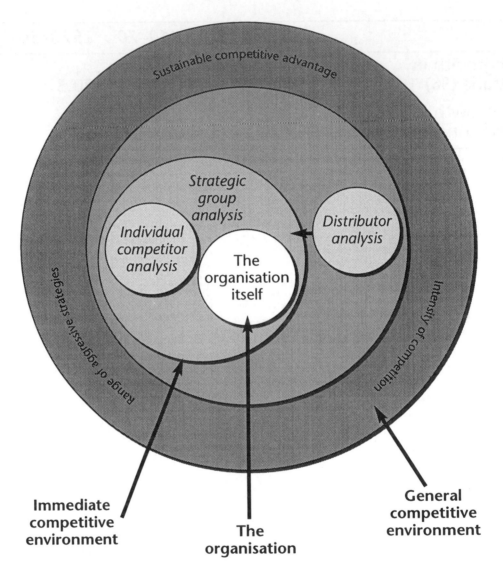

Immediate competitive environment

The organisation

General competitive environment

Note: There will be other strategic groups; only one is shown here. The organisation itself may also be a member of other strategic groups with other products or services.

Fig 5.2

Analysing the aggressive strategies undertaken by competitors

```
┌─────────────────────────────────┐
│       Market intelligence       │
└─────────────────────────────────┘
                 │
                 ▼
┌─────────────────────────────────┐
│    Clarification of objectives   │
└─────────────────────────────────┘
                 │
                 ▼
┌─────────────────────────────────┐
│       Choosing the enemy        │
└─────────────────────────────────┘
                 │
                 ▼
┌─────────────────────────────────┐
│   The four main attack strategies │
└─────────────────────────────────┘
                 │
                 ▼
┌─────────────────────────────────┐
│      Innovatory strategies      │
└─────────────────────────────────┘
                 │
                 ▼
┌─────────────────────────────────┐
│   Conclusions: Attack or defend  │
└─────────────────────────────────┘
```

Exhibit 5.2

The four main attack strategies

1 Head-on against the market leader

- Unless resources are sustained, the campaign is unlikely to be successful.
- Attack where the leader is weak.
- Pick a narrow front to open up the campaign.

2 Flanking or market segmentation

- Choose a flank that is relatively undefended.
- Aim to take a significant market share.
- Expect to invest in the flank for some years.
- Pricing and value for money are often distinguishing features of a successful flank.

3 Occupy totally new territory, that is, where there is no existing product or service

- Innovate if possible.
- Seek market niches.

4 Guerrilla, that is, a rapid sortie to seize a short-term profitable opportunity

- Relies on good information to identify opportunities.
- Fast response needed and rapid withdrawal after success.
- Important not to stand and fight leaders on their own ground but pick new areas.

Corporate Strategy Overhead Transparency Masters Pitman Publishing © Aldersgate Consultancy Limited 1997

Exhibit 5.3

The analytical process for strategic groups

1 Identify the competitive characteristics that specify strategic groups: for example, geographic coverage, product range, product quality, price ranges such as high/medium/low, common customers, etc.

2 Identify the leading pairs of independent variables associated with 1 above.

3 Plot the pairs as a matrix or as a two-variable map.

4 Assess which competitors should be grouped together using the two variables. Alternatively, identify competitors but leave them as individual companies.

5 Plot the groups or individual competitors as positions on the map.

6 Draw circles centred at the group or competitor with the radius or area representing turnover for the competitor or group.

Corporate Strategy Overhead Transparency Masters Pitman Publishing © Aldersgate Consultancy Limited 1997

Table 5.2

Some possible sustainable competitive advantages in different areas of business

High technology	Services	Small business	Manufacturing market leader
● Technical excellence	● Reputation for quality of service	● Quality	● Low costs
● Reputation for quality	● High quality and training of staff	● Prompt service	● Strong branding
● Customer service	● Customer service	● Personalised service	● Good distribution
● Financial resources	● Well-known name	● Keen prices	● Quality product
● Low-cost manufacturing	● Customer-oriented	● Local availability	● Good value for money

Table 6.1

Typical customer profiles

	Domestic consumer	Large industrial	Large private service	Not-for-profit charity	Public service	Small business	Strategic implications
Example	Unilever ice cream	Airbus aircraft	McDonald's restaurants	UNICEF	Health service hospital	Hairdresser or local builder	
Nature of demand	Primary	Derived or joint	Primary	Primary	Primary	Derived or joint	
Selling message	Immediate satisfaction: status can be important	Economic and non-economic needs	Immediate service: quality is part of service	Driven by belief in charity	As private service, but tempered by public service guidelines	As large industrial, but may place greater value on personal service	Major areas of difference may require industry-level strategies
Customer needs	Customers can be grouped into those with similar needs: segmentation	Each customer different	Customers grouped as in domestic	Customers may be grouped but individual service also important	Customers may be grouped but individual service also important	Customers may be grouped but many will be different	Strategies for segments and individual buyers
Purchase motivation	Individual or family	Buy for company	Will partly be driven by location, style	Receive for others and self	Receive for others and self	Local and national service	Major areas of difference may require industry-level strategies
Product	Branding, possibly low technical content	Perhaps technically sophisticated	People providing service are part of product	People providing service are part of product	People providing service are part of product. Also technical content	Possible technical content. Also possibly high and personal service	Technical sophistication in some areas. People as part of service in others

Fig 6.1

Analysing customer strategy: the main elements

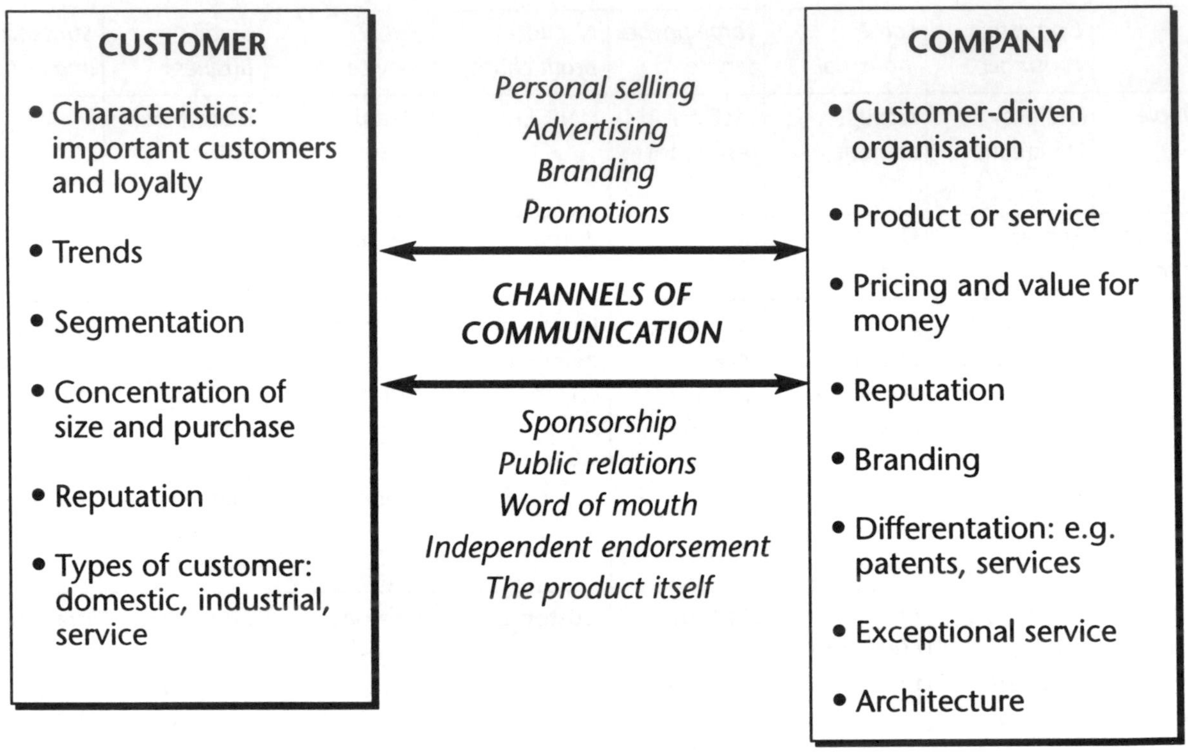

CUSTOMER		COMPANY
• Characteristics: important customers and loyalty	*Personal selling* *Advertising* *Branding* *Promotions*	• Customer-driven organisation
• Trends		• Product or service
• Segmentation	**CHANNELS OF COMMUNICATION**	• Pricing and value for money
• Concentration of size and purchase		• Reputation
• Reputation	*Sponsorship* *Public relations* *Word of mouth* *Independent endorsement* *The product itself*	• Branding
• Types of customer: domestic, industrial, service		• Differentation: e.g. patents, services
		• Exceptional service
		• Architecture

Exhibit 6.1

Some examples of customer-driven strategy

Understanding the customer

Direct customer contact at many levels

Widely disseminated research on key customer findings, e.g. on segmentation

Knowledge of why customers choose the organisation

Responsiveness of the organisation to customer needs

Regularly receive and act upon customer satisfaction surveys

Responsive to customer complaints and suggestions

Track key customer data on company image

Provision of real value for money

Monitor quality relevant to the positioning of products in the market place

Conduct comparative surveys of competitive prices and service offerings

● Rewards inside the organisation based on performance with customers

Fig 6.3

Basic considerations in strategic price setting

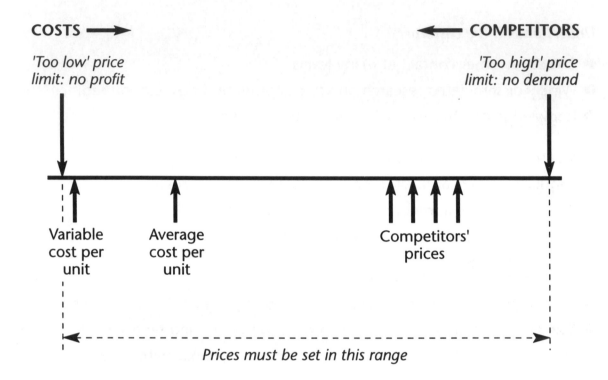

Fig 6.4

Two strategic pricing routes compared

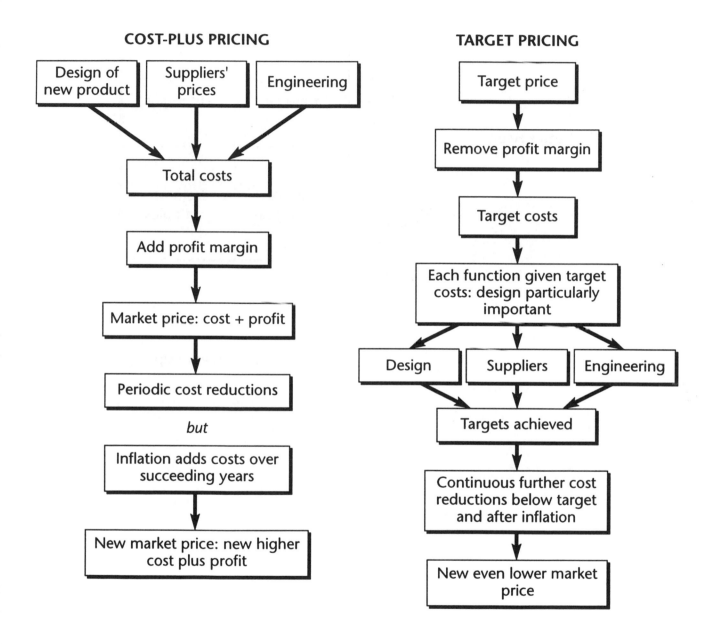

COST-PLUS PRICING

Design of new product | Suppliers' prices | Engineering

→ Total costs

→ Add profit margin

→ Market price: cost + profit

→ Periodic cost reductions

but

Inflation adds costs over succeeding years

→ New market price: new higher cost plus profit

TARGET PRICING

Target price

→ Remove profit margin

→ Target costs

→ Each function given target costs: design particularly important

→ Design | Suppliers | Engineering

→ Targets achieved

→ Continuous further cost reductions below target and after inflation

→ New even lower market price

Fig 6.5

Customer/competitor matrix

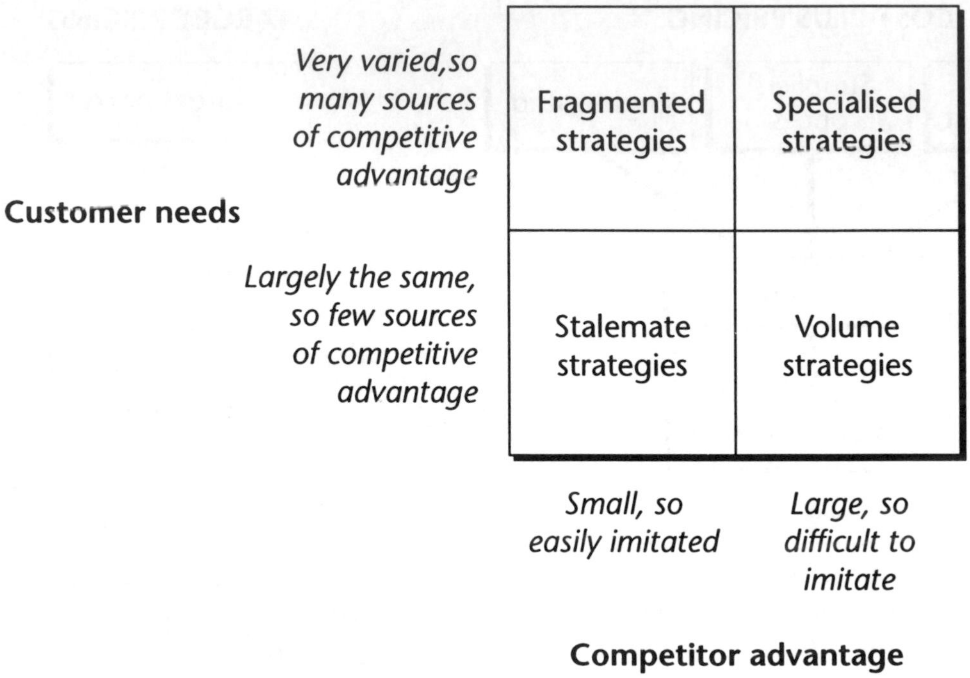

	Small, so easily imitated	Large, so difficult to imitate
Very varied, so many sources of competitive advantage	Fragmented strategies	Specialised strategies
Largely the same, so few sources of competitive advantage	Stalemate strategies	Volume strategies

Customer needs

Very varied, so many sources of competitive advantage

Largely the same, so few sources of competitive advantage

Small, so easily imitated   *Large, so difficult to imitate*

Competitor advantage

Exhibit 6.3

Levitt's justification of increased internationalisation

- Price competition is important and persuasive for customers.
- It is possible to change national tastes if prices are low enough.
- Globalisation will emerge from a standardisation of products and services.
- Tariffs and quotas will not protect national industries against the international attack.
- Major economies of scale are possible and will lead to increased international price competition.
- Global branding is meaningful and attractive to customers.

Fig 7.1

Adding value through resources

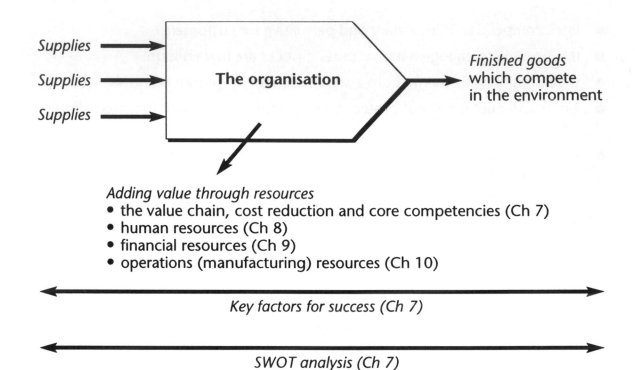

Supplies →

Supplies → **The organisation** → *Finished goods which compete in the environment*

Supplies →

Adding value through resources
- the value chain, cost reduction and core competencies (Ch 7)
- human resources (Ch 8)
- financial resources (Ch 9)
- operations (manufacturing) resources (Ch 10)

←——————————————————————→
Key factors for success (Ch 7)

←——————————————————————→
SWOT analysis (Ch 7)

Fig 7.2

Cost profiles – costs as a percentage of sales

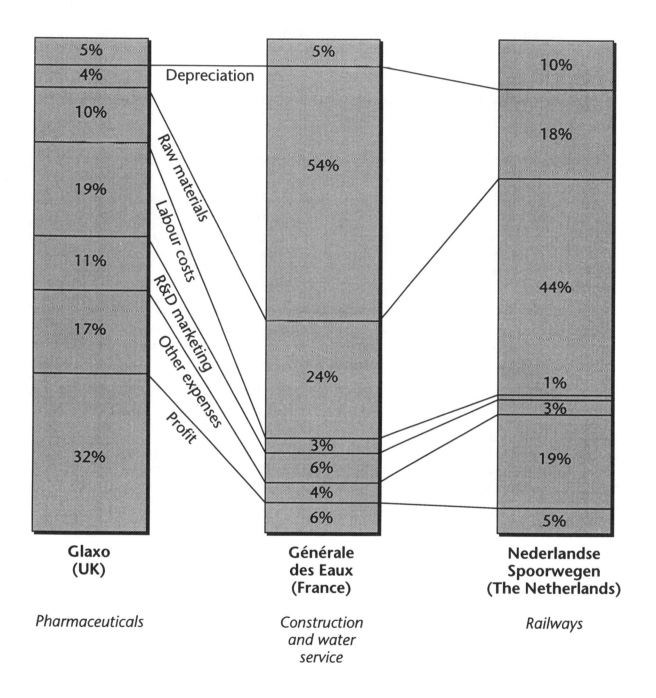

Glaxo (UK)	Générale des Eaux (France)	Nederlandse Spoorwegen (The Netherlands)
Pharmaceuticals	*Construction and water service*	*Railways*

Depreciation · Raw materials · Labour costs · R&D marketing · Other expenses · Profit

Exhibit 7.1

Identifying key factors for success

Note that key factors for success are directed at *all companies in an industry*, not just the target company for strategy development.

1 Customers
Who are our customers? Who are our potential customers? Are there any special segments that we dominate? Why do customers buy from us? And from our competitors?

- *Price.* Is the market segmented by high, medium and economy pricing? (Example: European ice cream.)
- *Service.* Do some customers value service while others simply want to buy the product? (For example, top class fashion retailers versus standard clothing shops.)
- *Product or service reliability.* Is product performance crucial to the customer or is reliability useful but not really important? (For example, heart pace makers and pharmaceuticals.)
- *Quality.* Some customers will pay higher prices for actual or perceived quality differences. Does this provide a route to success? (For example, organic vegetables.)
- *Technical specifications.* In some industrial and financial services, technical details will provide major attractions for some customers. Is this relevant to the organisation? (For example, specialist financial bond dealers.)
- *Branding.* How important is branding for the customer? (For example, Coca-Cola and Pepsi Cola.)

2 Competition
Who are our competitors? What are the main factors in the market that influence competition? How intense is competition? What is necessary to achieve market superiority? What resources do competitors possess that we lack and vice versa?

- *Cost comparisons.* Which companies have the lowest costs? Why? (For example, Toyota until the mid-1990s.)
- *Price comparisons.* Which companies have high prices? (For example, Daimler Benz does not make cheap cars.)
- *Quality issues.* Which companies have the highest quality? Why? How? (For example, Xerox (USA) in the light of fierce competition from Japanese companies such as Canon.)
- *Market dominance.* Which companies dominate the market? (For example, Nestlé with strongest coffee product range in the world and the largest market share.)
- *Service.* Are there companies in the industry that offer superior service levels? (For example, industrial markets, such as those served by Asea Brown Boveri, which need high levels of service to operate and maintain sophisticated equipment.)
- *Distributors.* Which companies have the best distributive network? Lowest costs? Fastest delivery? Competent distributors that really know the product or service? (For example, major glass companies such as St Gobain (France) and Pilkington (UK).)

Fig 7.3

Value added by a pharmaceutical company such as Glaxo plc

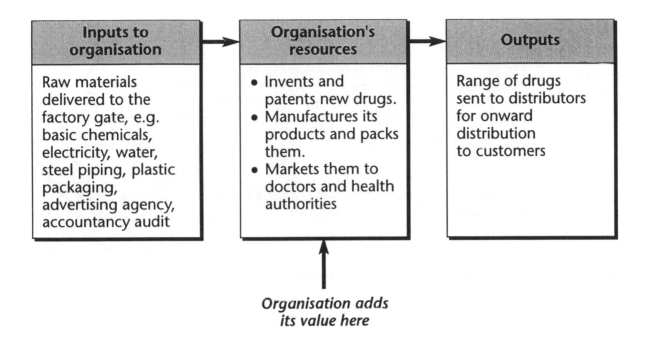

Inputs to organisation	Organisation's resources	Outputs
Raw materials delivered to the factory gate, e.g. basic chemicals, electricity, water, steel piping, plastic packaging, advertising agency, accountancy audit	• Invents and patents new drugs. • Manufactures its products and packs them. • Markets them to doctors and health authorities	Range of drugs sent to distributors for onward distribution to customers

Organisation adds its value here

Fig 7.4

The value chain

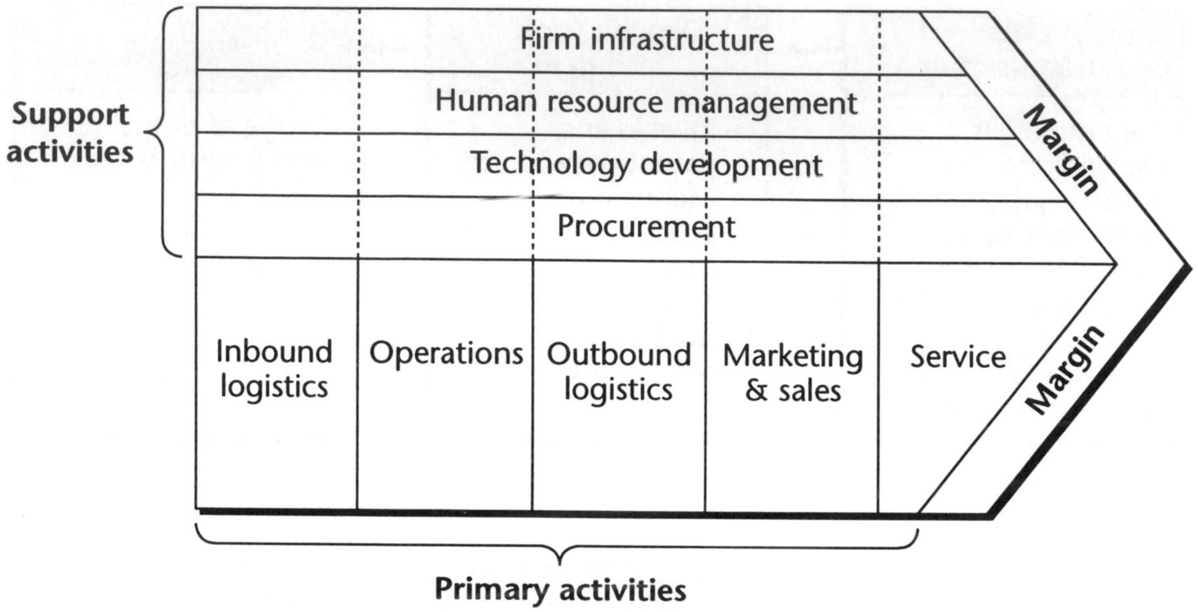

Support activities	Firm infrastructure				
	Human resource management				
	Technology development				
	Procurement				
	Inbound logistics	Operations	Outbound logistics	Marketing & sales	Service

Margin

Margin

Primary activities

Source: Reproduced with the permission of The Free Press, a Division of Simon & Schuster Inc, from *Competitive Advantage: Creating and Sustaining Superior Performance* by Michael E Porter. Copyright © 1985 by Michael E Porter.

Fig 7.5

The value system

(a) Single-industry firm

(b) Diversified firm (with several different business units, each with its own value chain)

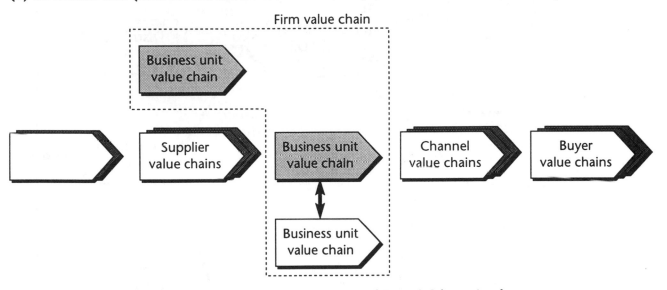

Source: Reproduced with the permission of The Free Press, a Division of Simon & Schuster Inc, from
Competitive Advantage: Creating and Sustaining Superior Performance by Michael E Porter.
Copyright © 1985 by Michael E Porter.

Fig 7.6

Linkages between the value chain and value system

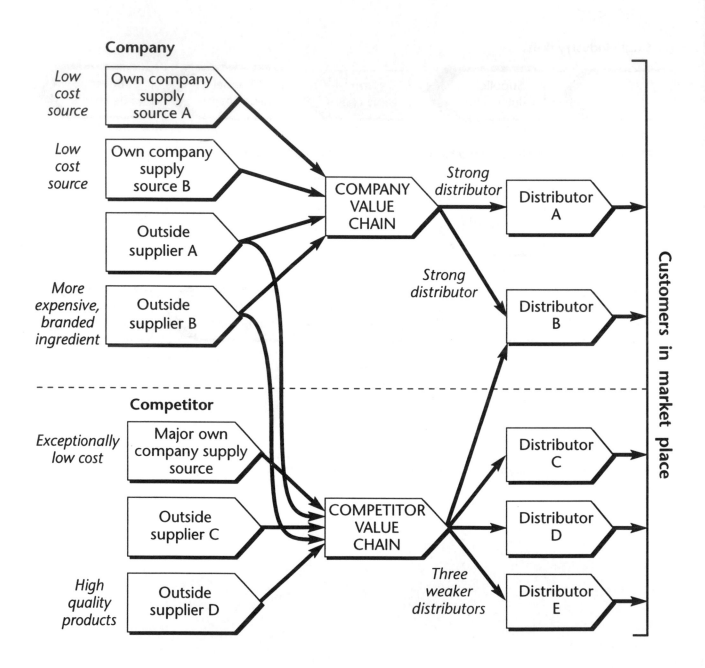

Fig 7.7

How the experience curve can deliver lower costs

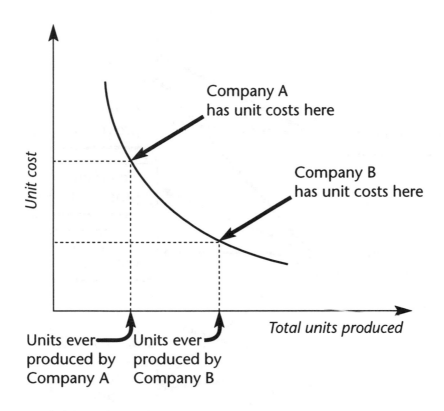

Fig 7.8

How core competences can link to the main business areas

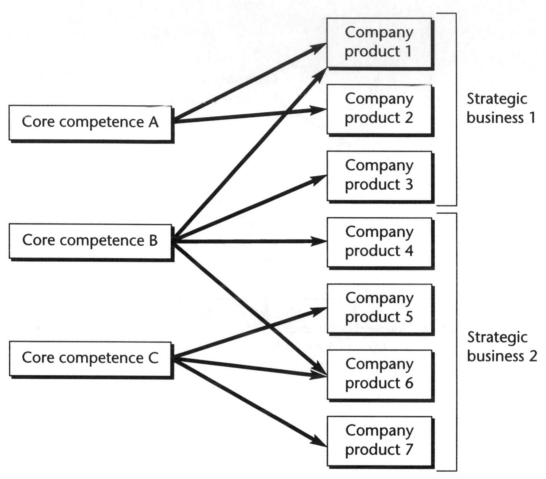

Table 7.2

Some possible factors in a SWOT analysis

Internal

Strengths	Weaknesses
● Market dominance	● Share weakness
Core strengths	● Few core strengths and low on key skills
Economies of scale	● Old plant with higher costs than competition
Low-cost position	● Weak finances and poor cash flow
Leadership and management skills	● Management skills and leadership lacking
● Financial and cash resource	● Poor record on innovation and new ideas
● Manufacturing ability and age of equipment	● Weak organisation with poor architecture
Innovation processes and results	● Low quality and reputation
● Architecture network	● Products not differentiated and dependent on few products
● Reputation	
Differentiated products	
Product or service quality	

External

Opportunities	Threats
New markets and segments	● New market entrants
New products	● Increased competition
Diversification opportunities	● Increased pressure from customers and suppliers
Market growth	● Substitutes
● Competitor weakness	● Low market growth
● Strategic space	● Economic cycle downturn
Demographic and social change	● Technological threat
Change in political or economic environment	● Change in political or economic environment
New takeover or partnership opportunities	● Demographic change
● Economic upturn	● New international barriers to trade
International growth	

Fig 8.1

The relationship between resources, culture, change and power

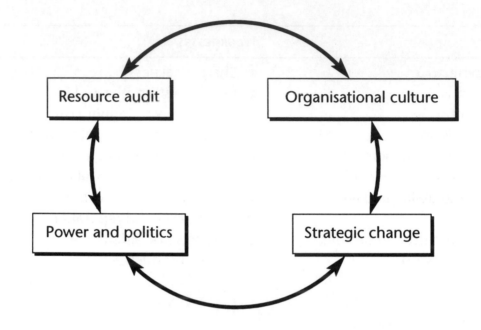

Exhibit 8.1

Human resource audit

People in the organisation

- Employee numbers and turnover

- Organisation structure

- Structures for controlling the organisation

- Use of special teams, for example for innovation or cost-reduction

- Level of skills and capabilities required

- Morale and rewards

- Employee and industrial relations

- Selection, training and development

- Staffing levels

- Capital investment/employee

- Role of quality and personal service in delivering the products or services of the organisation

- Role of professional advice in delivering the product or service

Role and contribution of human resource strategy

- Relationship with corporate strategy

- Key characteristics of human resource strategy

- Consistency of human resource strategy across an organisation with several divisions

- The responsiveness of human resource strategy to changes in business strategy and the environment

- The role of human resource strategy in *leading* change in the organisation

- The monitoring and review of human resource strategy

- The time frame for the operation of human resource strategy

Fig 8.3

Analysing the main elements of organisational culture

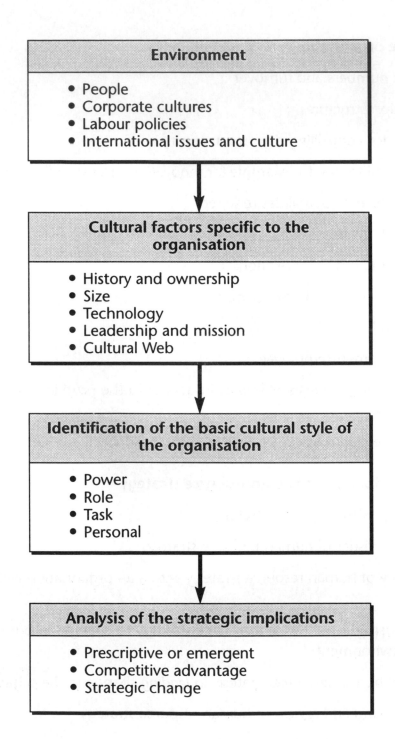

Fig 8.4

Developing the Cultural Web

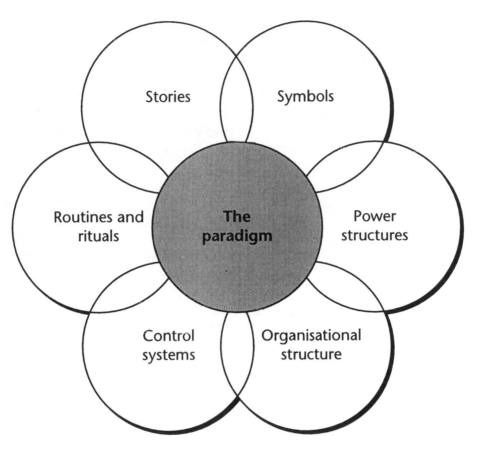

Source: Johnson, G (1992) 'Managing Strategic Change: Strategy, culture and action', *Long Range Planning, 25, pp 28–36.*

Table 8.1

Conclusions on the four types of culture

	Prescriptive or emergent strategy	Delivery of competitive advantage	Ability to cope with strategic change
Power culture	Presciptive	Enhanced but individuals may miss competitive moves	Depends on individual or group at centre
Role culture	Prescriptive	Solid, slow and substantive	Slow, will resist change
Task culture	Emergent	Good where flexibility is important	Accepted and welcomed
Personal culture	Possibly emergent	Depends on individual	Depends on individual

Corporate Strategy Overhead Transparency Masters Pitman Publishing © Aldersgate Consultancy Limited 1997

Fig 8.5

The analysis of strategic change in organisations

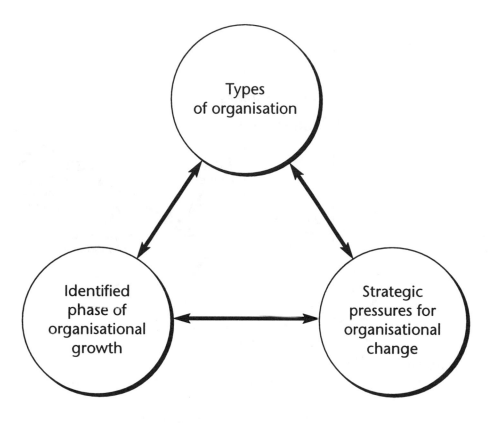

Fig 8.6

The five phases of growth

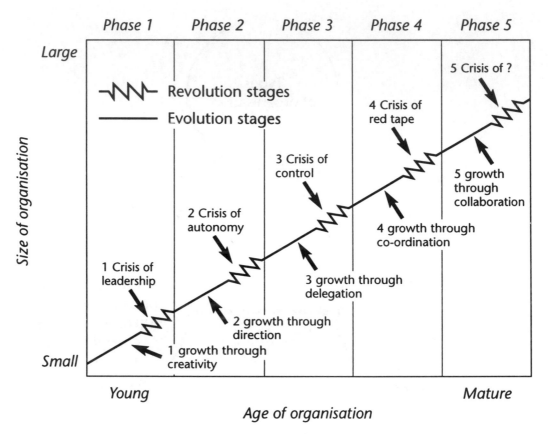

Source: Reprinted by permission of *Harvard Business Review*. 'Evolution and Revolution as Organisations Grow' by L Greiner, July – August 1972. Copyright © 1972 by the President and Fellows of Harvard College; all rights reserved.

Fig 8.7

The political network of an organisation

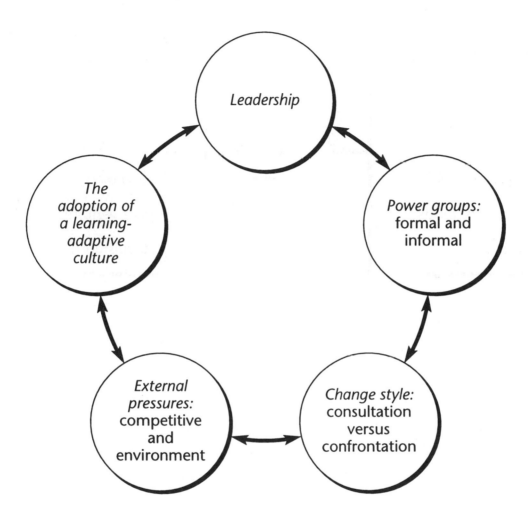

Fig 9.1

The relationship between financial resources and the resulting strategies

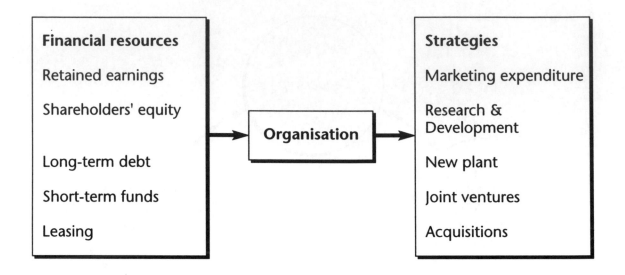

Financial resources

Retained earnings

Shareholders' equity

Long-term debt

Short-term funds

Leasing

Organisation

Strategies

Marketing expenditure

Research & Development

New plant

Joint ventures

Acquisitions

Fig 9.2

Sources of finance at Heineken (1994)

Strategic significance

Reserves and retained profits	40%	• Cheap and non-controversial • Typically the largest source of finance for many companies • Finances the majority of new strategic initiatives
Shareholders	13%	• Useful when major new strategic initiative • But changes ownership, so risky
Provisions for tax and pensions	15%	• Funds will be needed, so not really useful for strategy
Debt: long-term	7%	• Low at Heineken: could be higher
Debt: short-term	25%	• 'Short-term' means repayable inside one year, so only a temporary solution for major strategic initiatives

Table 9.3

Sources of capital in some of Europe's leading brewers

Source of funds	Heineken	Danone/ Kronenbourg*	Carlsberg
Reserves and retained earnings	40%	22%	33%
Shareholders	13%	24%	10%
Provisions for tax, pensions	15%	7%	16%
Debt: long-term	7%	23%	15%
Debt: short-term	25%	24%	26%
Total	100%	100%	100%
Total capital	US$ 5125 m	US$ 14863 m	US$ 2954 m

Source: Company annual reports
*Note that capital is used for non-beer trading, which is the majority of total turnover at Danone/Kronenbourg.

Table 9.5

Financial and strategic objectives

Financial objectives	Strategic objectives
Faster revenue growth	● Bigger market share
● Faster earning growth	● Higher, more secure industry rank
Higher dividends	● Higher product quality
Wider profit margins	● Lower costs relative to key competitors
Higher returns on invested capital	● Broader or more attractive product line
Stronger bond and credit ratings	● Stronger reputation with customers
Bigger cash flows	● Superior customer service
A rising stock price	● Recognition as a leader in technology and/or product innovation
● Recognition as a 'blue chip' company	● Increased ability to compete in international markets
A more diversified revenue base	● Expanded growth opportunities
● Stable earnings during recessionary periods	● Higher salaries and other employee benefits

Source: Thompson, A and Strickland, A, *Strategic Management*, 9th edition. © Richard D Irwin, a Times Mirror Higher Education Group, Inc. Company, Burr Ridge, IL, USA, p31. Adapted with permission of the publisher.

Fig 9.3

Using DCF to assess a typical new strategy

Example: US$3 million approved investment in new beer-brewing facility

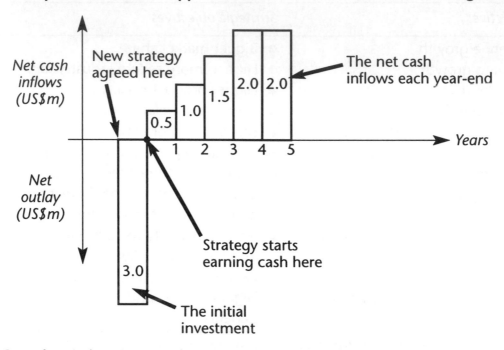

Cost of capital: Project needs to earn a minimum 10%
so use 10% discount factor and discount tables

DCF calculation

End of year	Discount factor	×	Cash inflow		Present value (US$m)
1	0.9091	×	0.5	=	0.455
2	0.8264	×	1.0	=	0.826
3	0.7153	×	1.5	=	1.073
4	0.6831	×	2.0	=	1.366
5	0.6208	×	2.0	=	1.242
	Present value of cash inflows				4.962
	Less: net outlay initially				3.000
	Net present value				US$1.962 million

Source: Adapted from Glautier, M W E and Underdown, B (1994) *Accounting Theory and Practice*, Pitman Publishing. © Guardjust Ltd and B Underdown 1994.

Fig 10.1

Analysing operations management

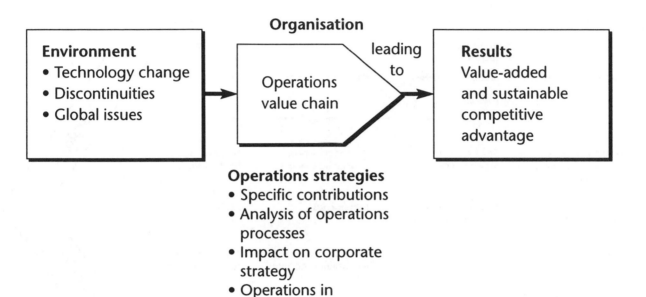

Fig 10.3

The operations value chain

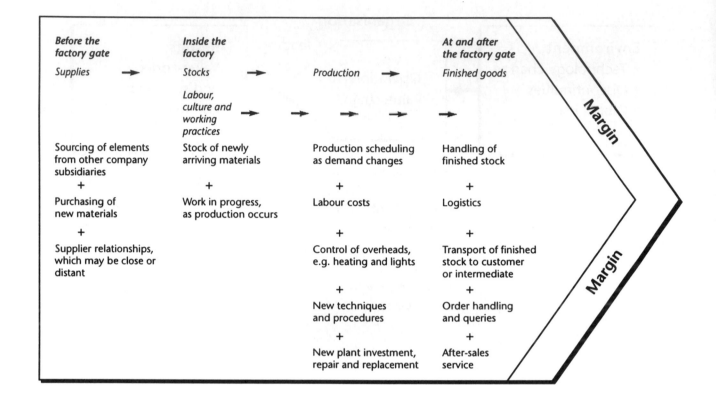

Before the factory gate	Inside the factory		At and after the factory gate
Supplies →	Stocks →	Production →	Finished goods
	Labour, culture and working practices → → → → →		
Sourcing of elements from other company subsidiaries	Stock of newly arriving materials	Production scheduling as demand changes	Handling of finished stock
+	+	+	+
Purchasing of new materials	Work in progress, as production occurs	Labour costs	Logistics
+		+	+
Supplier relationships, which may be close or distant		Control of overheads, e.g. heating and lights	Transport of finished stock to customer or intermediate
		+	+
		New techniques and procedures	Order handling and queries
		+	+
		New plant investment, repair and replacement	After-sales service

Margin

Margin

Table 10.2

Criteria for the relevance of manufacturing strategy to corporate strategy

Strategic area	Issues to be explored
Organisation objectives	Possible impact? Some strategies may be more important than others.
Added value	To what extent does the strategy add significant value?
'What if?' questions	Explore what would happen if certain conditions were changed and assess the impact on objectives – e.g. what would happen if we were able to reduce supply prices by 10%? Would this have a substantial impact or not make much difference?
Key factors for success	In Chapter 7, we explored this area. They may well guide the selection of the most appropriate manufacturing strategies.
Human resource implications	Operations strategy often involves change in working practices, responsibilities and reporting relationships. Some strategies may be difficult to operate unless these human factors are explored against the organisation's human resource objectives.

Table 10.4

The five main differences between services and products

Distinguishing features at the point of service	Description	Example	Impact on operations strategic analysis
Intangibility	Cannot be seen or tasted like a product	● Bank counter service ● Airline booking	More difficult to define but important for setting standards. Hence, difficult to analyse
Inseparability	● Cannot be separated from the person of the seller ● Consuming and selling may be undertaken at virtually the same time	● Telephone selling of car insurance ● McDonald's 'Big Mac'	● High reliance on the people delivering the service ● Need for careful selection and training
Heterogeneity	● Difficult to standardise service output ● Reliant on human element	● Hospital in-patient care ● Reception welcome at Holiday Inns Hotel	Decision on whether it is necessary, desirable or even possible to standardise service
Perishability	Services cannot be stored	● Empty hotel room ● Telephone call not made	● Concept of stock may be irrelevant ● Strategy needs to address issue of immediate utilisation of service
Ownership	Customer may not own what is being consumed	Cinema, night club, football stadium	No physical need for logistics and transport

Fig 10.4

The operations value chain in a service industry
(the areas that have changed from manufacturing are highlighted in bold type)

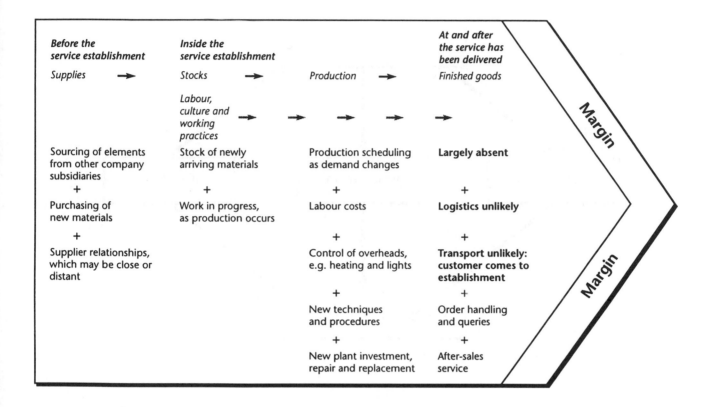

Before the service establishment	Inside the service establishment		At and after the service has been delivered
Supplies →	Stocks →	Production →	Finished goods
	Labour, culture and working practices → → → → →		
Sourcing of elements from other company subsidiaries	Stock of newly arriving materials	Production scheduling as demand changes	**Largely absent**
+	+	+	+
Purchasing of new materials	Work in progress, as production occurs	Labour costs	**Logistics unlikely**
+		+	+
Supplier relationships, which may be close or distant		Control of overheads, e.g. heating and lights	**Transport unlikely: customer comes to establishment**
		+	+
		New techniques and procedures	Order handling and queries
		+	+
		New plant investment, repair and replacement	After-sales service

Margin

Margin

Corporate Strategy Overhead Transparency Masters Pitman Publishing © Aldersgate Consultancy Limited 1997

Fig 11.1

The purpose of the organisation: developing the background issues

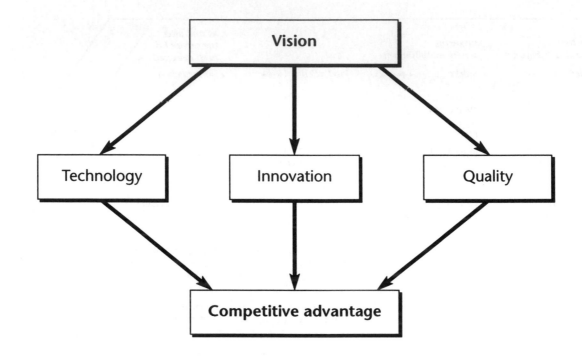

Table 11.1

Five criteria for judging the organisation's investigation of its vision

Criterion	Indicative area to be investigated
Foresight	What imagination and real vision is shown? Over what time frame?
Breadth	How broad is the vision of the changes likely to take place in the industry? And of the forces that will lead to the changes?
Uniqueness	Is there an element of uniqueness about the future? Will it cause our competitors to be surprised?
Consensus	Is there some consensus within the organisation about the future? If not, there may be a problem if too many different visions are pursued at once.
Actionability	Have the implications for current activity been considered? Is there basic agreement on the immediate steps required? Have the necessary core competences and future market opportunities been identified?

Source: Reprinted by permission of Harvard Business School Publishing from *Competing for the Future* by G Hamel and C K Prahalad. Boston, MA, 1994, p122. Copyright © 1994 Gary Hamel and C K Prahalad; all rights reserved.

Fig 11.2

Technology/product portfolio matrix

	Mature technologies	New technologies
New products	Possible growth opportunities in new areas	Embryonic, new stars
Mature products	Cash cows	New possible opportunities and, importantly, competitive threats

Exhibit 11.1

The controlled chaos approach to generating innovation

- *Atmosphere and vision* – with chief executives providing support, leadership and projecting clear, long-term ambitions for their company.

- *Small, flat organisation* – not bureaucratic, but flexible.

- *Small teams of innovators* – multi-disciplinary groups of idea makers.

- *Competitive selection process* – with innovatory ideas selected from a range in the company, and encouragement and support, not penalties, for the losing team.

- *Interactive learning* – random, even chaotic, consideration of ideas from many sources and from a range of industries.

Fig 11.5

The relationship between quality and profit

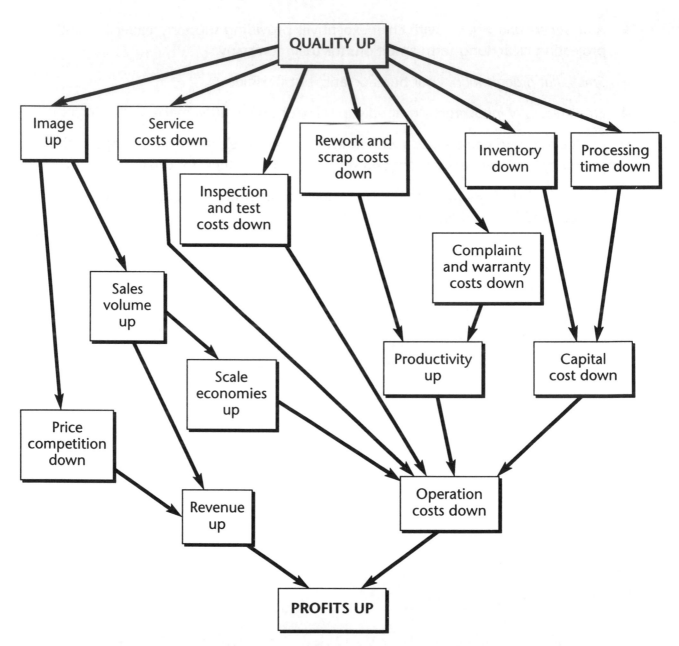

Source: Gummesson, Evert, 'Service Productivity: A Blasphemous Approach' . In *Proceedings from The 2nd International Research Seminar in Service Management*, Institut d'Administration des Entreprises (IAE), Université d'Aix-Marseille, France, June 1992. Reproduced with permission.

Fig 12.1

Developing the organisation's mission and objectives

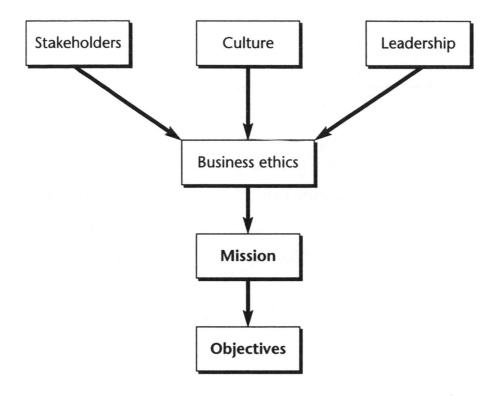

Table 12.1

Stakeholders and their expectations

Stakeholder	Expectations	
	Primary	Secondary
Owners	Financial return	Added value
Employees	Pay	Work satisfaction, training
Customers	Supply of goods and services	Quality
Creditors	Creditworthiness	Payment on time
Suppliers	Payment	Long-term relationships
Community	Safety and security	Contribution to community
Government	Compliance	Improved competitiveness

Source: Adapted with permission from Cannon, T (1994) *Corporate Responsibility*, Pitman Publishing.

Fig 12.3

Example of the best-fit approach to leadership analysis

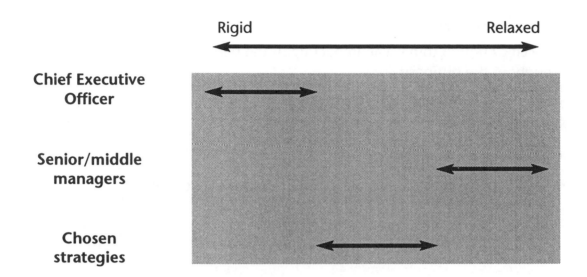

- **Chief Executive Officer** prefers a structured style, possibly even dominance.

- **Senior/middle managers** like to be given more personal initiative and responsibility.

- **Chosen strategies** are tightly defined in some areas, but allow some managerial initiative.

Conclusion: The three areas do not 'fit' – change is needed.

Exhibit 12.3

Some criteria for judging mission statements

A mission statement should:

- be specific enough to have an impact upon the behaviour of individuals throughout the business;

- reflect the distinctive advantages of the organisation and be based upon an objective recognition of its strengths and weaknesses;

- be realistic and attainable;

- be flexible enough to take account of shifts in the environment.

Fig 13.1

Developing resource-based strategic options

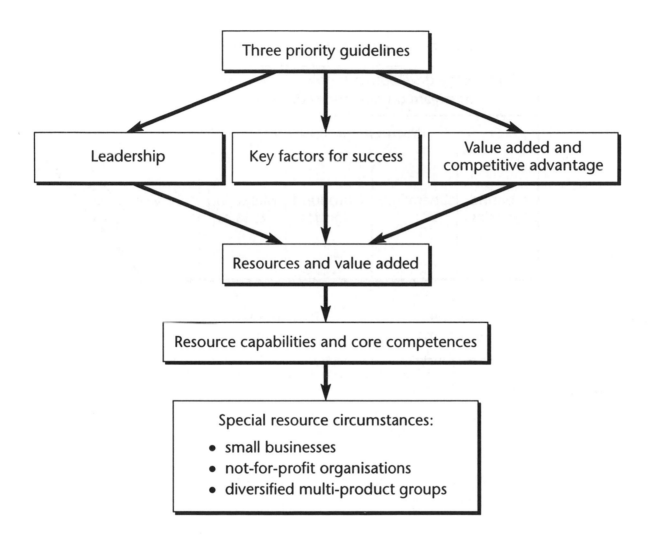

Fig 13.2

Value chain: upstream and downstream resources

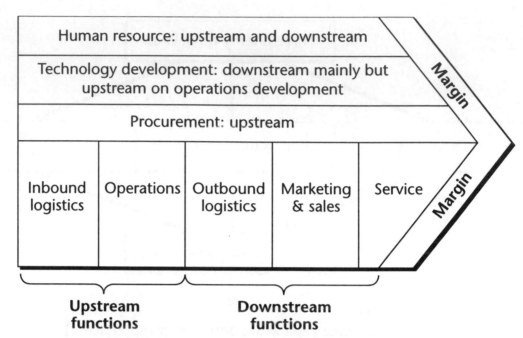

Human resource: upstream and downstream

Technology development: downstream mainly but upstream on operations development

Procurement: upstream

| Inbound logistics | Operations | Outbound logistics | Marketing & sales | Service |

Margin

Upstream functions   **Downstream functions**

Source: Reproduced with the permission of The Free Press, a Division of Simon & Schuster Inc, from *Competitive Advantage: Creating and Sustaining Superior Performance* by Michael E Porter. Copyright © 1985 by Michael E Porter.

Table 13.1

The location of the main source of value added in different single-product industries

Main resources	Examples of industries	Location: Primarily upstream or downstream?
Raw material extraction	Coal, oil, iron ore	Upstream
Primary manufacture to produce standardised output	Paper and pulp, iron and steel, basic chemicals	Upstream
Fabrication of primary manufacture	Paper cartons, steel piping, simple plastics	Upstream
Further added value through more complex manufacture, patents and special processes	Branded packaging, cars, specialist plastic products	Downstream
Marketing and advertising	Branded products	Downstream

Exhibit 13.1

Possible resource options associated with upstream and downstream activities

Upstream resource strategies might include:

- Increased standardisation of products

- Investment to lower the costs of production

- Operations innovation to lower the costs of production or improve the quality

- Capital investments that add value

- Developing a customer base from a wide range of industries that require a common product without variation.

Downstream resource strategies might include:

- Varied products targeted at particular market segments

- R&D and product innovation to add more value

- Advertising investment and branding

- New increased services to add value.

Fig 13.3

Resource-based strategy options

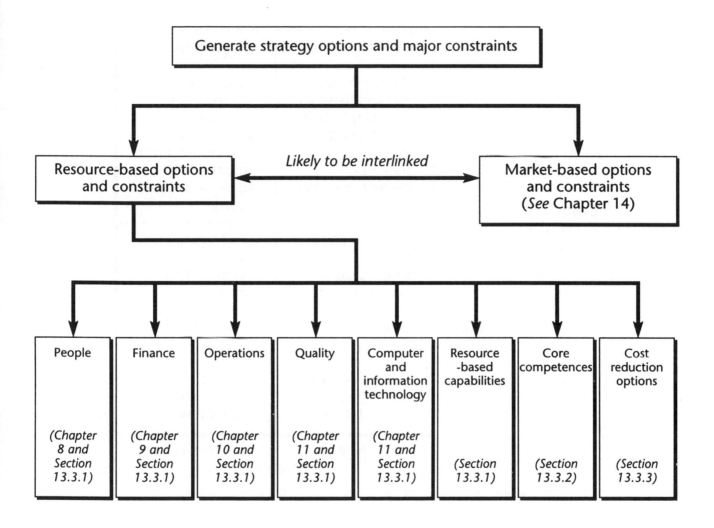

Fig 13.4

Strategic opportunities suggested by core competences

	Existing MARKET	**New**
New CORE COMPETENCE	*Premier plus 10* What new core competences will we need to build to protect and extend our franchise in current markets?	*Mega-opportunities* What new core competences would we need to build to participate in the most exciting markets of the future?
Existing	*Fill in the blanks* What is the opportunity to improve our position in existing markets by better leveraging our existing core competences?	*White spaces* What new products or services could we create by creatively redeploying or recombining our current core competences?

Source: Reprinted by permission of Harvard Business School Publishing from *Competing for the Future* by G Hamel and C K Prahalad. Boston, MA, 1994, p227. Copyright © 1994 Gary Hamel and C K Prahalad; all rights reserved.

Fig 13.5

Cost reduction stratergy options

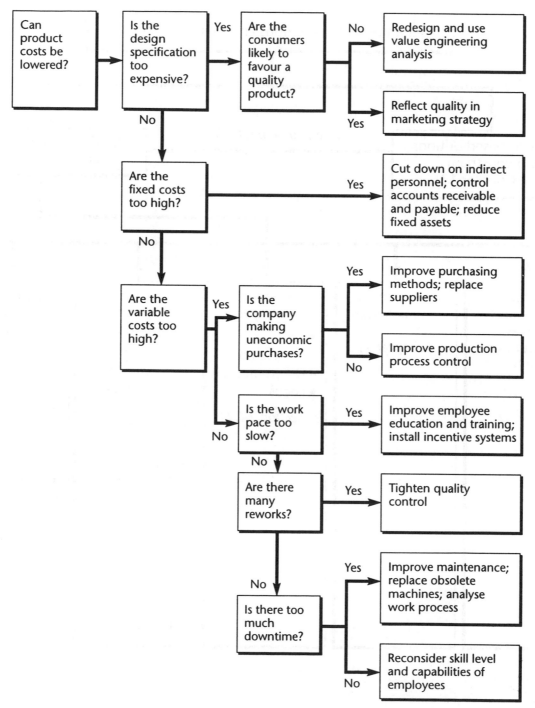

Source: Ohmae, K (1983) *The Mind of the Strategist*, Pan, pp24 and 25. Copyright © 1983 McGraw-Hill, Inc.

Fig 14.1

Market-based strategy options

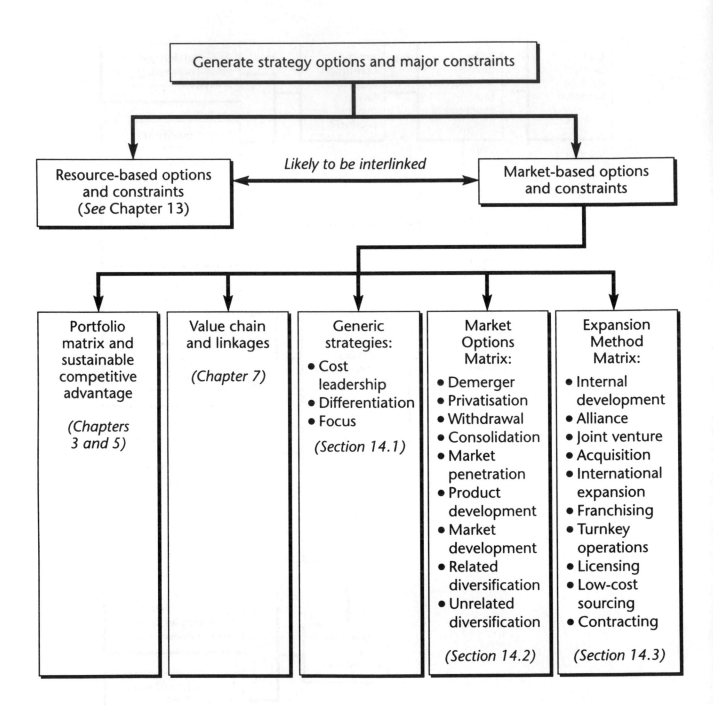

Generate strategy options and major constraints

Resource-based options and constraints
(*See* Chapter 13)

Likely to be interlinked

Market-based options and constraints

Portfolio matrix and sustainable competitive advantage

(Chapters 3 and 5)

Value chain and linkages

(Chapter 7)

Generic strategies:
- Cost leadership
- Differentiation
- Focus

(Section 14.1)

Market Options Matrix:
- Demerger
- Privatisation
- Withdrawal
- Consolidation
- Market penetration
- Product development
- Market development
- Related diversification
- Unrelated diversification

(Section 14.2)

Expansion Method Matrix:
- Internal development
- Alliance
- Joint venture
- Acquisition
- International expansion
- Franchising
- Turnkey operations
- Licensing
- Low-cost sourcing
- Contracting

(Section 14.3)

Fig 14.2

Generic strategy options

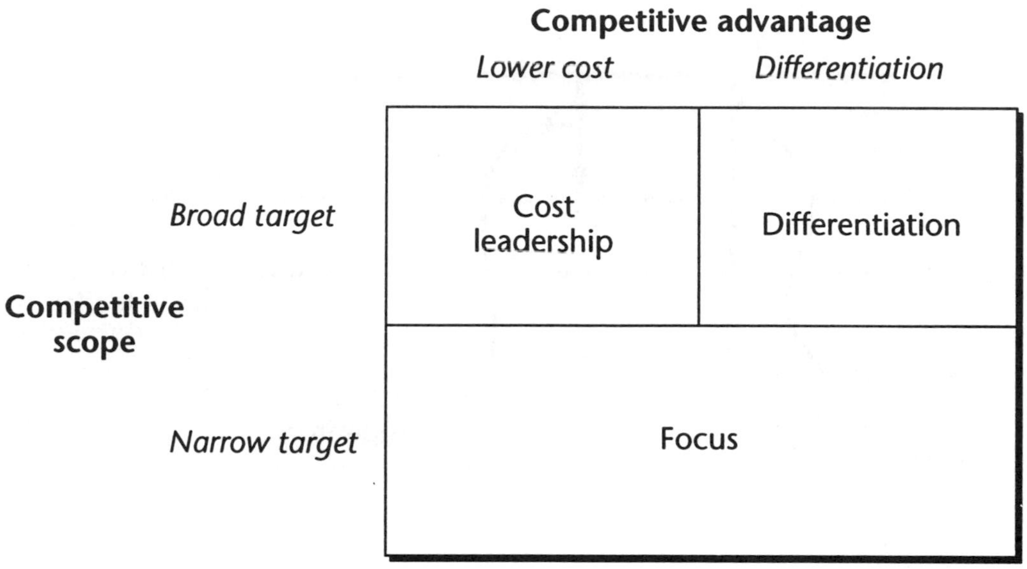

Competitive advantage

Lower cost   *Differentiation*

	Lower cost	**Differentiation**
Broad target	Cost leadership	Differentiation
Narrow target	Focus	

Competitive scope

Source: Reproduced with the permission of The Free Press, a Division of Simon & Schuster Inc, from *Competitive Advantage: Creating and Sustaining Superior Performance* by Michael E Porter. Copyright © 1985 Micheal E Porter.

Fig 14.3

How low-cost leadership delivers above-average profits

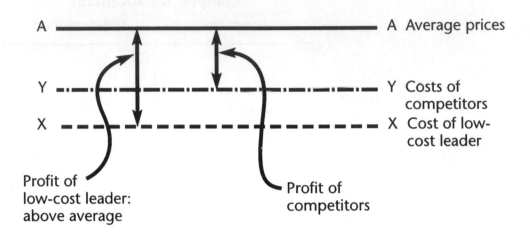

Profit per unit = Price – Costs per unit

A ————————————————— A Average prices

Y —·—·—·—·—·—·—·—·—·— Y Costs of competitors

X – – – – – – – – – – X Cost of low-cost leader

Profit of low-cost leader: above average

Profit of competitors

Fig 14.4

How differentiation delivers above-average profits

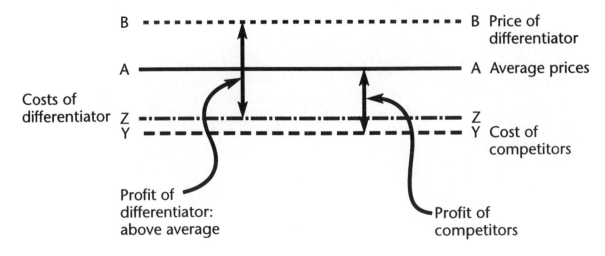

Profit per unit = Price – Costs per unit

B ·············· B Price of differentiator

A ————————————————— A Average prices

Costs of differentiator Z ═══════════════ Z

Y – – – – – – – – – – Y Cost of competitors

Profit of differentiator: above average

Profit of competitors

Fig 14.5

Generic strategies in the European ice cream industry

Competitive scope		Competitive advantage: *Lower cost*	Competitive advantage: *Differentiation*
	Broad target	**Cost leadership** Unilever	**Differentiation** • Mars ice cream • Nestlé?
	Narrow target	**Cost focus** Economy ice cream made by small, local ice cream companies with low overheads	**Differentiation focus** Super-premium, e.g. Häagen-Dazs

Fig 14.8

Market Option Matrix

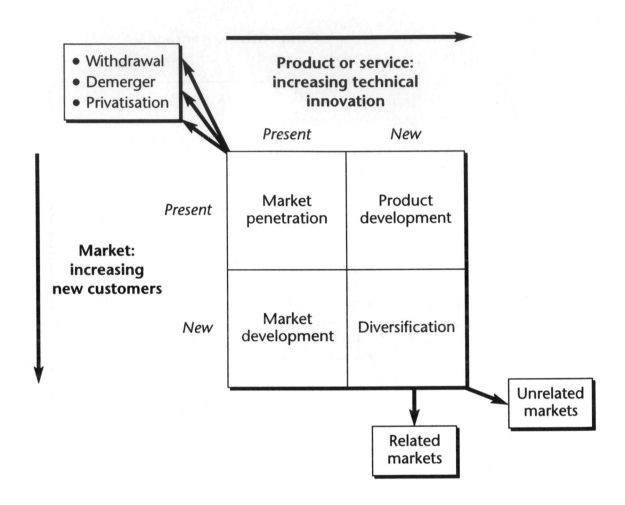

Fig 14.9

Expansion Method Matrix

Company

	Inside	*Outside*
Home country	• Internal development	• Merger • Acquisition • Joint venture • Alliance • Franchise
International	• Exporting • Overseas office • Overseas manufacture • Multinational operation • Global operation	• Merger • Acquisition • Joint venture • Alliance • Franchise • Turnkey • Licensing

Geographical location

Note: All the above methods must add value to the organisation if they are to justify their costs.

Fig 15.1

Selecting from the options: strategy evaluation and selection

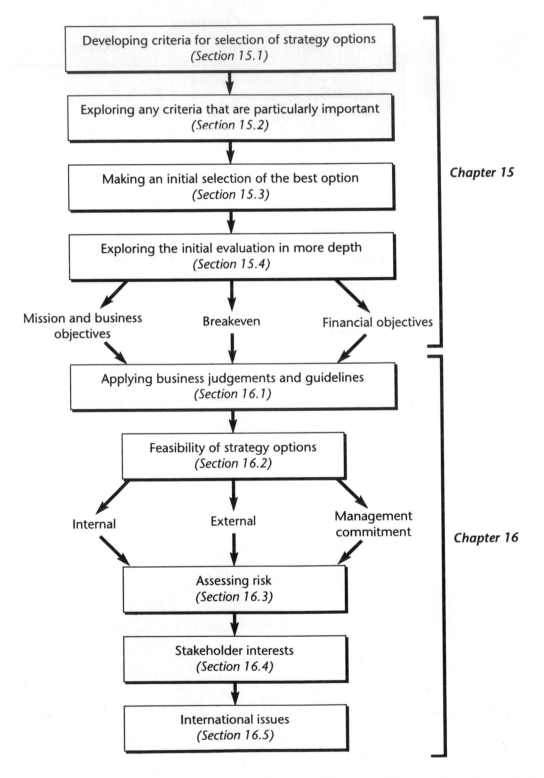

Developing criteria for selection of strategy options
(Section 15.1)

Exploring any criteria that are particularly important
(Section 15.2)

Making an initial selection of the best option
(Section 15.3)

Exploring the initial evaluation in more depth
(Section 15.4)

Mission and business objectives

Breakeven

Financial objectives

Chapter 15

Applying business judgements and guidelines
(Section 16.1)

Feasibility of strategy options
(Section 16.2)

Internal

External

Management commitment

Chapter 16

Assessing risk
(Section 16.3)

Stakeholder interests
(Section 16.4)

International issues
(Section 16.5)

Corporate Strategy Overhead Transparency Masters Pitman Publishing © Aldersgate Consultancy Limited 1997

Fig 15.2

Selection criteria and proposed strategies

Strategies need to be consistent with the mission and objectives

Consistent	**Inconsistent**
Mission and objectives	Mission and objectives
↑	⋮
Strategy	Strategy

Strategies need to be suitable for the organisation and its environment

Suitable
Environment   Organisation
Strategy

Unsuitable
Environment   Organisation
Strategy

Strategy assumptions must be valid and tested where possible

Valid	**Invalid**
Strategy assumptions	Strategy assumptions
✔ Tested	✘ No test possible

Strategies must be feasible if they are to be successful

Feasible
Internal resources ←→ Strategy ←→ Management commitment
↕
External

Infeasible
Internal resources ⋯ Strategy ⋯ Management commitment
⋮
External

Strategies must involve an acceptable level of business risk

Business risk
Acceptable risk
↕
Strategy

Business risk
Unacceptable risk
↕
~~Strategy~~

Strategies need to be attractive to the organisation's stakeholders

Attractive to stakeholders
Shareholders ←→ Strategy ←→ Employees
↕
Management

Unattractive to stakeholders
Strategy
Shareholders ⋯ ⋯ Employees
⋮
Management

Corporate Strategy Overhead Transparency Masters Pitman Publishing © Aldersgate Consultancy Limited 1997

Fig 15.3

Are some criteria more important than others?

Criteria in commercial organisations

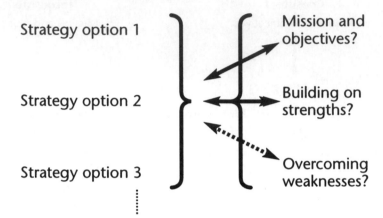

Strategy option 1

Strategy option 2

Strategy option 3

Mission and objectives?

Building on strengths?

Overcoming weaknesses?

Criteria in not-for-profit organisations

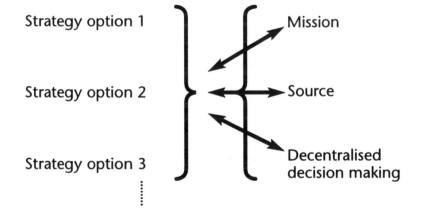

Strategy option 1

Strategy option 2

Strategy option 3

Mission

Source

Decentralised decision making

Table 15.1

Comparison of possible criteria in commercial and not-for-profit organisations

Commercial organisation	Not-for-profit organisation
● Quantified	● Qualitative
● Unchanging	● Variable
● Consistent	● Conflicting
● Unified	● Complex
● Operational	● Ambiguous
● Clear	● Non-operational
● Measurable	● Non-measurable

Table 15.2

Differences in perspective on mission and objectives

Level in organisation	Perspectives on mission and objectives	
	Strengths	Weaknesses
Corporate headquarters	• Clearly perceives overall group picture • Strong on core competences and synergies across group • Able to allocate resources across the whole group • Financial perspectives in terms of gearing and cash management • Group and global direction strong	• Makes limited distinction between the different business activities across the group • More difficult to identify market opportunities, niche segments, etc. • Differences in culture and national or regional variations ignored
Strategic Business Units	• More focussed strategy • Clearer on customers and competitors • Able to identify specific market opportunities • Can apply human resource management policies specific to that SBU or industry	• Synergy and core competences weaker • Corporate overview and links more difficult • Cash and currency management • Shareholder interests
Individual project, e.g. acquisition	• Easiest to evaluate at outset and judge success later • Focus on special opportunity • Clear, specific appraisal	• Links across corporate structure weaker • Synergy, core competences need to be defined and strengthened

Exhibit 15.1

Ten steps towards an initial strategy evaluation

1 Screen out any *early no-hopers* that are highly unlikely to meet the objectives.

2 Estimate the *sales* of each of the remaining options based on market share, pricing, promotional support and competitive reactions.

3 Estimate the *costs* of each of the remaining options.

4 Estimate the *capital and other funds* necessary to undertake each option.

5 Calculate the *return on capital employed* for each option.

6 Calculate the *breakeven* of each option.

7 Calculate the *net cash flow* effects of each option.

8 Evaluate whether the *projected sales levels* imply exceptional levels of market share or *unusually low costs*. Are these reasonable? Real strategic weaknesses can emerge here.

9 Assess the likely *competitive response* and its possible impact on each strategy option.

10 Assess the *risks* associated with each option (*see* Chapter 16).

Fig 16.1

Aspects of the strategy selection process

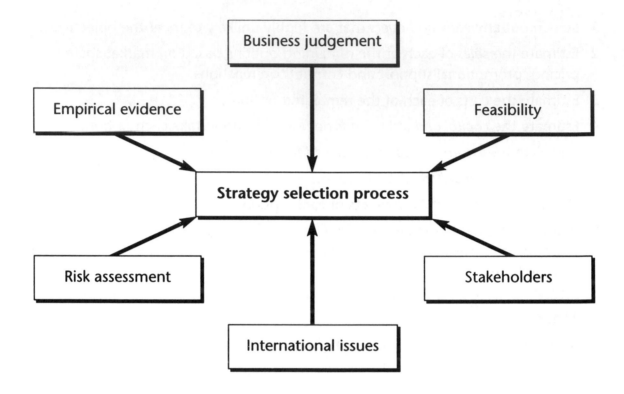

Fig 16.2

Possible strategic choice in fragmented industries

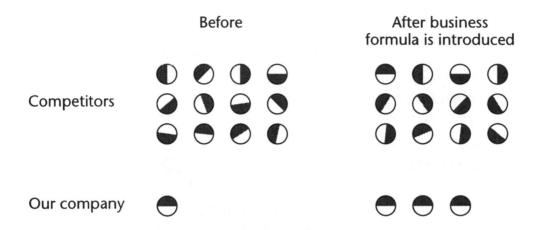

	Before	After business formula is introduced
Competitors		
Our company		

Fig 16.3

Possible strategic choice in emerging industries

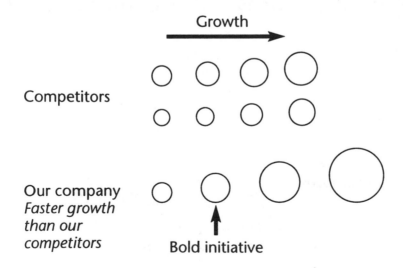

Growth

Competitors

Our company
*Faster growth
than our
competitors*

Bold initiative

Corporate Strategy Overhead Transparency Masters Pitman Publishing © Aldersgate Consultancy Limited 1997

Fig 16.4

Possible strategic choice in a mature market for a company that is not the market leader

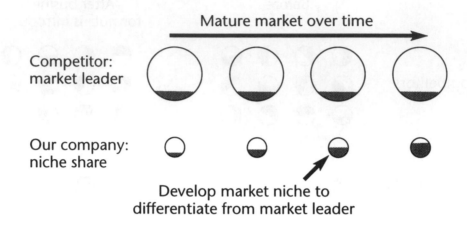

Mature market over time

Competitor: market leader

Our company: niche share

Develop market niche to differentiate from market leader

Fig 16.5

Possible strategic choice in a declining market for a company that is not the market leader

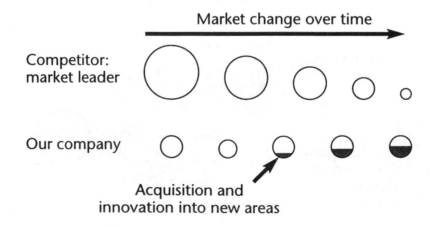

Market change over time

Competitor: market leader

Our company

Acquisition and innovation into new areas

Table 16.1

Evaluation using The Lifecycle Portfolio Matrix

Maturity / Competitive position	Embryonic	Growing	Mature	Ageing
Clear leader	**Hold position** Attempt to improve market penetration *Invest slightly faster than market dictates*	**Hold position** Defend market share *Invest to sustain growth rate (and pre-empt potential competitors)*	**Hold position** Grow with industry *Reinvest as necessary*	**Hold position** *Reinvest as necessary*
Strong	**Attempt to improve market penetration** *Invest as fast as market dictates*	**Attempt to improve market penetration** *Invest to increase growth rate (and improve position)*	**Hold position** Grow with industry *Reinvest as necessary*	**Hold position** *Reinvest as necessary or reinvest minimum*
Favourable	**Attempt to improve position selectively** Penetrate market generally or selectively *Invest selectively*	**Attempt to improve position** Penetrate market selectively *Selectively invest to improve position*	**Maintain position** Find niche and attempt to protect it *Make minimum and/or selective reinvestment*	**Harvest, withdraw in phases, or abandon** *Reinvest minimum necessary or disinvest*
Defensible	**Attempt to improve position selectively** *Invest (very) selectively*	**Find niche and protect it** *Invest selectively*	**Find niche or withdraw in phases** *Reinvest minimum necessary or disinvest*	**Withdraw in phases or abandon** *Disinvest or divest*
Weak	**Improve position or withdraw** *Invest or divest*	**Turn around or abandon** *Invest or disinvest*	**Turn around or withdraw in phases** *Invest selectively or disinvest*	**Abandon position** *Divest*

Source: Reproduced with permission from Arthur D Little. Copyright © Arthur D Little, Inc 1996.

Table 16.2

Contributions to the variance of profitability across business units

Source within corporation	Contribution to the total profitability of the corporation
Corporate ownership	0.8%
Industry effects	8.3%
Cyclical effects	7.8%
Business unit specific effects	46.4%
Unexplained factors	36.7%
Total across corporation	100%

Source: Rumelt, R (1991) 'How much does industry matter?' *Strategic Management Journal*, March, pp 64–75, John Wiley, New York. Reproduced with permission of John Wiley & Sons Ltd.

Table 16.3

PIMS data showing that both quality and market share drive profitability

Relative quality	Relative market share		
	Low to 25%	Medium	High above 60%
Inferior	7	14	21
Roughly equal	13	20	27
Superior	20	29	38

Numbers inside matrix are the return on investment expressed as a percentage.

Source: PIMS Associates Ltd, 1996.

Table 16.4

The PIMS relationship between marketing activity and market share

Relative market share	Market/Sales ratio			
	Low	5%	10%	High
Low 25%	18	15	9	
60%	20	20	21	
High	33	32	33	

Numbers inside matrix are the return on investment expressed as a percentage.

Table 16.5

Evidence showing that heavy investment as a percentage of sales drags down profitability and high productivity only offsets part of this effect

Productivity*	Investment/Sales ratio		
	Low to 40%	Medium	High above 60%
Low to US$60	23	14	4
Medium	35	22	11
High above US$90	41	28	15

*Productivity is defined as value added per employee in US$ thousands, 1995.
Numbers inside matrix are the return on investment expressed as a percentage.

Source: PIMS Associates Ltd, 1996.

Table 16.6

The performance of mergers

Method of evaluation	Major studies	Conclusions
1 Subjective opinions of company personnel	Hunt *et al* (1987)	Around half were successful
2 Whether acquired business is retained in the long term	Ravenscraft and Scherer (1987)	More divested than retained
3 Comparison of overall profitability before and after the merger	Meeks (1977), Mueller *et al* (1980), Ravenscraft and Cosh *et al* (1990), Scherer (1987)	Nil to negative effect
4 Effect on stock market valuation	Franks and Harris (1986), Franks, Harris and Mayer (1988)	Positive initial impact

Source: Kay, J (1993) *The Foundations of Corporate Success*, Oxford University Press, Chapter 10. Reproduced with permission.

Table 16.7

The balance between global expansion and national responsiveness

Pressure for global strategy	These are not mutually exclusive ⟵ ⟶	Pressure for international strategy but also responsiveness to national variations
● Global or multinational customers		● Differing customers or customer segments by nation or region
● Global or multinational competitors		● Differing competitors or distributors by nation or region
● High levels of investment or technology that need large sales for recovery, e.g. in production, branding or R&D		● Need to adapt product extensively to meet national needs
● Need to cut costs by seeking low labour sources		● Pressure from governments for national activity, e.g. tariff or quota restrictions on global activity
● Global sourcing of raw materials or energy		● National purchasing of key supplies essential

Exhibit 16.1

Ten-point checklist on internal feasibility

1   *Capital investment required.* Do we have the funds?

2   *Projection of cumulative profits.* Is it sufficiently profitable?

3   *Working capital requirements.* Do we have enough working capital?

4   *Tax liabilities and dividend payments.* What are the implications, especially on timing?

5   *Numbers of employees and, in the case of redundancy, any costs associated with this.* What are the national laws on sacking people and what are the costs?

6   *New technical skills, new plant and costs of closure of old plant.* Do we have the skills? Do we need to recruit or hire temporarily some specialists?

7   *New products and how they are to be developed.* Are we confident that we have the portfolio of new products fully tested on which so much depends? Are they real breakthrough products or merely a catch-up on our competition?

8   *Amount and timing of marketing investment and expertise required.* Do we have the funds? When will they be required? Do we have the specialist expertise such as advertising and promotions agency teams to deliver our strategies?

9   *The possibility of acquisition, merger or joint venture with other companies and the implications.* Have we fully explored other options that would bring their own benefits and problems?

10 *The communication of the strategy.* How are these areas to be communicated to all those involved? Will we gain the commitment of the managers and employees affected?

Exhibit 16.2

Four-point checklist on external feasibility

1 How will our *customers* respond to the strategies we are proposing?

2 How will our *competitors* react? Do we have the necessary resources to respond?

3 Do we have the necessary support from our *suppliers*?

4 Do we need *government* or *regulatory* approval? How likely is this?

Exhibit 16.3

Two examples of the connection between international objectives and strategy selection

1 *Objective*   International expansion because the home market is mature

     Key factors for success   Include economies of scale

     Implication   Retain home-base production to obtain increased economies of scale

     Strategy choice   Select low-cost strategy based on production economies of scale from home-base factory and then export production

     Example   BMW car production is still based largely in Germany, but sales are international

2 *Objective*   International expansion because trade barriers are high

     Key factors for success   Need to obtain distribution inside the barrier, as well as economies of scale in production

     Implication   Need to set up manufacturing operation inside trade barrier

     Strategy choice   Select country that represents a useful entry point behind the trade barriers, but also allows good communications with the home country

     Example   Nissan and Toyota cars have set up operations in the UK and Spain behind the trade barriers represented by the European Union

Fig 17.1

Finding the strategic route forward

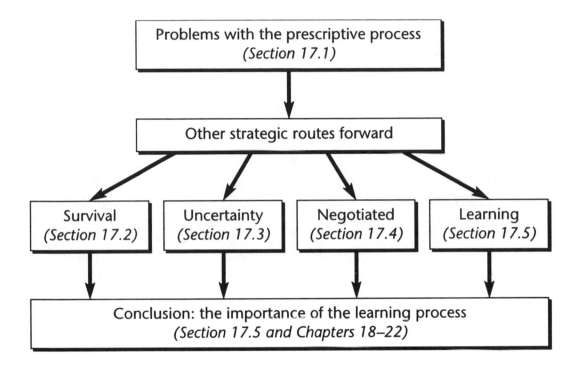

Table 17.1

The prescriptive model of the corporate strategy process

Who typically undertakes what in the prescriptive model?	Typical outline of the prescriptive model of the corporate strategy process	Discussion in this book
Chief Executive Officer	Mission and objectives	Chapters 11 and 12
Corporate planning team plus probably the SBU in its own product or service area	Environmental analysis	Chapters 3, 4, 5 and 6
SBU plus possibly the corporate planning team	Resources analysis	Chapters 7, 8, 9 and 10
SBU	Strategy options generation	Chapters 11, 13 and 14
Group in co-operation with the SBU	Strategy selection	Chapters 15 and 16
SBU	Implementation	Included within Part 6

Exhibit 17.1

Examples of inertia against change in company environments

Internal inertia

- Existing investment in plant and machinery.
- Previous experience and history of the company.

For example, in European telephone companies the existing bureaucracy which had been built up during many years in government ownership was very difficult to shift.

External inertia

- Barriers to entry and exit from an industry.
- Difficulty and cost of acquiring information on how the environment itself might be changing.

For example, European telephone companies' existing investment in exchanges and telephone equipment, coupled with external government restrictions that would prevent new companies entering until 1998, had created an inertia to change within the industry.

Table 17.3

The survival-based strategy process compared with the prescriptive process

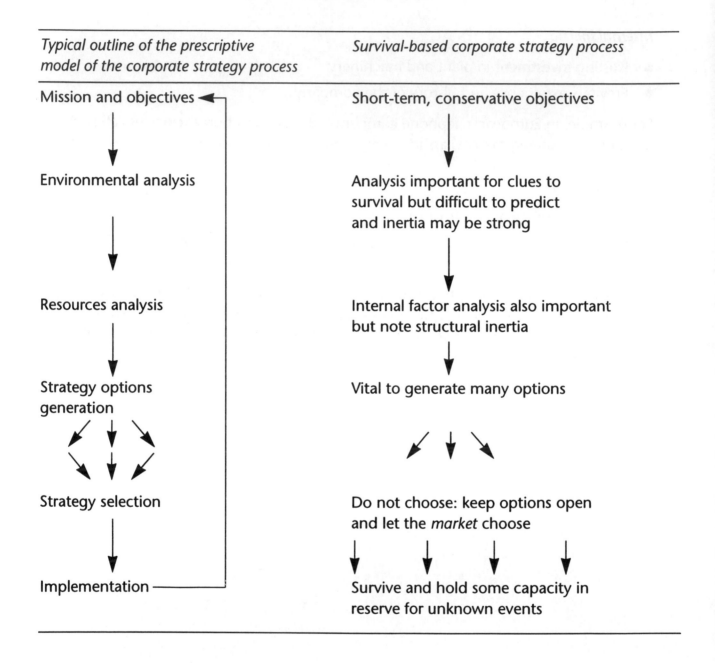

Typical outline of the prescriptive model of the corporate strategy process	Survival-based corporate strategy process
Mission and objectives	Short-term, conservative objectives
Environmental analysis	Analysis important for clues to survival but difficult to predict and inertia may be strong
Resources analysis	Internal factor analysis also important but note structural inertia
Strategy options generation	Vital to generate many options
Strategy selection	Do not choose: keep options open and let the *market* choose
Implementation	Survive and hold some capacity in reserve for unknown events

Table 17.4

Comparison of the uncertainty-based route with the prescriptive process

Typical outline of the prescriptive model of the corporate strategy process	Uncertainty-based strategy process	Flow process
Mission and objectives	Short-term only: possibly some strategic intent with innovation as a stated aim	?
Environmental analysis	Unpredictable: waste of time	
Resources analysis	Important to be aware of internal factors but the analysis will not have the predictive thrust of the prescriptive approach	No clear flow process ?
Strategy options generation	Options generation is irrelevant since the outcomes are unknown and unpredictable	Chaotic only with constant monitoring of the environment
Strategy selection	Strategy selection is also irrelevant but spontaneous. Small groups and learning mechanisms might be involved in short-term selection	?
Implementation	Informal, destabilising networks are useful. It may also be worth holding some resources in reserve because of the unknown	Flexible response from informal groups depending on the opportunities that emerge

Table 17.5

Comparison of the negotiation-based process with the prescriptive process

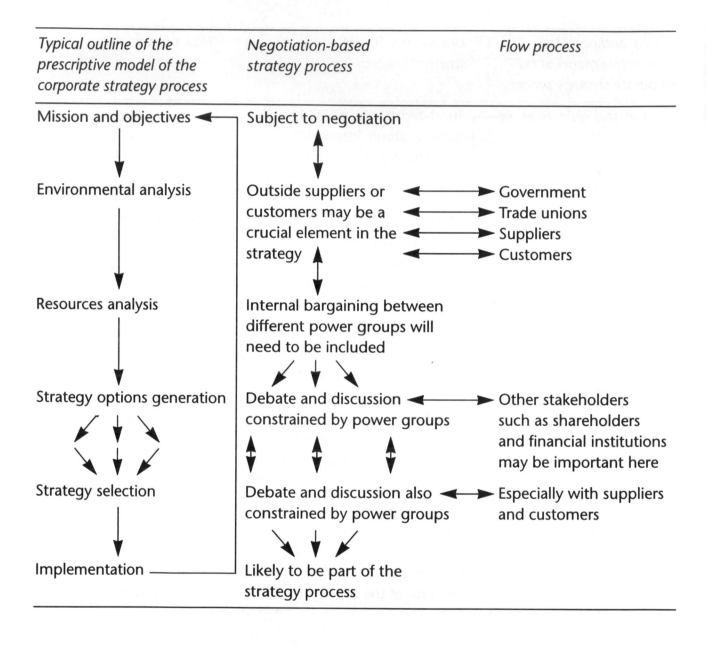

Typical outline of the prescriptive model of the corporate strategy process	Negotiation-based strategy process	Flow process
Mission and objectives	Subject to negotiation	
Environmental analysis	Outside suppliers or customers may be a crucial element in the strategy	Government Trade unions Suppliers Customers
Resources analysis	Internal bargaining between different power groups will need to be included	
Strategy options generation	Debate and discussion constrained by power groups	Other stakeholders such as shareholders and financial institutions may be important here
Strategy selection	Debate and discussion also constrained by power groups	Especially with suppliers and customers
Implementation	Likely to be part of the strategy process	

Exhibit 17.3

The five learning disciplines

- *Personal mastery* – not only developing personal goals but also creating the organisational environment that encourages groups to develop goals and purposes.

- *Mental models* – reflecting and speculating upon the pictures that managers and workers have of the world and seeing how these influence actions and decisions.

- *Shared vision* – building commitment in the group to achieve its aims by exploring and agreeing what these aims are.

- *Team learning* – using the group's normal skills to develop intelligence and ability beyond individuals' normal abilities.

- *Systems thinking* – a method of thinking about, describing and understanding the major forces that influence the group.

Source: Based on the writings of Peter Senge

Fig 18.1

Analysing the relationships between strategy, structure and style

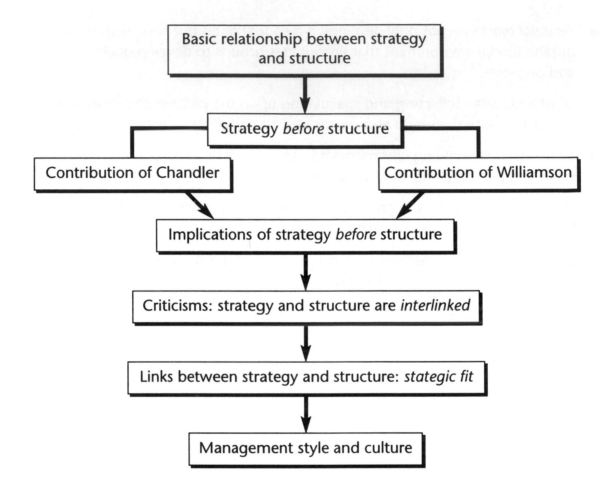

Basic relationship between strategy and structure

Strategy *before* structure

Contribution of Chandler

Contribution of Williamson

Implications of strategy *before* structure

Criticisms: strategy and structure are *interlinked*

Links between strategy and structure: *stategic fit*

Management style and culture

Fig 18.3

Two perspectives on strategy and structure

(a) The prescriptive approach

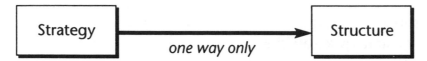

(b) The emergent approach

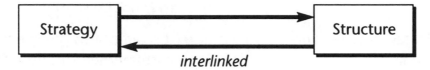

Exhibit 18.1

The balancing considerations between centralisation and decentralisation

Advantages of centralisation	Elements favouring decentralisation
● It is possible to produce a consistent strategy across the organisation	● Enables a strong response to local circumstances
● The greater likelihood of economies of scale	● When decisions are very complex or localised, centralised decision making may not be sensible
● It facilitates co-ordination of sub-units	● It is difficult to provide high-quality customer services from the centre
● Simpler control systems than with a decentralised structure	● Provides opportunities to develop general management talent
● Faster decision making, with less compromise	● Motivates staff in locations outside the centre
● Limited geographic distance between HQ and subsidiary	● A more diversified product range
● High degree of inter-relationship between sub-units	● A stable environment
● High technology content	● It is appropriate when unit is unimportant to the centre
● Resource allocation by the centre is much simpler	

Exhibit 18.2

Summary of the five main criticisms of the strategy-first, structure-afterwards process

1 Structures may be *too rigid, hierarchical and bureaucratic* to cope with the newer social values and rapidly-changing environments of the 1990s.

2 *The type of structure* is just as important as the business area in developing the organisation's strategy. It is the structure that will restrict, guide and form the strategy options that the organisation can generate. A learning organisation may be required and power given to more junior managers. In this sense, strategy and organisational structure are inter-related and need to be developed at the same time.

3 *Value-chain configurations* that favour cost cutting or, alternatively, new market opportunities may also alter the organisation required.

4 *The complexity of strategic change* needs to be managed, implying that more complex organisational considerations will be involved. Simple configurations such as a move from a functional to a divisional structure were only a starting point in the process.

5 *The role of top and middle management* in the formation of strategy may also need to be reassessed: Chandler's view that strategy is decided by the top leadership alone has been challenged. Particularly for new innovative strategies, middle management and the organisation's culture and structure may be important. The work of the leader in empowering middle management may require a new approach – the collegiate style of leadership.

Corporate Strategy Overhead Transparency Masters Pitman Publishing © Aldersgate Consultancy Limited 1997

Exhibit 18.3

A comparison of the early and late twentieth century business environments

Early twentieth century	Late twentieth century
● Uneducated workers, typically just moved from agricultural work into the cities	● Better educated, computer-literate, skilled
● Knowledge of simple engineering and technology	● Complex, computer-driven, large scale
● The new science of management recognised simple cause-and-effect relationships	● Multi-faceted and complex nature of management now partially understood
● Growing, newly-industrialising markets and suppliers	● Mix of some mature, cyclical markets and some high growth new technology markets and suppliers
● Sharp distinctions between management and workers	● Greater overlap between management and workers in some industrialised countries

Fig 18.6

The six basic parts of every organisation

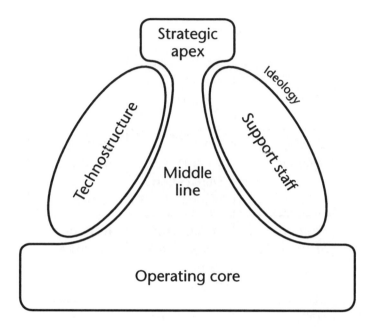

Source: *The Structure of Organisations*, by H Mintzberg © 1979.
Reproduced by permission of Prentice-Hall, Inc., Upper Saddle River, New Jersey.

Exhibit 18.5

Mintzberg's configuration of organisations and the way they operate

Mintzberg's strategic configurations	Background: see Part 2 of this book		Structures and linkages		Example
	Environmental analysis	Resource analysis	Key part of organisation	Key co-ordinating mechanism	
Entrepreneurial organisation	Simple/ dynamic	Small, young Duplication of jobs	Strategic apex: the boss or owner	Direct supervision	Small computer service company
Machine organisation	High growth or cyclical	Older, large Defined tasks, techno-structure	Techno-structure	Standardisation of work	Computer assembly or car plant
Professional organisation	Stable, complex, closed to outsiders	Professional control by managers	Operating core	Standardisation of skills	Management consultancy or hospital
Divisionalised structure	Diverse	Old and large Strong links possible Standard criteria for resource allocation	Middle line	Standardisation of outputs	Fast-moving consumer goods group
Innovative organisation*	Complex and dynamic	Often young, complex work, experts involved	Support staff	Mutual adjustment	Advertising agency
Missionary organisation	Simple, static	Ideologically driven co-operative Small groups within total	Ideology	Standardisation of norms	Charity or social work

* Note that innovative organisation is called an *adhocracy* in some texts and versions of the above.

Fig 19.1

The implementation process

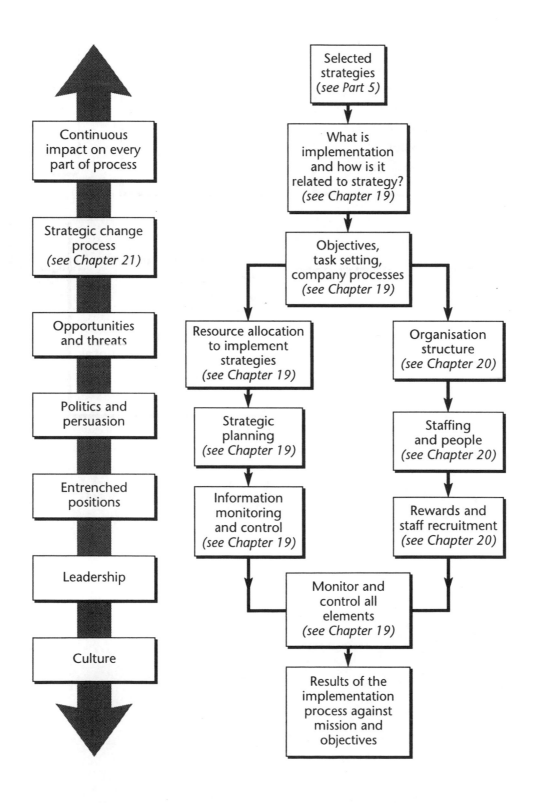

Continuous impact on every part of process

Strategic change process (*see Chapter 21*)

Opportunities and threats

Politics and persuasion

Entrenched positions

Leadership

Culture

Selected strategies (*see Part 5*)

What is implementation and how is it related to strategy? (*see Chapter 19*)

Objectives, task setting, company processes (*see Chapter 19*)

Resource allocation to implement strategies (*see Chapter 19*)

Organisation structure (*see Chapter 20*)

Strategic planning (*see Chapter 19*)

Staffing and people (*see Chapter 20*)

Information monitoring and control (*see Chapter 19*)

Rewards and staff recruitment (*see Chapter 20*)

Monitor and control all elements (*see Chapter 19*)

Results of the implementation process against mission and objectives

Fig 19.2

The basic implementation process

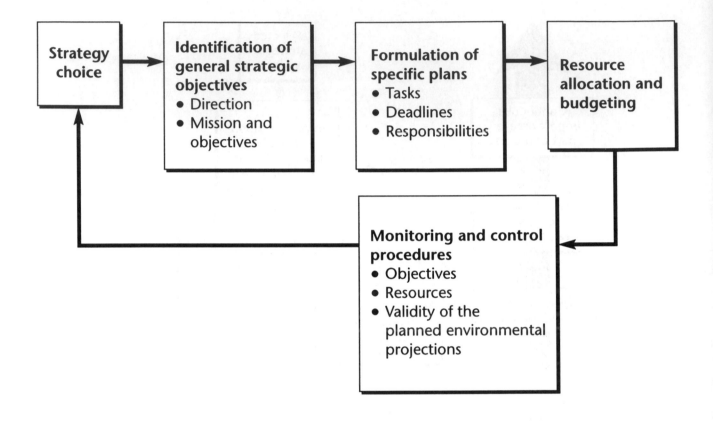

Table 19.1

How the nature of the activity affects the implementation

Activity	Typical implications for implementation	Typical implications for monitoring and control
Ongoing, existing activity	● General plans only ● Predictable outcomes within limits	● Monitor major variations only ● Monitoring undertaken against the experience of previous years and against the objectives for the plan (not necessarily the same)
New activity	● Careful, detailed plans ● Perhaps incremental or selective ● Staged release of funds for the strategy	● Monitor the programme in depth ● Use detailed progress reports ● Go beyond outline numbers into detailed discussions to understand the reasons

Exhibit 19.1

Three emergent perspectives on the implementation process

- Implementation must involve many parts of the organisation.

- Implementation needs to be seen as an ongoing activity rather than one major event with a finite outcome.

- Implementation needs to be flexible and responsive to outside and internal pressures.

Fig 20.1

Organisation structure and people issues

```
┌─────────────────────────────┐
│    Basic considerations      │
└─────────────────────────────┘
              │
              ▼
┌──────────────────────────────────────┐
│ Six main types of organisational structure │
└──────────────────────────────────────┘
              │
              ▼
┌──────────────────────────────────────┐
│ Organisational structures for innovation │
└──────────────────────────────────────┘
              │
              ▼
┌──────────────────────────────────────────────┐
│ Building the most appropriate organisational structure │
└──────────────────────────────────────────────┘
              │
              ▼
┌──────────────────────────────────────────────┐
│ Motivation and staffing in strategy implementation │
└──────────────────────────────────────────────┘
              │
              ▼
┌──────────────────────────────────────┐
│ International strategy and structure │
└──────────────────────────────────────┘
```

Exhibit 20.1

Examples of the connection between purpose and organisational design

Purpose	Implications for organisational design
'Ideas factory' such as an advertising or promotions agency	Loose, fluid structure with limited formalised relationships. As it grows in size, however, more formal structures are usually inevitable
Multinational company in branded goods	Major linkage and resource issues that need carefully co-ordinated structures, e.g. on common suppliers or common supermarket customers for separate product ranges
Government civil service	Strict controls on procedures and authorisations. Strong formal structures to handle major policy directions and legal issues
Non-profit-making charity with a strong sense of mission	Reliance on voluntary members and their voluntary contributions may require a flexible organisation with responsibility devolved to individuals
Major service company such as a retail bank or electricity generating company	Formal structures but supported by some flexibility so that variations in demand can be met quickly
Small business attempting to survive and grow	Informal willingness to undertake several business functions such as selling or production, depending on the short-term circumstances
Health service with strong professional service ethics, standards and quality	Formalised structure that reflects the seniority and professional status of those involved while delivering the crucial complex service provisions
Holding company with subsidiaries involved in diverse markets	Small centralised headquarters acting largely as a banker with the main strategic management being undertaken in individual companies

Fig 20.2

The functional organisation structure

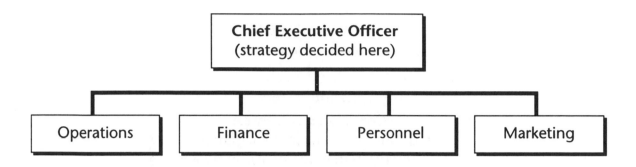

Exhibit 20.2

Advantages and disadvantages of the functional organisation structure

Advantages	Disadvantages
● Simple and clear responsibilities	● Co-ordination difficult
● Central strategic control	● Emphasis on parochial functional areas in strategy development rather than company-wide view
● Functional status recognised	● Encourages inter-functional rivalry
	● Strategic change may be slow

Fig 20.3

The multi-divisional organisational structure

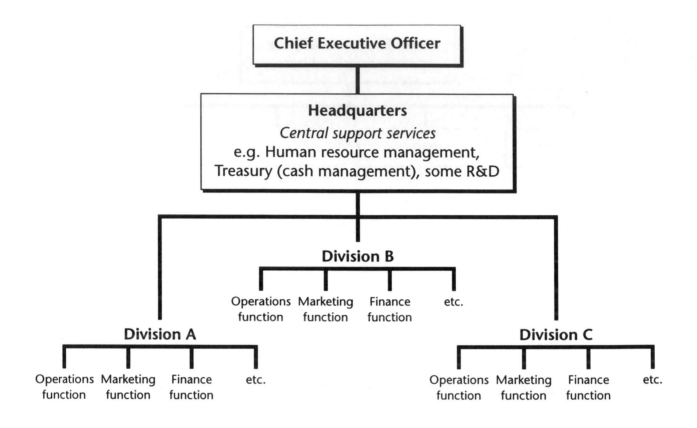

Exhibit 20.3

Advantages and disadvantages of the multi-divisional organisational structure

Advantages	Disadvantages
● Focusses on business area	● Expensive duplication of functions
● Eases functional co-ordination problems	● Divisions may compete against each other
● Allows measurement of divisional performance	● Decreased interchange between functional specialists
● Can train future senior managers	● Problems over relationships with central services

Fig 20.4

The holding company organisational structure

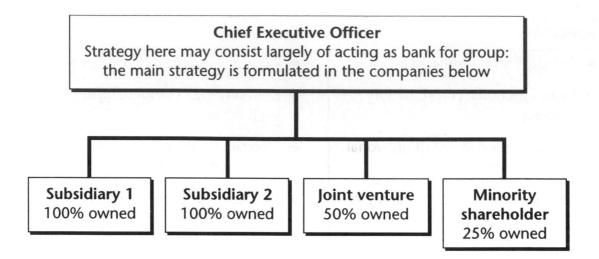

Chief Executive Officer
Strategy here may consist largely of acting as bank for group: the main strategy is formulated in the companies below

| Subsidiary 1 100% owned | Subsidiary 2 100% owned | Joint venture 50% owned | Minority shareholder 25% owned |

Exhibit 20.4

Advantages and disadvantages of the holding company organisation structure

Advantages	Disadvantages
● Allows for the complexity of modern ownership	● Little control at centre
● Taps expertise and gains new co-operations	● Little group contribution beyond 'shareholding/banking' role
● New market entry enhanced	● Problems if two partners cannot co-operate or one partner loses interest
● Spreads risk for conglomerate	● May have very limited synergy or economies of scale

Fig 20.5

The matrix organisation structure

Chief Executive Officer

	Product group 1	Product group 2	Product group 3
Geographical area 1			
Geographical area 2		*Strategy perhaps decided in each of the matrix groups and perhaps at the centre*	
Geographical area 3			

Exhibit 20.5

Advantages and disadvantages of the matrix organisation structure

Advantages	Disadvantages
● Close co-ordination where decisions may conflict	● Complex, slow decision-making: needs agreement by all participants
● Adapts to specific strategic situations	● Unclear definition of responsibilities
● Bureaucracy replaced by direct discussion	● Can produce high tension between those involved if teamwork of some parts is poor
● Increased managerial involvement	

Exhibit 20.6

Guidelines for organising innovative project teams

1 *Flexible structures* that allow experts not just to exercise their skills but to break through conventional boundaries into *new* areas.

2 *Co-ordination* within the team needs to be undertaken by experts with a technical background in the area, rather than a superior with authority from outside.

3 *Power* in the team needs to be distributed among the experts, where appropriate. they progress their innovative ideas.

Exhibit 20.7

Five pointers to encourage innovation

1   Publicise and take pride in existing achievements.

2   Provide support for innovative initiatives, perhaps through access to senior managers, perhaps through project teams.

3   Improve communication across the enterprise by creating cross-functional activities and by bringing people together.

4   Reduce layers in the hierarchy of the organisation and give more authority to those further down the chain.

5   Publicise more widely and frequently company plans on future activity, giving those lower down a chance to contribute their ideas and become involved in the process.

Exhibit 20.8

Nature of business activity and organisational structure

Nature of business	Likely organisational structure
Single business	Functional
Range of products extending from a single business	Functional but monitor each range of products using separate profit and loss accounts
Separate businesses within group with limited links	Divisional
Separate businesses within group with strong links	Matrix (or divisional with co-ordination if matrix is difficult to manage)
Ideas factory	Innovative structure
Unrelated businesses	Holding company
Related businesses owned jointly or by minority shareholdings	Holding company

Fig 20.6

Global and national responsiveness requirements for international organisations

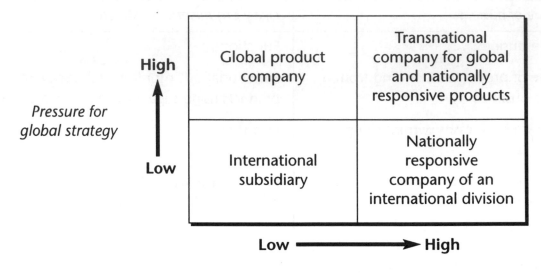

Fig 21.1

Managing strategic change

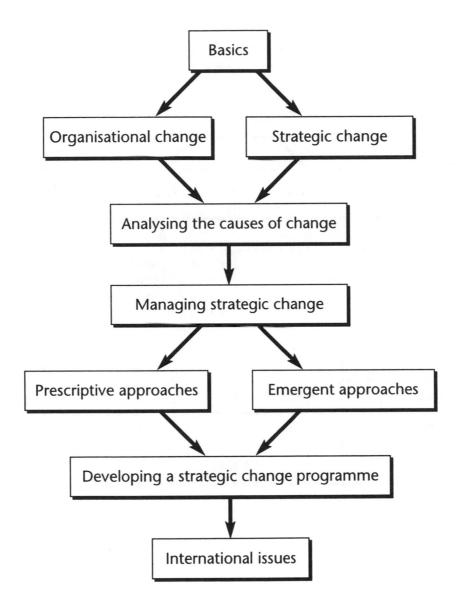

Fig 21.2

People and pressure points for influencing strategic change

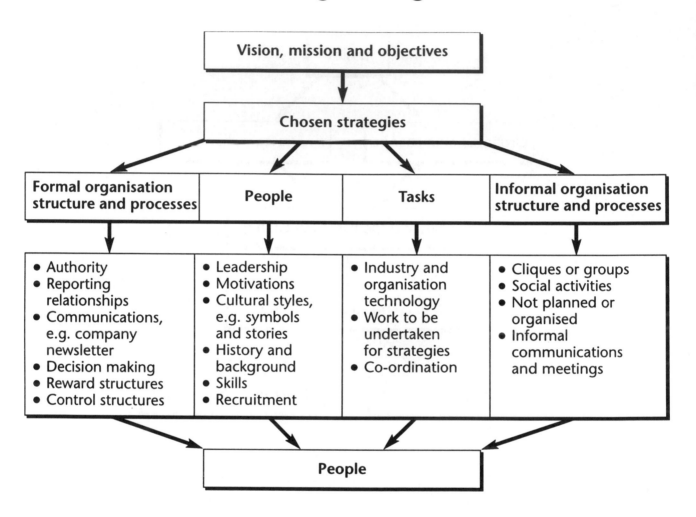

Fig 21.3

Some time costs associated with the strategic process

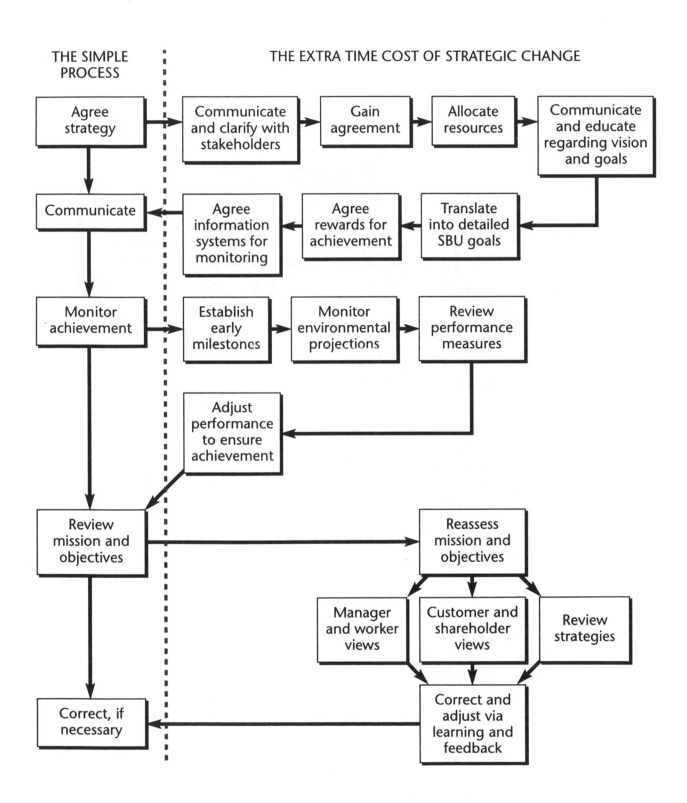

THE SIMPLE PROCESS

THE EXTRA TIME COST OF STRATEGIC CHANGE

- Agree strategy
- Communicate and clarify with stakeholders
- Gain agreement
- Allocate resources
- Communicate and educate regarding vision and goals
- Communicate
- Agree information systems for monitoring
- Agree rewards for achievement
- Translate into detailed SBU goals
- Monitor achievement
- Establish early milestones
- Monitor environmental projections
- Review performance measures
- Adjust performance to ensure achievement
- Review mission and objectives
- Reassess mission and objectives
- Manager and worker views
- Customer and shareholder views
- Review strategies
- Correct, if necessary
- Correct and adjust via learning and feedback

Fig 21.5

The five factors in the successful management of strategic change

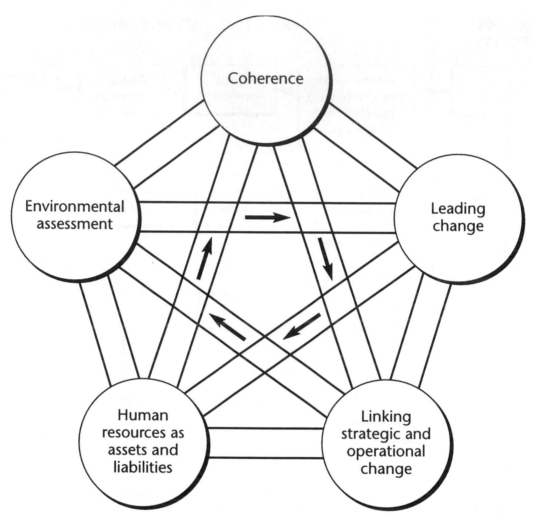

Source: Pettigrew, A and Whipp, R (1991) *Managing Change for Competitive Success*, Blackwell Publishers, Oxford, p104. Reproduced with permission.

Fig 21.6

Characteristics of the five central factors

	Environmental assessment	Leading change	Linking strategic and operational change	Human resources as assets and liabilities	Coherence
PRIMARY CONDITIONING FEATURES	1 Availability of key people 2 Internal character of organisation 3 Environmental pressures and associated dramas 4 Environmental assessments as a multi-function activity	1 Building a receptive context for change; legitimation 2 Creating capability for change 3 Constructing the content and direction of the change	1 Justifying the need for change 2 Building capacity for appropriate action 3 Supplying necessary visions, values and business direction	1 Raising HRM consciousness 2 Use of highly situational additive features to create positive force for HRM change 3 Demonstrating the need for business and people change	1 Consistency 2 Consonance 3 Advantage 4 Feasibility
SECONDARY MECHANISMS	5 Role of planning, marketing 6 Construction of purposive networks with main stake-holders 7 Use of specialist task-forces	4 Operationalising the change agenda 5 Creating the critical mass for change within senior management 6 Communicating need for change and detailed requirements of the change agenda 7 Achieving and reinforcing success 8 Balance continuity and change 9 Sustaining coherence	4 Breaking emergent strategy into actionable pieces 5 Appointment of change managers, relevant structures and exacting targets 6 Re-thinking communications 7 Using the reward system 8 Setting up local negotiation climate for targets 9 Modifying original visions in light of local context 10 Monitoring and adjustment	4 *Ad hoc*, cumulative, supportive activities at various levels 5 Linking HRM action to business need with HRM as a means not an end 6 Mobilising external influences 7 Devolution to line 8 Construction of HRM actions and institutions which reinforce one another	5 Leadership 6 Senior management team integrity 7 Uniting intent and implementation 8 Developing apposite knowledge bases 9 Inter-organisational coherence 10 Managing a series of inter-related changes over time

Source: Pettigrew, A and Whipp, R (1991) *Managing Change for Competitive Success*, Blackwell Publishers, Oxford, p106. Reproduced with permission.

Fig 21.8

Change options matrix

Three main areas of strategic change	Areas of people activity			
	Formal organisation structure	**People**	**Tasks**	**Informal organisation structure**
Technical and work changes from the strategy to be undertaken	• Organisation of work and reporting • Strategy and structure	• Selection, training • Matching of management style with skills • Routines	• Consider environment, technology, learning, competitor activity • Learn and carry out new tasks	• Understand and monitor • Feed with 'good news'
Cultural changes Style of company, history, age, etc.	• Managerial style • Mintzberg's subcultures (Chapter 15) • Handy's cultures (Chapter 8)	• Individual and corporate values matched • Management of groups and teams • Leadership choice	• Symbols, stories • Unfreezing • Make role models of key people • Clarify values • New recipes	• Awards, symbols • Develop networks • Encourage useful groups • Develop social activities
Political changes Interactions and power inside the organisation	• Formal distribution of power • Balance of power between departments	• Use available skills and networks • Match with new strategies • Incentives and rewards	• Lobbying • Develop structures • Influence formal and informal groups	• Attempt to manage • Make contacts • Network and circulate

Exhibit 21.1

Resistance to change

Why people resist change	Overcoming resistance
● Anxiety, e.g. weaknesses revealed or loss of power or position	● Involving those who resist in the change process itself
● Pessimism	● Building support networks
● Irritation	● Communications and discussion
● Lack of interest	● Use of managerial authority and status
● Opposition strategy proposals	● Offering assistance
● Different personal ambitions	● Extra incentives
	● Encouraging and supporting those involved
	● Use of symbols to signal the new era

Table 21.2

Politics in organisations

Objective	Activities undertaken to achieve the objective	Reaction by superiors or rivals to the activities
Resist change or resist authority	● Sabotage ● Rebellion	● Fight back ● Institute new rules and regulations
Build power	● Flaunt or feign expertise ● Attach oneself to superior ● Build alliances with colleagues ● Collect subordinates: empire build ● Control resources	● Call bluff ● Find heir ● Reorganise department ● Reclaim control of resources
Defeat rival	● Battles between units ● Battles between staff and line ● Expose mistakes (we all make them)	● Good leadership should provide balance
Achieve fundamental change in strategy, authority and leadership	● Form power group of key executives ● Combine with other areas above ● Inform on opponent ● Leak damaging material to public media	● Intelligence essential ● Recognise and cultivate those who are particularly influential ● Seek out rival power groups ● Respond with own leaks

Fig 22.1

Combining the elements together

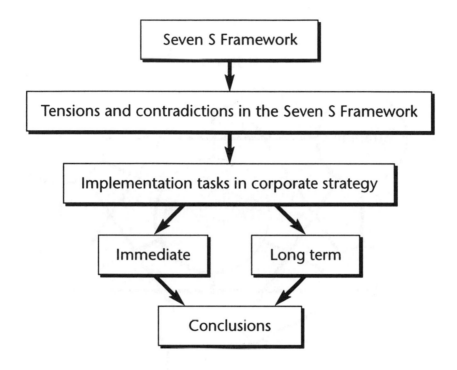

Fig 22.2

The Seven S Framework

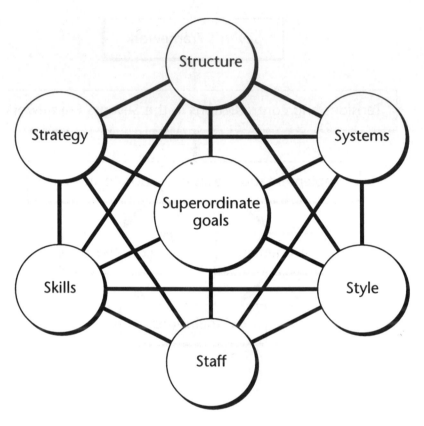

Exhibit 22.1

Qualities of excellent companies
(Peters and Waterman)

- *Operate on loose-tight principles.* The best companies were both tightly controlled from the centre and yet, at the same time, encouraged entrepreneurship.

- *Incline towards taking action.* There may be analysis, but there is always a bias towards practical and fast solutions where possible.

- *Close to the customer.* The best companies offered customers quality, reliability and service.

- *Innovative autonomy.* Responsibility is moved to individuals who are encouraged to be as innovative as possible.

- *Simplicity of organisational form.* Organisation structures work better when clear, simple and with well-defined lines of authority and responsibility. Matrix management structures were not to be encouraged because they were too complex. When organisations were organised simply, they were more able to combine quickly into effective teams, task forces and project groups.

- *The importance of the people resource, not just as an abstract concept but as individuals to be respected.* The better companies not only made tough demands on individuals but also treated them as individuals to be trained, developed and given new and interesting challenges.

- *Clarity regarding the organisation's values and mission.* In the best companies, many employees were clear both about the company's values and about *why* such values had been chosen. Better companies made a significant attempt to communicate, debate and seek to inspire all within the organisation.

- *Stick to the knitting.* Organisations may diversify into other related areas but the companies that do best are the ones that concentrate on their core skills. Companies should not move into unrelated areas.

In addition, three other elements of excellent companies can be identified from the Peters and Waterman research that are consistent with other areas of this book:

- *Excellent companies have flexible organisation structures.* This flexibility enables them to respond quickly to changes in the environment.

- *Excellent companies have quite distinctive cultures.* The company culture integrates the organisation's desire to meet its defined mission and objectives with two other important areas: serving customers and providing satisfying work for its employees.

- *Successful strategy emerges through purposeful, but essentially unpredictable, evolution.* Excellent companies are learning organisations that adapt their strategy as the environment changes through experimentation, challenge and permitting failure.

Source: Adapted from Peters, T and Waterman, R (1982). *In Search of Excellence,* HarperCollins, New York. (Copyright 1982 by Thomas J Peters and Robert H Waterman Jr. Reprinted by permission of HarperCollins Publishers.)

Exhibit 22.2

Tensions and contradictions in the 'Seven S' elements (Pascale)

Strategy	*Planned*	*Opportunistic*
Structure	**Elitist** organisations tend to coalesce into groups which are often based on functions: focus is needed to drive strategy forward	**Pluralist** organisation structures are essential if teamwork and cross-functional activities are to be undertaken
Systems	**Mandatory** systems are used to ensure that meeting formats and reports are always prepared to an agreed standard	**Discretionary** systems are necessary if the organisation is not to be swamped with form-filling that will drive out entrepreneurial initiative
Style	**Managerial** style is essential for the administration necessary to keep the organisation operating smoothly	**Transformational** style is needed for the quantum leaps in performance that are essential for major new initiatives
Staff	**Collegiality** is important in large companies to obtain team spirit and support colleagues, but peer pressures to conform can be strong	**Individualism** is important where new ideas or heretical solutions to existing problems are required. It may be necessary to challenge the existing order
Shared values*	**Hard minds** are needed to deliver the bottom-line profit	**Soft hearts** are needed when issues such as responsibility for the environment, customers and employee rights are under discussion
Skills	**Maximise** skills essentially concentrate work activity on doing better what the organisation already does well	**Metamise** skills are involved when it is important to develop new skills that move competences to a completely new level

Source: Adapted from Pascale, R (1990) *Managing on the Edge,* Viking Penguin, London, pp 16 and 17.

* Note that Pascale used the Peters and Waterman revision.

Exhibit 22.3

Factors that drive strategic stagnation and renewal (Pascale)

Fit – *the consistencies, coherence and congruence of the organisation.* Specifically, this is the fit between objectives, strategies and identified elements of change. For example, a strategy of increased customer service will not 'fit' if funds are withdrawn from the customer service department and reward systems are defined simply by short-term profits. This is similar to the concept of *coherence* explored in Chapter 21.

Split – *the variety of techniques that can be employed to develop and sustain the autonomy and diversity of large organisations.* An example would be setting up profit-accountable subsidiaries or profit centres. This concept includes both divisionalisation and the multifunctional task forces to encourage innovation, as described in Chapter 20.

Contend – *the constructive conflict that every organisation needs.* For example, conflict generated between different functional areas needs to be channelled productively, not suppressed. Resolution of such conflicts is an ongoing management task.

Transcend – *given the inevitable complexities of the above three areas, organisations need an approach to management that will cope with the difficulties.* This cannot be achieved by compromise but needs a totally different mindset (or paradigm) that copes with conflict and uses it to move the organisation forward.

Source: Adapted from Pascale, R (1990) *Managing on the Edge*, Viking Penguin, London, pp 16 and 17.

Exhibit 22.4

Some key guidelines on strategy implementation and control

Problems of successful implementation tend to focus on how well or badly the organisation's reporting proves to be.

Problems arise:

- where implementation cuts across traditional organisational units;
- when information monitoring is poor;
- when an organisation resists change;
- when rewards for performance are geared to past performance rather than future action.

For successful implementation:

- allocate clear responsibility and accountability;
- pursue a limited number of strategies;
- identify the required actions and gain agreement from those who will implement them;
- produce 'milestones' so that it is clear earlier rather than later if implementation is off-course;
- above all, secure the active support of the chief executive.

Fig 22.3

The principle of the strategic staircase

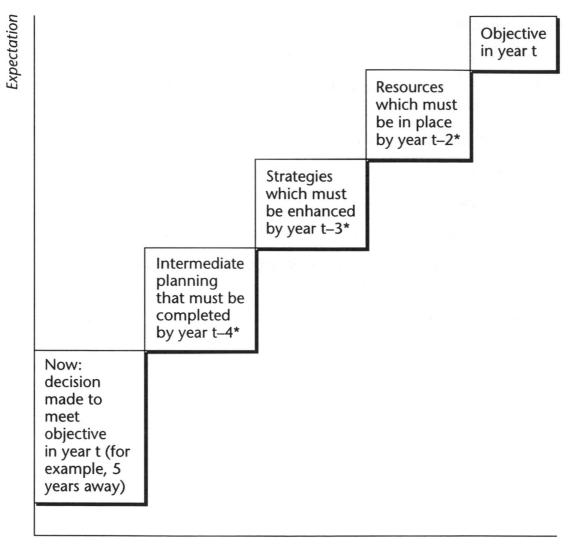

Note: The year numbers (t–1, t–2, etc.) are only examples.

Corporate Strategy Overhead Transparency Masters Pitman Publishing © Aldersgate Consultancy Limited 1997

Exhibit 22.5

Projecting the future strategic environment: some possible issues

- Globalisation and global competition.
- Increasing ease, speed and low price of communications.
- Privatisation of government holdings and increase in market competition: deregulation.
- Environmental 'green' concerns.
- Mergers and acquisitions, and increasing alliances.
- Technological discontinuities.
- Excess production capacity in some industries, e.g. cars.
- Changing customer expectations: affluence, instant satisfaction, technological games and electronic shopping.
- Downsizing to smaller company units.
- Working from home instead of the office.